CANALS & CAMPAIGNS

GKSM as a Lieutenant, RE, aged about thirty

CANALS & CAMPAIGNS

*An Engineer Officer in India
1877 – 1885*

Major General Sir George Scott Moncrieff
KCB, KCMG, CIE, RE

PUTNEY, LONDON
1987

Published by the British Association
for Cemeteries in South Asia (BACSA)

Secretary: Theon Wilkinson
76½ Chartfield Avenue
London SW15 6HQ

Copyright 1987, Miss Martha Scott Moncrieff

All rights reserved. No part of this publication may be reproduced, stored in a retrieval system, or transmitted in any form or by any means, electronic, mechanical, photocopying, recording or otherwise, without the prior permission of the copyright owner.

ISBN   0 907799 20 5

Cover: designed by Rosemarie Wilkinson

Maps: adapted by Rosemarie Wilkinson

Printed by The Chameleon Press
5-25 Burr Road,
Wandsworth,
London SW18 4SG

Contents

Illustrations and Maps		iii
Foreword		v
Introduction		vi

Chapter

1 **The Voyage**   1
Embarking at Portsmouth – Arrival at
Bombay – Journey to Roorkee

2 **Roorkee and the Bengal Sappers**   9
Camp life – Station life – Local leave
to Hardwar, Dehra Dun and Mussoorie –
Long leave to Kashmir

3 **The Swat River Canal**   21
To Swat; with the Guides at Mardan –
Engineering work at Narrai – Visits
to Peshawar and Abazai – War clouds

4 **Afghan Campaign – Ali Musjid**   35
At war and advance into Afghanistan –
Action at Ali Musjid – Campaign road
building, then back to Swat

5 **Afghan Campaign – Jallalabad**   44
To the front again, Dakka and Jallalabad –
To Gandamak on leave – Peace treaty and
return to India

6 **Abazai**   56
Canal duties and social life – News of
Kabul massacre and on the war path again

7 **Afghan Campaign – Kuram and Kabul**   62
Joining General Roberts in the Kuram Valley –
On to Kabul and road making at Butkhak –
Fortifying Butkhak – Night withdrawal

Chapter		
8	**Afghan Campaign – Butkhak and Sherpur** Beseiged – Defence works and road making – Life at Kabul; news of Kandahar disaster and back to Peshawar	80
9	**Hill Station Life, 1879-82** Kasauli and military works – Simla and its society	93
10	**Lucknow** Executive Engineer and life in the city – Viceroy's visit; durbar of the Talukdars; sport on the Ganges; Cawnpore – Benares and transfer to Railway Works	102
11	**Sinde-Peshin Railway** The start at Nari (Narrai) and Baberkach – Survey of route between Harnai and Quetta	112
12	**Work on the Railway** Through the Chappar Rift – The Quetta Week and work on the line to Quetta	118
13	**Three Months Leave** Simla; fishing at Hardwar; Roorkee for Christmas; Delhi – Jaipur; Amber; Hansi to Karnal via Jhind	125
14	**Floods and Fever** Return to Narrai and work on the railway; a train disaster; a huge flood; down with fever; invalided to England	131

Epilogue   136

Appendix – The Frontier Railways of India
(Three lectures delivered by author in 1885)

	Lecture 1	The railway network of the Punjab	138
	Lecture 2	The Harnai route; the Chappar Rift; the temporary Bolan line	150
	Lecture 3	Technical points in the construction of the line: bridges and tunnels, fuses and gunpowder, plate-laying and flood protection	162

Illustrations and Maps

GKSM as a Lieutenant, RE, aged about thirty   Frontispiece

Swat River Suspension Bridge, built with the   23
assistance of Bengal Sappers Pontoon Section
Swat River Trestle & Crate Bridge, length 420 yards,
built by 1st and 6th Companies Bengal Sappers

Bridge over Sakar Nulla on Mardan/Dargai Road   27
(Capt. HC Norton with civil labour)

Group of RE officers at Safed Sang (Gandamak)   49
Major-General Maunsell and others (see caption)

6th Company Sappers & Miners at Safed Sang   51

Bridge at Safed Sang with Bengal Sappers (top)   55
First portion of bridge on Kabul River (lower)

5th Company Sappers Bridge over Kabul River (top)   79
Another 5th Company bridge (lower)

A halt in the shade of a Minar at Kabul   88

Mussoorie, showing the Camel's Back and the   101
Roller Skating Rink

The Chatter Manzil, Lucknow; used as a Club   104

Maj-General Sir George Scott Moncrieff,KCB,KCMG,CIE,RE
at the end of his long career (taken about 1912)   137

Maps

Skeleton Plan of Ganges Canal   8

Campaign in Afghanistan, 1878-1879   34

Afghanistan and North-West Frontier   111

GKSM's map of Sinde-Peshin Railway   149

Notes on sources of illustrations

The photograph of GKSM in the frontispiece and facing the epilogue come from the family

The photographs of the bridges and scenes in Afghanistan and North-West Frontier come from the albums of Lieutenants Ancrum and Dove, both RE officers serving in the same campaigns as the author - from the Royal Engineers Library, Chatham (see also the Foreword)

The photographs of Mussoorie and Lucknow come from a private collection

NB The drawings and copies of prints that occur throughout are from:

(a) The Ganges Canal, by TG Glover, published in Roorkee in 1867 (and copies obtained by kindness of the RE Library, Chatham)

(b) Afghanistan and its late Amir with some account of Baluchistan; compiled from Bellew, Hunter's Gazeteer of India, Wheeler's The Amir Abdur Rahman, The Statesman's Year Book, etc; Madras, 1902

Foreword

This is the ninth of a series of books published by BACSA, for BACSA members with a wider public in mind and particularly those with an interest in the Indian Army, the Sappers and Miners and their works whether on canals, railways, roads or fortifications.

"Canals and Campaigns" is a personal account of one Engineer, George Scott Moncrieff, during the first eight years of his career. It is an edited and abridged version of the handwritten narrative in the India Office Library and Records and his daughter, Martha, explains in the Introduction how it came to be written.

There is also, as a separate section in the Appendix, the author's detailed description of the building of the Frontier railways of India given in the form of three lectures and published in 1885 in "The Professional Papers of the Royal Engineers", Volume II. Paper IX.

The illustrations come from a variety of sources to give a visual impact of some of the people and places, canals and railways referred to in the text, but only the two portraits are his own. A debt of gratitude must be expressed to Major JT Hancock, the Librarian of the Royal Engineers Library, Chatham, for his help in locating a number of contemporary photographs in their collection and arranging for their reproduction.

Honorary Secretary
BACSA

Introduction

George Kenneth Scott Moncrieff spent three separate periods of his life in the Indian sub-continent. 1) Born in 1855, he spent his early childhood in the province of Bihar. 2) After education in Britain (Edinburgh Academy) and training at Woolwich and Chatham, he returned to India as Lieutenant in the Royal Engineers, aged twenty-one. This is the phase, lasting till he was almost thirty, of which his own detailed account still exists and is presented here. 3) Later with the rank of Major, he served for a further five years (1899-1904) during Lord Curzon's Viceroyalty, in the then North-West Frontier Province, now Pakistan.

Though he kept a diary all through his soldiering days, in fact until his life's end in 1924, he still found time to write this fuller narrative for the benefit of his children. The diaries were useful for reference, though most of the entries are very brief.

The task must have occupied him during a time of what he called 'enforced leisure' after a minor operation, and perhaps continued in early mornings thereafter. He wrote rapidly - the diaries are interleaved with thin blotting paper - and seldom erased or altered anything.

He begins by recalling a time when, having leave, he was visiting Lucknow with his uncle, Colonel Sir Colin Scott Moncrieff, who was also an RE officer. Though far apart in rank and age, this colonel and subaltern were on excellent terms and obviously enjoyed each other's company. Several instances occur in the narrative showing Uncle Colin's kindness to his nephew and the latter's appreciation.

From that time, he writes, Lucknow seemed somehow to have 'a flavour of home', and this helps to explain his resolve to put into words some of his own early experiences so that his children could share in them.

His story begins on the night he left his mother's home in Edinburgh, 26th December 1876.

St Andrews
1987

MCSM

1
The Voyage

It was regular Christmas weather, snow on the ground and more in the air. I remember the last I saw of mother and sisters was standing at the door of the house with a foreground of trodden snow and a background of bright gaslight in the lobby with holly decorations and warmth and brightness. It was an awful night however and I thought it was a curious introduction to a voyage to the gorgeous East. The train stuck fast in the snow between Carstairs and Beattock and a howling wind was blowing. However, we got on eventually and I reached Portsmouth that afternoon in rain and slush. Several of my brother officers were going out in the same ship with me and we all put up together at the same hotel.

There were also there some lads going out to join their regiments in India. I found one of them gaily walking off to report himself to the military authorities at Portsmouth in uniform, but with a neat umbrella over his head! Poor lad, he did not understand that an umbrella is not 'regulation'.

HMS CROCODILE was taking out on this occasion the 12th Lancers, two batteries of Horse Artillery and drafts of nearly every cavalry regiment in India. There were besides a number of doctors and veterinary surgeons, young sub-lieutenants of infantry and a few stray artillerymen and engineers, not in command of any drafts.

I slept on board the night before sailing. I had handed over all my baggage, as ordered, to the loading party and saw nothing more of it during the voyage. The staff-officers in charge of the embarkation were very busy seeing that everybody was in their right place and I heard one lady say to her husband, "My dear I am the senior lady on board and have therefore the right to sit next to the Captain besides having my choice of berth." She went to the distracted staff-officer stating her claims and insisting that he should see that she had her proper place next to the Captain. This lady during the rest of the voyage would talk to nobody under the rank of (military) Captain, so I never had the pleasure of her acquaintance.

Next morning Friday 28th the last arrivals came on board and friends came to bid last farewells.

The band struck up 'Auld Lang Syne' and we all gave three hearty cheers for the Old Country as the screw revolved and the huge vessel moved slowly away from the quay.

Down the Solent and into the Channel, HMS CROCODILE moved, and the usual effects of wind and waves were soon felt by many on board. I myself was not wholly free from such qualms, and dined off two oranges and a ship's biscuit. However, the next morning I was quite ready for a hearty breakfast.

It was certainly very rough, emphatically what sailors call 'dirty' weather. On the morning of Sunday 31st December we were fairly in the Bay of Biscay and had the usual Divine Service on the lower deck.

Every morning we had what are called divisions on the quarter deck. All hands not on duty were mustered and inspected by the naval officers, and the military officers and men of the watch had to be present. Then the chaplain came and read the Psalms for the day and the beautiful prayers authorised for those at sea. All this to the accompaniment of waves and wind. At times it was hard for us landlubbers to keep our feet, the ship rolled so much. Of course all the sailors swayed gracefully with the motion of the ship. Once the chaplain was dislodged by a more violent lurch than usual and went flying headlong into a group of stalwart tars, his prayer book falling in the water at the leeside of the deck. We irreverent soldiers laughed but the sailors picked up the good man, put him on his legs again with his prayer-book open at the right place and he went on from where he had stopped quite as a matter of course.

The Captain of the ship was a martinet of the old school and never took the slightest notice of us youngsters except to rebuke us when necessary. We generally saluted him in the mornings, which he received with calm dignity and without acknowledgement. The first lieutenant was a different man - genial and pleasant to everybody, as indeed were all the other naval officers.

A troopship has three decks, the first with cabins for the ship's captain, the colonel commanding the troops, the ladies and the naval officers. Next, under the saloon and lighted from it, were so-called 'horse-boxes' for the junior officers. I slept in one of these with two companions. The lowest deck of all, below the water-line, was known as 'pandemonium'.

The 1st of January 1877, on which Her Majesty was proclaimed Empress of India at Delhi was in the wild Atlantic a day of storm and tempest. I was the military officer of the middle watch, ie from midnight to 4 am and a weird and lonely time I spent holding on to a rope and looking at the inky blackness all round. The huge ship was heaving and plunging against a south-west wind. Every minute the screw would be elevated out of the water and whirled round with increased velocity, the next minute plunged into the water again and checked. The naval officer of the watch said to me cheerily, "If that screw shaft gives we are done for". He then explained that we were off the coast of Portugal where there are high dangerous rocks, that if the steam machinery broke down our sails would be useless and the ship unmanageable and hence there was only the machinery between us and destruction. This was very cheerful news! My duties as military officer of the watch were to visit the sentries of the various decks at certain intervals. Poor sea-sick wretches they were very miserable specimens of the British soldier. It was difficult picking one's way about from deck to deck and on one occasion I fairly lost my balance and got pitched on to the top of a snoring trooper whose dreams I rudely dispelled.

But after every storm comes a calm and in due time we reached still water near the Straits of Gibraltar, two days late, however. We had a splendid view of the famous rock and passed through the Strait with all our sails spread about midday. Fortunately for all, we had perfect weather and favourable breezes the whole way to Malta.

Then life on board began to assume a more merry aspect. Faces that had not been seen since Portsmouth began to venture on deck, fair ladies sat in deck chairs with work or books, and the usual ship games were produced, such as playing quoits with coils of rope thrown into a bucket. We were gliding along the northern coast of Africa, sufficiently near to make it worth one's while to examine it through glasses to discover trees, houses, etc and here and there we passed small craft of quaint aspect recalling tales of Algerian pirates.

Early on the morning of the 9th of January we came in sight of Malta. Little gaily painted boats with dark Maltese boys surrounded us at once. Letters and telegrams were brought on board, hawkers came selling sponges and lace and filagree, and we all made up parties to go ashore.

We stayed twenty-four hours in Malta, a visit full of enthralling interest while coaling was done on the ship. After re-embarking, nothing unusual happened on the way to Port Said - a squalid town on the flat with no striking appearance - but everyone looked forward eagerly to travelling down the Suez Canal, which in 1877 was comparatively new (opened in 1869).

The vast size of our vessel made the Canal appear small. We seemed to take up nearly the whole width. The great ship moving slowly along raised in front of her a great wave and caused a corresponding trough behind, the result being much <u>wash</u> of the canal banks and I should think considerable destruction. <u>Dredgers</u> to meet this continual wasting were passed here and there. Beyond the banks the scenery was flat desert. In the lagoons on either side countless flamingoes, storks and cranes waded about, and perhaps one might see an occasional string of camels with attendants or a solitary jackal among the sand hills, beyond these however no signs of life or of vegetation. We went thus slowly on our way for an entire day till in the evening we reached the Bitter Lake at or near Ismailia, where we anchored. It was a lovely evening, and the sunset one of the most beautiful I ever beheld.

At Suez we could not go ashore because of quarantine; and once in the Red Sea, we found that the hottest part of the voyage had begun. Those who had white clothing put it on. Those who had blue serge uniforms wore that. I had in my ignorance provided myself with neither so had to get along as best I could in my ordinary patrol jacket. At nights sleeping in the cabins was, as a rule, out of the question. Most people slept either on deck, or on the stern sheets of the lower deck, which was what I did and was very pleasant. We had a sail bath in the mornings, a great institution. This was a big sail about ten feet square and three feet deep slung in the fore part of the ship and filled with sea water in which one could plunge one's heated body with much pleasure and not have to wait for one's turn as in the other bath room. The early mornings were always jolly and cool. We were allowed to go about the deck then very lightly dressed with feet bare, while the sailors were washing the decks.

This part of the voyage was wearisome, and all looked forward to arriving at its end. We had got to know one another pretty well. Later, I learned the subsequent fate of some of my fellow-passengers, for instance Captain C of the 9th Lancers; he was a superb dandy, always appeared in a clean shirt, wore gloves on deck, and had more luggage than any man on board. In the Afghan war he took his men into battle wearing their peace-time uniforms and was persuaded with difficulty to let them have padded coats against the bitter cold. But his courage was unequalled, and in that battle he fell mortally wounded.

In contrast, the only baggage of his cabin-mate Captain B was one small portmanteau. He had travelled all over Central Asia disguised as a Chinese (with British eyes and features?), had been to Khiva, and was on his way to Simla to interview the Viceroy. Later it was learned that he had done so, had gone off again to explore, and returned after two or three years. But no one believed his stories, and he had to leave the Army.

A captain in the 10th Hussars was 'a queer red-faced fellow with a sardonic grin, but a kindly nature'. He was 'found dead in a railway carriage in England'.

These and many other particulars I learned twelve years later when I met with no fewer than seven of the former passengers of HMS CROCODILE at the Curragh in Ireland. Early in the morning of 9th February land was sighted, and by 12 noon we had anchored in Bombay harbour.

**   **   **   **   **

Fantastically shaped mountains in the distance - forest country between - and close at hand one of the noblest cities in the world rising from the blue water; such was my first impression. How eagerly we had looked forward to this first sight of the country we were travelling to, the mighty empire of Hindustan. Bombay's magnificent situation that nature gave her has been improved by a master architect, Sir Bartle Frere whose far-seeing artistic brain conceived the group of public buildings near the sea front as well as many others.

My aunt Mrs Ballard, sister of Uncle Colin, was married to the man in charge of the Mint in Bombay. They were away on furlough at this time, but she had arranged with Colonel White (taking temporary charge of the Mint) to put her nephew up on his arrival. So while my fellow travellers dispersed, mainly to clubs and hotels, I found my way to the Whites' bungalow and was made welcome. Already two young officers were sharing the premises.

It was a pretty little one-storied house with a thatched roof and broad veranda, standing in a well-wooded and well-kept garden full of tropical plants and creepers. One was struck at once with the cool interior of the house - no carpets, matting only and Persian rugs, no doors nor windows, but openings in the walls in which hung chicks or screens of thin bamboo rods tied together at the ends. Of course there were really doors too which would be shut if necessary, though I don't think they ever were.

In the bedrooms the chief furniture was a light bed with a framework of mosquito curtains standing in the middle of the room, perhaps a chest-of-drawers and a few cane-bottomed chairs. Leading out of each bedroom was a bathroom where all materials for washing and dressing, a big wooden tub and two or three large earthenware jars of water, with a little hole in the wall at the floor level to carry off all the water spilt or splashed on to the cool masonry floor. All this was to be part of my daily life now for eight years more or less but this was my first introduction to it.

I went to collect my belongings at the Carnac Bunder that afternoon, but was only able to claim a box of books and one of cartridges, both useful in their way but not immediately so. The next day I went again, and found everything, except a case of new saddlery which never turned up in spite of all enquiries. This was a heavy blow; it had been very expensive and I was poor. However, the week in Bombay was very pleasantly spent. Colonel White showed me over the Mint, where ingots of silver were being turned into new, bright, clean silver 'Empress' rupees. I received invitations to dinner, rode borrowed horses, rowed and sailed in the harbour. But as there was no word of the missing saddles I decided to push on to Roorkee without delay. Here I expected to meet my uncle.

** ** ** ** **

The railway journey up country was of course full of interest, everything of the commonest character being worthy of attention. I was much disappointed with the country as we got north. The luxuriance of the tropics had disappeared. nothing seemed to remain but flat country, well-wooded it is true but with trees of no significance, the people poor and thin, dwelling in squalid villages of mud houses where man seemed to be raised very little above the animals which shared the village with him.

On the second morning I reached Allahabad. The train was late so I missed the mail up country and was detained for twelve hours. It was raining hard and miserably cold. I felt very wretched; however I spent the day pleasantly enough on a voyage of discovery at what was to be seen. The chief sight was the fort situated at the junction of the Ganges and Jumna and from the rampart walls the view of these two great rivers flowing together in a united current over a wide open country is a very fine one.

I proceeded with my journey that night past Cawnpore towards Meerut. A letter put in my hands at one station from Uncle Colin bade me arrange to get out at a place called Muzaffarnagar where he said he would meet me, so I arranged that I should be discharged there with all my luggage, the guard telling me we would arrive there about 9 pm. At Meerut a helmeted head was put into the carriage, which had a pair of black eyes that searched all round the carriage and then a voice said, 'Is Mr Moncrieff here?' It turned out to be, much to my pleasure, my cousin Dr Bob Pringle who with Susie Willcocks had come down to the station to see if they could see me. (Susie was also a cousin.) She had been married a few months before and was looking very well. Her husband was then Executive Engineer in charge of one of the divisions of the Ganges Canal. Bob Pringle was the Inspector of Vaccination for the whole of the district. In winter his headquarters were at Meerut, in summer at Mussoorie in the hills, so he secured for himself and family a delicious climate all the year round. His camp that night was some way out of Meerut, so he came in the train as far as the next station. He was in great spirits and it was most amusing to hear him.

We reached Muzaffarnagar eventually and in the dark night I got out with all my worldly possessions. It was a small wayside station. A number of natives got out too, speaking of course a language unknown to me and indeed the only man who knew English in the place was the stationmaster. I asked if he knew where Major Moncrieff could be found. He said he had never heard of him, where did he live? I said he was marching down the Ganges Canal, perhaps if I could get a conveyance I might drive and find out his camp. (Refreshing innocence! I imagined that cabs would be in waiting for the train and that good roads would abound in the country as at home.) The stationmaster said he thought that would hardly do, but he would enquire whether there were any canal officers' camps in the neighbourhood. Yes it turned out that among the native passengers who had arrived by train was one, the servant of a canal officer whose camp was not far off. The man had been to get supplies from Meerut and would show me the way to his master's camp. So off I started in the darkness with this man and before long we reached some tents. Here it was intimated to me that the gentleman was dining out at a neighbouring bungalow. I went on there, to see if I could get any information and entered a dining room where two gentlemen were sitting smoking at the fire. One of these was the canal officer, a French gentleman, the other was a civilian Mr Ross Scott, brother of Buchanan Scott, afterwards a very dear friend of mine. Scott insisted on my staying all night with him, when he heard of my state of the case. As my uncle was evidently nowhere near he thought it would be my best plan just to go on to Roorkee next day and not wait. So next day I went on. Nowadays there is a railway to Roorkee, then however, and for many years afterwards, one had to get out at a station called Saharanpur and drive some thirty or forty miles. I did this in a dak ghari or post chaise, a vehicle in which one can lie down at full length and sleep comfortably (though I did not know that then) while relays of horses take one speedily along the road. I suppose they will soon be things of the past.

I arrived at Roorkee late at night on the 9th February, at the dak bungalow or staging inn. I had left the greater part of my luggage at Saharanpur to follow me by cart, but I had enough to supply immediate wants with me. And thus I had arrived at the end of my journey.

Bombay 1852

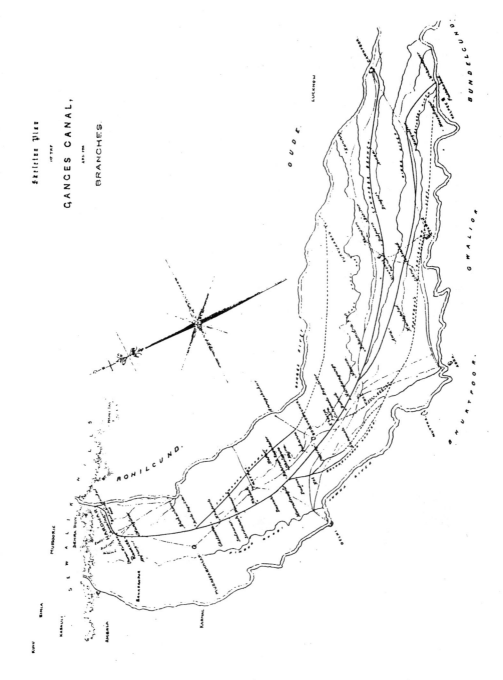

2
Roorkee and the Bengal Sappers

I was up very early the next morning, got a light breakfast and prepared to go up to the barracks and report my arrival. When packing my baggage I became aware of a familiar figure entering the room and a cheery voice exclaimed, 'Hullo Georgie, here you are at last!' It was Uncle Colin, booted and spurred, just going to start on a march down the canal of which he, as the Superintendent Engineer, was then making an inspection. He had been delayed by rain from going sooner and had sent me a second letter not to get out at Muzaffarnagar which had never reached me, and so in despair of my coming he was going off alone. He took me up in his dogcart first to the mess, introduced me to Captain Blood, RE and several others, got ten days leave for me and carried me off with him.

Then I had ten days delightful experience of the easy camp life of northern India. Let me try and describe what I now look back upon with so much pleasure. We rose early in the mornings just as it was getting light and after a cup of tea and toast started off on our march, walking briskly for the first mile or two to get the chill out of one's limbs then mounting our horses and riding across country and along irrigation channels for twelve or sixteen miles to our next halting place, usually a canal bungalow (ie a house built for the purpose of giving accommodation to irrigation officers) where we found all our baggage ready and breakfast ready to be served. All the baggage had gone on to this place overnight except what we actually required for use during the night.

Then my uncle would do his office work till dusk, while I would take a gun and roam in search of sport. For two or three days we left the beaten tracks and went into the Kadir or land on the margin of the Ganges, a district of lake and marsh, of scrubby bush and broken ground, tenanted by wild boars and leopards, deer, wildfowl, snipe and other game. What a glorious country! While Uncle Colin and the executive engineer of the district were away all day discussing plans of drainage and land improvement, I and another young engineer wandered about with our guns, blazing away at everything with fur or feather in our happy ignorance of what was game. We sometimes got a partridge or a few wild ducks, with perhaps a hare or a snipe but we shot these quite impartially with kites, plovers, parrots or anything else that presented itself.

The life generally was a most delightful one and not the least pleasant part by any means was the association with my uncle. We had so much in common, our family, our profession, our friends, that for me at least it was a pure pleasure to have a long chat with him and I cannot but think it was a mutual feeling. I saw more of him during that first year in India than ever I did again and the warm feeling of affection has never, I am sure, been allowed to cool.

Eventually we reached Meerut where were our Pringle cousins and the Willcocks's. I made Will Willcocks' acquaintance then, an acquaintance which speedily ripened into friendship.

The ten days however came to an end at last and I returned to Roorkee to begin my work there regularly. My uncle's kindness did not cease with the hospitality he showed me then. He said that if my father had been alive he would certainly have made me a present of a horse on my starting in the country. He, Uncle Colin, was going to do this. He gave me Sultan, and as this brave old steed was my constant companion for five years I think I must tell here something about him.

One day in May my bearer (native valet) came to say that a horse had come for me. I went out and there saw the most thoroughbred little Arab I ever saw. In height only just over fourteen hands he would be reckoned a pony at home yet he did not look small. From his small beautifully shaped head to his long white silky tail he looked an aristocrat in every line and feature. A broad forehead, a large and intelligent eye, broad neck, round compact barrel and beautiful clean limbs, all marks of the true Arabian. He was then seventeen years old and had been bought for me from Colonel Brownlow, RE who found the horse too difficult for him to manage. In colour he was a 'flea bitten' grey, a very good 'caste' colour for an Arab and I have not the least doubt he was of the very purest blood.

I found him as pleasant to ride as he was handsome to look at, but before very long found out that his weak point was bolting and had my difficulties with him. I used generally to ride him to parade in the mornings, but one morning I had occasion to go not to the regular parade ground but to the field work ground which was in another direction. Sultan positively refused to go - until at last getting impatient I struck him, with the little cane in my hand, a smart cut over the shoulders. He started, gave a plunge, and away at full gallop for the parade ground but with his rider determined that he should not go to the parade ground. The actual result was a devious mid-way course over roads and ditches, finally stopping at the orderly room where as my helmet was off with the chin-strap however still held between my teeth I was the subject of some chaff from my brother officers. I adjusted my head gear and again turned my horse's head towards my object. I got him part of the way all right but he wheeled again and bolted straight for his stable. Round my compound was a low mud wall with a ditch on the far side. He took this slanting and kicked heavily on landing, sending me over his head into my helmet whence my bearer extricated me, while the horse, who was in this case the conqueror regained his stall.

On another occasion I was, on a very hot evening, on my way back from bathing in the canal; and being in a bit of a hurry pushed Sultan into a canter over the grass near the church. This canter became a gallop and I found I could not hold him. In front of us was a road with young trees newly planted, round each of which was a circular wall some four feet high and perhaps twelve feet in diameter. I put the horse straight at one of these thinking he would either stop or swerve or in some way let me get a pull - a mad idea, which fortunately the horse was too good for. He simply pulled himself together and cleared the whole thing at a bound! Like the hunting Frenchman I did not remain, and old Sultan got back to the stables by himself, once more the conqueror. Some seven years afterwards I was walking with another man along that same road. I stopped opposite a tall young tree on the side of the road. 'What are you looking at?' said my companion. 'I jumped over that tree and its protecting walls some seven years ago on an Arab horse,' I said. My companion looked very incredulous but said nothing.

However Sultan was not always to be the master. Within six months my horse and I were on perfect terms. I could hold him easily in the fastest gallop and steady him at any obstacle. It was a rare pleasure to ride him then, feel him working up to his bit and enjoying the fun of it. Brave old horse! If Whyte-Melville's famous words are true then truly I do expect you to give me joyous greeting in the land of the hereafter.

The Roorkee Bridge (looking upstream, Ganges Canal)

Roorkee itself, a small, pretty station some seventeen miles from the Sewalik hills, owes its existence to a huge aqueduct carrying the Ganges Canal over the Solani river. The Government had set up large workshops and a civil engineering college at this point, and it had become the headquarters of military engineers throughout India, augmented after the Mutiny by half a British infantry battalion.

The duties being light, the hills near and the countryside full of game, the place became popular with RE officers. The CRE was Colonel Maunsell, a fine old soldier who had been severely wounded in the Mutiny; his wound was generally supposed to be the cause of a slight eccentricity, but he was beloved by all. Besides the colonel, his second-in-command and his adjutant, there were about twenty junior officers, about sixty European NCOs and seven companies of (non-european) Bengal Sappers and Miners.

I was given the choice whether to apply for appointment in 1) the Public Works Department 2) Railways 3) Irrigation 4) General Military duties. I thought it prudent to wait a while before deciding and meanwhile set myself to learn Hindustani, in which language I passed the first examination after six months.

But after that the idleness began to be wearisome and I was not sorry when I eventually did leave Roorkee to take up harder work and greater responsibility.

The outlet for energy on the part of the officers was sport. A keener lot of sportsmen it would be difficult to find than the senior RE officers then at Roorkee. The mess was quite a marvel of hunting trophies. Twenty-five varieties of horns adorned the mess room walls; tiger, leopard and bear skins covered the floors. The letter box was formed of a tiger's head, the hat racks were stag's horns. Every week - generally I regret to say on Sundays - during the cold weather there was organised a hunt for the mighty boar, and there never was wanting game for the mess table, during the cold season at all events. There was fishing too. I have caught 24lb weight of mahseer - the Indian salmon - in the course of an afternoon within a few miles of the cantonment.

This leisure time was happily enough spent by officers, but it was quite different with the European NCOs. They had neither the means nor the desire for field sports. One way was open to them - among others -for whiling away the time, and that was drink. An enormous number of men at that time were periodically either stupidly or actively drunk, to their moral and physical ruin.

There was a temperance society of which I was President, and which held weekly meetings. It did some good, more than I thought at the time, though many were left untouched. This work brought me into touch with

Gilson Gregson, a Baptist missionary, whose whole-hearted efforts later resulted in one-sixth of the whole British fighting force joining the association.

The general tone of Roorkee, however was not religious. There was little immorality or open vice, but simply neglect of Christian duty such as Sunday worship. Attendance at cantonment Chapel was miserably small. I used often to go on Sunday evenings to worship with the Methodists, whose young American pastor became a firm friend.

When there was so little work to be done, leave was of course easy to obtain. One was entitled to two months in the year, but 'station leave' up to ten days was readily granted. Two fellows went for a six months tour in Tibet, another went shooting for six months in Kashmir, and so on; during the hot weather, numbers at Roorkee dwindled considerably.

The Workshops, Roorkee

The first leave I took was early in April for a day or two to see the Hardwar Fair. Hardwar, some eighteen miles from Roorkee is where the Ganges issues from the hills, a clear swift and beautiful stream. It is a place of much sanctity among the Hindus who go there periodically to bathe, and at the beginning of April each year there is a regular religious festival. Combined with the festival is a horse fair where animals from all parts of the country are brought for sale, and consequently numbers of cavalry officers and others used to come to purchase remounts.

This horse fair was generally held on an island in the river, and to facilitate traffic it was customary for the sapper companies to make two pontoon bridges across from the mainland to this island. Two companies were sent annually for this purpose and as the neighbouring country abounded with game it was always a favourite duty with officers.

The horse fair itself was much like a horse fair anywhere else but the whole surroundings of the place, the wooded hills, the beautiful river, the picturesque temples, the crowds of earnest pilgrims, made a very interesting scene and I was very glad I had gone. The great engineering works at the head of the Ganges Canal are also at Hardwar and are most interesting. Between this place and Roorkee the Canal passes under rivers, through rivers, and over rivers by various triumphant works.

The next leave I took was for a few days with Will and Susie Willcocks on a visit to his old father and stepmother. Captain and Mrs Willcocks lived at Dehra Dun, a most beautiful little station forty-three miles from Roorkee between the Sewalik Hills and the Himalayas. The interval between these hill ranges is a valley about 1200 feet above sea level enjoying a fairly temperate climate and of amazing fertility and beauty. When I went there in April the hedgerows were one mass of rose blossoms among the feathery bamboos and the dark full foliage of the mango trees.

Captain and Mrs Willcocks were most kind and hospitable. He was a very interesting old man whose society I much enjoyed. He had begun life as a volunteer soldier in the Carlist war of 1836. After it he had gone home again, so full of military zeal that he enlisted in the Bengal Horse Artillery and came out to India about 1837, never to return home. He served through the first Afghan War and went to Kabul with Sir F Pollock. After that he got into the Public Works Department and was promoted to a commission. He married shortly after this (it was his second wife whom I met) and had five sons, all of whom got into the Government service in India, one a clergyman, one a doctor, two engineers, and a soldier, who at the time I write of was a cadet at Sandhurst, and afterwards became a very prominent officer.

Captain Willcocks was then Executive Engineer of the roads and canals in Dehra Dun, which was pretty easy work I fancy. The canals were only little tiny irrigation cuts. Close to his house was the headquarters of the 2nd Goorkha Regiment, a very crack corps. Will Willcocks and I did a little shooting chiefly at quail and jungle fowl, among the beautiful woods and valleys of the Dun. But we did not get much sport owing to the fact that the soldiers of the Goorkha Regiment are all keen sportsmen and prevent much game from accumulating near their lines.

One day however when shooting through a barley field with some clumps of furze in it I unexpectedly put up a splendid leopard. Much to my sorrow I had only No 10 shot in my cartridges so had the mortification of seeing the splendid beast bound away without getting a chance at him. He ran past the line of beaters or I think I should have had a crack at him; as it was, I reflected, I could scarcely expect to kill him dead with such small shot and if wounded he would go straight for the nearest man - a half-naked coolie.

We went for a few days to Mussoorie where John Willcocks was then at school, the same school where all the brothers had been educated. I was very much struck with Mussoorie; the houses are perched on the top of hills and ridges, as far as possible from the valleys. The only roads in the place are bridle paths, protected from the steep hillside or khud by railings. Hill ponies are ridden by most of the gentlemen and some ladies, though the latter could also be carried in jampans or litters on four men's shoulders.

Near Mussoorie is Landour, a convalescent depot where at 7000 feet above sea level British soldiers could recover strength after the heat of the plains. Later in 1877, and twice after that, I visited my Pringle cousins at Mussoorie.

I afterwards paid another visit to Dehra Dun in February 1878. The garrison of Roorkee was engaged in various sporting contests with that of Dehra, the sports lasting for a week. I rode the whole way this time. The first night I spent at a dak bungalow at the edge of the Sewalik Hills and remember I had a magnificent view of the sun setting far away over the plains of India in gorgeous colours. Next morning I started very early and rode old Sultan through the beautiful Mohan Pass of the Sewalik Hills where a first rate road connects Dehra Dun with the plains. It was a beautiful ride and most enjoyable. I was engaged to play in a two days' cricket match and I rode back after the match was over.

I may mention that the telephone had just been invented then. We rigged up one in our mess and another in the Goorkha mess at Dehra forty-five miles off and we used in the evenings to hold conversations with our brethren in arms at the other and relative to the day's sport.

The hot weather of 1877 will long be remembered for its intensity and the failure of the rain. In July when the monsoon usually had burst there were only a few little showers and then the heavens again became as brass and the earth like a brick kiln.

In northern India it was bad enough but in southern India it brought on one of the most awful famines in Indian history. Personally I saw nothing of it, but it was brought home vividly to me by the fact that Uncle Colin was sent to manage the relief works. He and I with some others had been planning an expedition to Kashmir. We had got all the necessary arrangements and were to form a party of five or six. Had it come off, it would have been truly charming. But it was not to be. I alone of the party went there, and though I enjoyed myself immensely, such enjoyment would undoubtedly have been enhanced by the society of the others who were to have come.

One day in August I got a letter from Uncle Colin (whom I was constantly seeing at Roorkee) telling me to come to Meerut at once, as he was off to Madras, and had been in Simla conferring with the authorities there as to what was to be done. When I got the letter I got two days' leave at once, rode into Saharanpur, got a lift in a goods train to Meerut and arrived at Uncle Colin's house about midnight several hours before he expected me. He was sleeping in the middle of his compound on a charpoy (or bed of the country) when I arrived; after greeting me he ordered another to be brought out for me and so five minutes after my arrival I was quietly asleep too under the stars. Next morning he told me that there had been difficulties in the administration of Mysore. The authorities there were not anxious to meet the Viceroy's views, and so Uncle Colin had been offered, in very flattering terms, the position of Chief Engineer for the famine relief works, a delicate post to fill, for it involved his relieving and practically superseding a senior officer of engineers then holding it. I did not see my uncle again for two years, during which time he fought the famine with philanthropic energy, and unquestionably saved the lives of many of the poor people there.

The Dhunowree Works (looking upstream, Ganges Canal, mile 13)

The Kashmir party was however at an end. I got leave for September and October and started with two servants and a little tent to avail myself of the 'pass' I had from the Government to travel in that foreign territory. I had a companion with me for the first ten days in a brother officer named Harrison who was travelling as far as the capital of Kashmir, Srinagar.

We travelled first by rail to a little town called Gujranwala some eighty miles north of Lahore and perhaps forty from Bhimber which is the first town in Kashmir territory and lies at the foot of the hills. This route for entering Kashmir sometimes called the Bhimber route and sometimes the Pir Panjal route, is the route which used to be traversed by the Mughal Emperors when they travelled from Delhi to spend their summers in Kashmir. Harrison and I spent a day or two - one being Sunday - in the somewhat dreary and hot dak bungalow at Gujranwala, our heavy baggage meantime getting on by easy stages to Bhimber. We caught it up by travelling in a mail cart the whole way and then for the next nine days we walked all our marches averaging about sixteen miles a day till we reached Srinagar. That nine days march was truly delightful. We crossed the ranges of mountains separating the plains of India from the Vale of Kashmir, each range higher than the one before, till at last we crossed the Pir Panjal pass at a height of 11,000 feet above sea level and began to descend. Our road was through beautifully wooded valleys and along clear flowing rivers, past old ruined temples and rest houses of bygone ages. Needless to say, the scenery was one of infinite variety and magnificence and the climate gradually grew colder and colder from the fearful heat of the plains to the bitter cold of the summit of the Pass.

At heights we put up in rest houses of different kinds, our servants cooked our food and our baggage was carried on the backs of coolies at the rate of 6d per stage for each load.

Srinagar itself has been called the Venice of Asia, but what an insult to the 'Bride of the Sea'. The only reason for the comparison is that in Srinagar much of the journeying to and fro is by boat, as in Venice. For natural situation Srinagar has many advantages. Beautiful mountains are all round. It is situated on the Jhelum, a broad and placid stream and the banks are well-wooded with poplars and planes or sycamore. The town has one or two fine buildings such as the Maharaja's palace, and there are four or five bridges over the Jhelum, all of wood, which are worth seeing, but for the most part squalor and misery are the leading characteristics of town and population. At the eastern end of the town the Maharaja has built many very pretty houses for the use of English visitors; he has also set apart a beautiful sycamore grove for their tents (where I pitched mine), given a nice piece of turf for games such as cricket and polo, and even supplied some ponies for the latter game from his own royal stables. So he has done everything in his power to encourage English people to come to his capital and stay as long as they like. The place was thronged with English folk all holiday seeking, some of them returning from shooting trips in the wild interior and I saw there at least one collection of trophies which made my mouth water! I engaged a shikari or native hunter to come with me, with a second man to clean and carry guns. The man I got was not a good man, and, as it turned out, he got me very little sport, but it was impossible at that late period of the season to get a really good man. All the best had been engaged long before and were away with their masters in the hills. And further, all the best shooting ground was taken up. I knew this would be so, and so did not anticipate any great sport.

The trade of Srinagar is shawls, embroidered work, metal work, and furs. I got a few specimens to send home, replenished my stock of provisions and then set off in a boat down the Jhelum - a very pleasant mode of travelling - to go to the Sinde Valley where I intended shooting. It was not the direct route but I had written to an old friend, Shirres of the Artillery, to meet me; and we had arranged to meet at a place down the river. However when I got there I found that he had changed his mind and gone elsewhere so I turned and went up the Sinde Valley by myself.

Some little distance below Srinagar the Jhelum enters a large lake called the Wular Lake, a lovely sheet of water at the foot of a mountain called Haramuk 22,000 feet high. There is another and smaller lake connected with this and up this one I travelled in my boat amid the most lovely scenery.

I stayed in the glens of the Sinde Valley for about four weeks living a life of healthy activity and great independence. One could encamp where one chose, and shoot where one chose with this restriction only -the sportsman's unwritten law - that if another sportsman had his tent pitched in any glen he was not to be disturbed in it. Living was very cheap only 1/6d a day, and that for the best of everything. The scenery of course was superb beyond all description and the climate most delightful.

How fortunate was I living there, while in Europe at that moment the deadly struggle was going on round Plevna, and in Mysore thousands were dying of famine, a famine which was to spread the following year to the fair valley where then I was.

The sport I had was not great. There were plenty of bears, who used to come out on the moonlight nights to eat the walnuts off the trees, and it was very exciting fun going after them but I did not shoot many; only two, though I lost four more wounded. For the latter part of my time I was chiefly occupied in stalking the great bara singh or red deer of the Himalayas, very good sport, but I had hard lines and only got one, which supplied my camp with excellent meat for about ten days!

Early in October there was a heavy fall of snow which forced me to quit my high camping ground and seek a milder climate. This snow was most unusual, for generally it does not come till November. The rice crop was still ungathered and for the most part spoilt by this snow, and my <u>shikari</u> expressed to me grave fears of scarcity in the following year which alas! were only too surely realised. The governing class in Kashmir, a small proportion of the population, are Hindus, aristocratic and handsome men (some quite fair) but most hard and tyrannical. The large bulk of the population are Muslims ground down to a degree of poverty and misery such as I have never seen in British India. I believe the grasping nature of the Hindus appeared during the famine year in more hideous prominence than ever.

On my return to Srinagar I found the Pir Panjal passes were blocked with snow so there was no alternative for me but to go back by the other route down the Jhelum to Murree and Rawal Pindi, a longer but easier way than the other. It was of course a pleasant variety.

I started down the Jhelum in a boat with all my belongings to go as far as that end of the Wular Lake where the Jhelum issues a swift and brawling torrent about as big as the Tay at Perth. There the road begins which goes to Murree and India, some ten marches. When I crossed the Wular Lake it was simply one mass of wild fowl all on their way from their breeding grounds in Central Asia to spend the cold weather in the plains of India. I went out in a small canoe and in a very short time bagged several 'for the pot'. Had I been intent on wanton slaughter I might have shot a large number. As it was with every shot I fired, thousands rose quacking in the air wheeling around me.

I was fortunate enough to meet another companion on my return journey in a Captain WH Johnstone, RE who was returning to India. We travelled very pleasantly together to Murree and Rawal Pindi.

The march was a very pleasant one through beautiful wooded hills along the banks of the rapid Jhelum. We followed the left bank for about eight days, putting up at nights in rest houses similar to those on the Pir Panjal route, until on the eighth day we crossed the river by a suspension bridge into British territory at a part of the road two stages from Murree. This is a hill station which was formerly the headquarters of the Punjab Government in summertime. I only stayed there for part of a day so did not see much of it. It appeared to me however that it was cleaner, the roads better and the trees more variegated than Mussoorie although the hills around were not so steep and high.

Three marches more from Murree and we reached Rawal Pindi, a large station on the plains. There I spent two days with many old artillery friends leaving by <u>dak ghari</u> on 29th October for Jhelum the terminus then of the railway and 100 miles from Lahore - at Jhelum the 32nd Pioneers were stationed. My cousin Alick Samuells and his wife were there and I dined with them, both very hearty and kind. The regiment was then just starting for Quetta. I arrived at Roorkee again on 31st October.

I spent the winter of 1877-78 in a very lazy fashion. I passed my examination (lower standard) in Hindustani shortly after my return from Kashmir so had no need to trouble myself with the 'black classics' just then. Regimental work and duty was of course the very lightest. I applied for an appointment on the Irrigation Department of the Public Works and got a reply that as a vacancy occurred I might get such, but the chance was remote. So I had no better prospect than cricket, shooting, hunting, fishing in the immediate present. And these I may say I applied myself to with much vigour. In addition to old Sultan on whom I had many a splendid gallop I had a little pony and a riding camel, the last a most useful animal capable of going long distances at a jog-trot and carrying a considerable amount of luggage. I used him much for shooting purposes, and I found that from his back I had an excellent coign of vantage from which to spy whether there were any herd of antelope about the adjacent country. I often went out after large game but was very unsuccessful. With small game however it was not so and I became a very fair shot at snipe.

I may mention here an instance of singular instinct on the part of Sultan. We were pig-sticking not far from a river noted for its dangerous quicksands, but which could be forded at certain established points known to the natives. I was outside a sugar cane field waiting for it to be beaten, when a pig broke cover some distance from me and made across the bed of the river, broken undulating ground covered with coarse grass and bushes. Of course I pursued at full speed when, coming to the top of some rising ground I saw below me a large pool of water perhaps fifteen yards broad of unknown depth and covered with weeds. I could not stop and the next minute Sultan and I were tumbling over one another in the water. He was out first and made for the river; when he got to its bank he paused and instead of going across he trotted up the bank for a good way until he came to one of the regular fords when he crossed and galloped straight home. He might have crossed at any point but in some way his instinct warned him not to try it.

I spent Christmas with my cousins Dr and Mrs Pringle at Meerut and he and I had a good gallop after the hounds there - for at Meerut there was a regular pack of fox hounds.

But it was with no regret that at last in February 1878 I got an order to proceed to the Swat River Canal being posted to the Punjab Irrigation Department as an assistant engineer. My orders were to proceed to Amritsar and report myself there to the Superintending Engineer Bari Doab Circle, in which Circle the Swat Canal was situated.

So I left Roorkee and the Bengal Sappers and Miners on the 3rd March 1878. regretted I believe by a good many people, at least so they were kind enough to say.

3
The Swat River Canal

In the extreme north-west of British India lies the Peshawar Valley, a roughly circular plain about sixty miles in diameter, which until 1853 was Afghan territory and is still inhabited by Afghans, or Pathans.

The plain is divided in two by the Kabul river, which after flowing eastwards through the Khyber Pass, leaves Peshawar city some twelve miles on its right and finally joins the great Indus at Attock. The Kabul river is itself joined by the Swat river, rising in the Hindu Kush mountains far in the north; this river enters the Peshawar plain at a place called Abazai. Here it is a clear and rapid stream about the size of the Tweed at Melrose.

That portion of the plain south of the Swat and Kabul rivers was always fertile and well cultivated. The northerly portion however, with equally good soil was (in 1878) bare and barren, thinly populated by a wild and fierce people who fought for the few fertile spots with the trans-border tribes. It was a scene of perpetual feuds and lawlessness.

I think it was in 1870 that Sir H Durand, then Lieutenant Governor of the Punjab, thought it would be a good idea to irrigate this part by a canal from the Swat River. An abundant supply of water was all that was needed to make the whole fertile. Surveys were accordingly started, but many engineering difficulties were discovered. Unlike other Indian canals which go along the country's watersheds, this one would have to <u>cross</u> all the natural lines of drainage, hence very large works would be required. Many plans and estimates had to be produced before it was decided which would be best to adopt.

Thus the work was not actually begun till 1876. The Executive Engineer in charge was Lieutenant SL Jacob, RE and his assistants were two RE Lieutenants. As the natives of the country devoted their attention entirely to war and agriculture and would not be induced to work as labourers, gangs of the humble coolie class were imported from the Punjab and worked at first <u>without any protection</u>, contrary I believe to Lieutenant Jacob's recommendation. A terrible catastrophe followed this careless policy. In February 1877 some seventy of these unfortunate men were massacred one night near Abazai and no trace could be found of the murderers, though I know now pretty well who was the instigator. The Punjab Government chose to attribute this partly to the overbearing manner of Lieutenant S, a very unjust charge, for although he certainly had a harsh manner with the natives still there was absolutely no evidence to connect any act of his with this deed. However the result was that pressure was put upon him to leave the canal and go to another department of the Public Works, and I was appointed to succeed him.

I left Roorkee on 2nd March 1878 and proceeded to Amritsar where I reported myself to the Superintending Engineer, a Mr Palmer -who by the way was the only civil engineer I regularly served under while in India. He was very courteous and told me I should have much interesting work to do, though as he evidently was very busy our interview was not a lengthy one. I occupied part of the day in a visit to the Golden Temple, the sacred place of the Sikhs. It is a little open building of pure marble inlaid with coloured stones in beautiful colours and devices, the whole roofed with a gold or at least gilded dome. It stands in the centre of a large tank of marble and is connected with one of the sides by a pier or bridge of marble. In the inside there is no idol, only the sacred book or 'granth', which a Sikh priest reads in a monotonous voice while the faithful come and present offerings of fruit or flowers. They had no objection to my presence in any part of the building as long as I divested myself of my boots and wore the slippers they provided for the purpose.

I went on that evening to Lahore where I spent a day or two at the hospitable home of Captain and Mrs Broadfoot. He was connected with relatives at home and I knew his sisters though I had never seen him before. He showed me all the sights of Lahore, its fort, palace and new public buildings, all interesting though not very striking. Then after leaving him I went by rail to Jhelum, dak ghari to Rawal Pindi where I passed a few hours with the RA fellows and dined at their mess, and then started after dinner by dak ghari for Nowshera, eighty miles off and about seventy miles from Peshawar.

When I awoke the following morning I found we had crossed the Indus and were close to Nowshera which we soon reached. Rows of bare looking barracks on either side of a dusty road constitute the whole station. A dreary looking place in every way. Here I had to cross the Kabul river and proceed in the best way I could fifteen miles to Hoti Mardan the headquarters of the Canal division and of the regiment of Guides. To accomplish this fifteen miles I tried an ekka, the pony-cart of the country, light but awfully uncomfortable for a European. This had first to be ferried across the river in a rather crazy-looking ferry boat and when we had safely reached the further shore we started on our drive.

The road first led up a low rocky hill from the summit of which I could see an immense bare plain in front with the road bare and straight crossing it for about ten miles in an unbroken line. It was a very dreary and very rough road. But the drive came to an end eventually and I found

Swat River Suspension Bridge, built with the assistance of Bengal Sappers Pontoon Section

Swat River Trestle & Crate Bridge, length 420 yards, built by 1st and 6th Companies Bengal Sappers

myself close to three very new-looking houses with evidence of recent work on paths and boundary fences. I stopped at one of these and found it was the Executive Engineer's office. One of the clerks (a native) came to show me the way to the other and as he went he told me that the people of the country were very fierce and blood-thirsty - poor man! The Hindu is a very peaceful creature.

I found a gentleman in the house who introduced himself to me as Lieutenant S. He told me Jacob would be coming soon to Narrai, a place where he suggested we should both set out for that evening. He took me to the Guides' mess, introduced me to the officers there and then in the afternoon we drove twelve miles to the Narrai fort along a road which was absolutely bare except for one small thorn tree about half way.

The Guides are rather a celebrated corps. They were raised originally by Sir Henry Lawrence for service on the northern Frontier, to be recruited from tribes having local knowledge and experience and commanded by picked officers of skill and courage. They consisted of two squadrons of cavalry and eight companies of infantry with about a dozen British officers. The uniform was drab with scarlet facings and the cavalry wore a blue turban. The latter were very poorly mounted and the whole always badly drilled, yet they were wonderful men to march and to fight. They could do fifty miles in the day easily and fight at the end of it. They had always complete transport and equipment so they could always move at any time when called upon. They had recently received the title of 'Queen's Own' of which they were not a little proud and it was thought in the army generally that they gave themselves too many airs. Certainly they had every reason to be proud of their regiment. They had made themselves very comfortable at Mardan. The mess was very pleasant and convenient and in the mess garden were a fine racket court, lawn-tennis courts, a swimming bath, a skating rink and gymnastic apparatus, besides a nice garden. All these we had the use of as honorary members of the mess. One curious custom prevailed - they always dined in plain clothes except when there was some special occasion. I do not know why this slovenly habit was allowed.

Narrai where I went with Lieutenant S was a small square mud fort in the middle of a flat and dreary plain, and close to one of the large masonry works on the Canal, viz;- the Narrai culvert. The fort had accommodation for a large number of work people and for animals, and in one corner was a small house of two stories, two rooms in each storey, which was to be my residence and office for long afterwards. It was anything but a cheerful place, the surroundings were most dreary. Jacob joined us there that night and the following day we returned to Mardan.

I found that my duties were to be as follows:-

Take charge of all the construction of nine miles of the canal and the forts adjacent; superintend all the supply of material for the work, and also help Jacob in making out a revised estimate of the cost of the whole, including the re-designing of some of the chief works, as the work on these nine miles had barely begun and as there were some very big masonry works. On this section it will be seen that I had a pretty fair programme of duty before me. I had also later on charge of the workshops at Mardan.

That evening as Jacob and I were going to mess we met two officers of the Guides, Major Wigram Battye and Major 'Bertie' Hutchinson, two very different men, but both splendid fellows. Alas! they both were cut off in the prime of life, both in the service of their Queen and country, and a little church at Mardan is now built to their special memory. Wigram Battye was a short well-made and very handsome man, the beau ideal of a light cavalry officer. Hutchinson was a big man, with a very quiet manner. We used to call him 'the long man', 'the gentle giant' and so on. I came to know and to like both these men very much and it is in accordance with their life and their death that my introduction to them should have been just as they were starting on a 'border raid'. Jacob had asked Battye 'What is the news?' to which he laughingly replied 'Oh I am full of news, if you were to prick my leg it would all burst out'. We noticed some of the troopers of the regiment assembling on the parade ground, though there was nothing in the conversation at mess that night to lead one to suppose that anything unusual was going to happen. However as it got dark all the officers went away and sure enough the whole regiment paraded and wandered off. Their destination was a refractory village beyond the border which they reached and surrounded by dawn. The tribesmen woke up to find themselves face to face with a powerful force and so after firing a shot or two they gave in, and the Guides returned next day having marched about fifty miles in the twenty-four hours.

These little expeditions occurred two or three times after I went first to the Frontier, gradually they became less necessary and I suppose they are now of rare occurrence. Bertie Hutchinson lost his life in one of them many years after this.

Night travelling in the Punjab

Very soon after this S went away and I began my regular work. I generally spent the greater part of the week along at Narrai, but on Fridays used to go in to Mardan, have a game at polo in the evening with the Guides (if we could not get up a game entirely of officers, some of the native troopers would play and were very good at it). Then on Saturdays I would have a regular long day at estimates with Jacob and his brother, a young Cooper's Hill engineer, who came up to help in these estimates. On Sundays we always had a pleasant day of rest, a swim in the morning in the bath at the mess garden and quiet reading in the forenoon before midday breakfast. Then in the afternoon we always had Divine Service in the ante-room of the mess, which the colonel of the regiment conducted, and then at night after dinner I generally rode back again to Narrai to begin work again on Monday mornings.

In the Guides' mess, though none of the men ever talked about religious matters, there was no profane language, no ribald stories. I never knew anything said there which would shock the most sensitive ears, by any officer of the regiment.

My work at Narrai was much more interesting than the compilation of the plans and estimates, though I was equally inexperienced in both. I had some large engineering works to carry out and looking back upon these works I often wonder how our engineers at home, surrounded by all sorts of machinery and appliances, would care to execute similar work where machinery was unknown. The materials at our disposal were very indifferent. Good stone was certainly to be had, though at some distance from the work. It had to be quarried by native labourers and carried to the site of the work on the backs of camels, bullocks and donkeys, so it could only be obtained in small blocks and of course as a large number of the above animals were required I had to make extensive arrangements for feeding time.

There was no water at the site of any of the works, so wells had to be sunk wherever a masonry work was required, sometimes to a very great depth. Then the only lime we had was what is technically known as fat lime, pure white stuff such as is only used in Europe for white washing. To give this lime the requisite binding quality brick dust (called surkhi) had to be manufactured. This is a very common substance in India, but I had never before heard of it and knew nothing about its manufacture until I found myself ordered to produce large quantities. To burn this in kilns, quantities of wood had to be obtained and that was a matter of some difficulty in a treeless barren land. But contracts were taken for the supply of it by native contractors who brought in loads of it on the backs of mules and bullocks for whom of course more fodder was required. Our lime kilns were in a wild and savage gorge of the mountains some sixteen miles from Narrai, where I had to go periodically - a jolly ride.

In spite of all these drawbacks in the way of poor material the engineering work was bold and effective. Concrete, which in England is almost invariably made with the best cement, was there made with our fat lime and I built at Narrai a concrete arch, semi-circular twenty-two feet span, 127 feet long, which was as strong and sound as any cement work I ever saw. Indeed I never saw another concrete arch of that size anywhere. But of course it was made with the utmost care and I never left the work for a day, for six weeks.

I had four horses or ponies in constant work. Every morning two of them were sent out ready saddled, and I rode from six to twelve miles on each - I rose at 4 or 5 am, was in the saddle and inspecting works till 9 when I came back and had a bath and breakfast. Then I worked at accounts till late in the afternoon when I used to take a short nap, have a cup of tea and out again on the works till it was dark. Then dinner and to bed early.

Besides the works and duty connected therewith I used to work at the Pushtu language. It was easy to pick up a colloquial knowledge of this as it was spoken all round me, but I aspired to a more perfect knowledge and so engaged a teacher in the shape of an old mullah or Muslim divine who gained a living as a teacher of Persian and Pushtu. I don't think he knew much about the former language however. He was a very fine looking man with a pleasant open face and strong physique. His beard was dyed a rich red, like many of the old men of the Afghans, (denoting a pilgrimage to Mecca).

I had much interesting talk with this old chap. We used to converse a great deal about religion and I learned much about the Muslim creed from him. It is a wonderful arrangement of natural devotion and of pandering to man's animal nature. In return I told him much about Christ and read him many passages of Scripture. I gave permission to the Muslims at Narrai to build a little mosque near the fort, where every day they assembled for prayer, and my friend was the chaplain so to speak (muezzin). He had a very rich voice and used to sing out the azan or call to prayer in a very sonorous manner five times a day. He was a very decent rider too and often accompanied me in my perigrinations.

Bridge over Sakar Nulla on Mardan/Dargai Road

The even tenor of my life that summer was thus filled up by hard but useful and healthy work and was only interrupted by an occasional flying visit to Peshawar or Abazai.

At Peshawar which was about thirty miles in a direct line from Mardan, were quartered two companies of the Bengal Sappers under Lieutenants Dove, Campbell and Talbot. I went in first in March to see Campbell. I found the place looking very pretty for in spring all sorts of garden flowers grow in profusion. It was a very large and well-wooded garrison cantonment, being situated about a mile (at the nearest point) from the native city which was very large and filled with all sorts of wild barbarians from Central Asia. The Mall or main road of the cantonment was a splendid thoroughfare about two miles long, a wide and beautifully kept road with rows of well-wooded gardens and houses on each side. The barracks there seemed all strong and substantial but private houses were built of mud bricks and with flat mud roofs. The first night I was in Peshawar staying with Campbell there was very heavy rain and in the middle of the night we were both awakened by the descent of a stream of mud through the roof! It was a matter of quite ordinary occurrence.

At Peshawar I made the acquaintance, always cherished with pleasure, of the missionaries Messrs Jukes and Hughes. The former had known my uncle William in Devonshire - the latter was, when I first visited Peshawar, at home on leave - they always had a warm and hospitable welcome for me when I went to Peshawar saying in the Afghan proverb 'My house is yours'. This hospitality they extended to all natives who came in to the city, so that in the Mission Compound one often saw very curious specimens of barbarous humanity. During the cold weather the missionaries often came and stayed with me, itinerating in the adjoining districts. I used after their example to read the gospel to the natives at Narrai on Sunday afternoons and talk to them about it.

Abazai was built by Lord Napier of Magdala about the year 1850 when he was Chief Engineer of the Punjab. It is a large fort of the old French bastioned type with a big square keep inside where the officers' quarters are situated. It was built on the left bank of the Swat River close to where the latter issues from the mountains and is at the extreme north-west corner of British India.

The headworks of the canal where the waters of the Swat River are drawn off in the canal for the irrigation of the great plain are situated in a gorge of the hills about two miles above Abazai, and it was the duty of Lieutenant Cather my brother assistant on the works, to construct the canal from this headwork to a place called Ziam nine miles from Narrai. I had charge of this sub-division at a later period. It had much more interesting work in it than even the one I had then charge of, for besides the headworks, there were forts for defence, there were two immense aqueducts where the canal passed over two mountain torrents, two super-passages where mountain torrents passed over the canal, and several culverts and bridges.

The scenery round Abazai was bold, though the heat in the months of June, July and August was intense. Cather however made himself very comfortable there. He was a very big powerful man, very like the typical John Bull, a first rate engineer, a capital horseman and a kindly pleasant fellow. In after years he gained much military fame in the Afghan, Egyptian and Burmese wars, and would no doubt have risen to the highest distinction but for his untimely death in Burma in 1889. At the time I speak of he was building a very nice house in the fort just over-looking the river, which I occupied in the following year.

Jacob went home on leave in the summer of 1878 for three months, and left Cather and me to work the canal by ourselves. Cather was quite in his element. He had four of Jacob's horses to look after besides five of his own and he used to experiment upon them all in tandem driving with me to the imminent risk of our bones, though we never had any smashes strange to say. During that time there were heavy rains and floods which did much damage to our works and kept us very busy; the excitement of fighting these floods was most fascinating and victories when we did achieve them most triumphant.

Meantime I got on with my Pushtu studies and could converse fluently enough with the people of the country. It helped me immensely in establishing confidence. Often I have ridden into a village unarmed and without escort to see the headman about some affair of business, and have been greeted by him with cordiality and hospitality. I made friends with one young khan or chief about my own age whom I used sometimes to go out shooting with and to whom I was as hospitable as possible when he came to see me. To refuse the hospitality of these most hospitable people would be a deadly affront though it was often difficult to enjoy it. I remember once I was offered a bowl of hot milk mixed with grease or fat. I had to shut my eyes and take a gulp, but it was dreadful! But sometimes the food they gave me was very acceptable to a hungry horseman. Omelettes cooked on a sort of cake or scone were a common dish, a fowl boiled with rice and spices was another - of course there were no knives or forks, but an attendant stood by with water to wash the hands as often as desired.

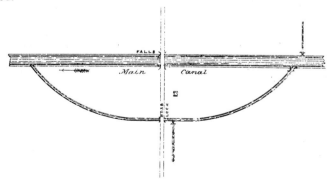

Still the dangerous element in the country was not wanting. We had a hospital at the works for the benefit of such of the men as got sick or met with accidents. One of the patients who was grateful for a cure told Cather that it had been settled that the three European Officers were to be killed and the murderers had each been appointed! Another time when I was riding from Ziam to Narrai nine miles along a road with low bushes on either side I was begged by a friendly native not to go as he knew there were men lying in wait for me. Of course I went, but nothing came of either of these threats. One night however an attempt was made on the life of a native groom in my service. who was leading old Sultan along the road. The man was badly wounded but he struck his assailant's horse over the head with a stick, and the animal bolted with the would be assassin into the surrounding darkness. All round one used to hear of blood feuds and murders, but I fear that was but the ordinary state of the tribes.

One day in August when I went into the Guides' mess at Mardan I found unusual excitement. "Have you heard the news? There is an Embassy to be sent to Kabul, Stewart and Wigram Battye are going with it and 100 sabres." This was the first cloud on the horizon of the great war with Afghanistan that lasted for two years more.

Whether the Government were right or not in sending a mission to Kabul in opposition to the wishes of the Amir I do not now care to say. But for some years past the Amir had hated and distrusted us and he was glad to welcome ostentatiously a Russian Embassy thinking it would annoy us. I dare say it was a trap deliberately set by the Russians. We had just gained a diplomatic victory over them at the Berlin Conference and they sent a mission to Kabul as a counter stroke of policy. The unfortunate Amir was induced to believe that the Russians would help him in the event of war, and he lived long enough, poor man, to find these ideas a chimera, and died in poverty a fugitive from his capital. after his troops had been defeated in two decisive battles.

Preliminaries for the British Embassy which was to be forced on the Amir were speedily settled. Sir Neville Chamberlain was to be the Ambassador, Major Cavagnari his Chief Political Officer; three officers of the Guides and a squadron of 16th Bengal Lancers formed the escort.

On 11th September we had a farewell dinner for them all at the Guides' mess. Thirteen of us were present, ten being Guides' officers. Wigram Battye who sat next to me, told me how he had always longed to see Kabul and now had a chance of doing so. Poor fellow, he never got there - he was killed in action the following spring. His two companions reached Kabul, but both lost their lives there, cut off in the full vigour of manhood. But such is a soldier's life.

It was impossible not to be infected to a certain extent with the prevailing excitement. We all knew that if the Embassy were not accepted or in any way insulted there would be a likelihood of war, and we knew that warlike preparations were going on all over the country. My friend Campbell at Peshawar had no subaltern in his company and I determined if it came to military operations that I should apply to return to military duty and serve under my old school companion and brother officer.

Towards the end of September the Embassy started. But they had barely entered the Khyber Pass when only sixteen miles from Peshawar they were stopped by the Commandant of the fort of Ali Musjid who informed them that he had positive orders from the Amir not to let them pass. The Embassy therefore returned to Peshawar and all the frontier tribes must have chuckled at the British Lion retreating with his tail between his legs. The Government of the day sent word to the Amir that they would give him two months till 20th November to reconsider his decision and if by that time he still refused to accept the Embassy they would declare war against him.

Meantime warlike preparations were made everywhere. Two divisions under Generals Stewart and Biddulph went by Multan to Quetta in the south, another division under General Roberts was to assemble at Kohat and Thull, while a fourth division under General Sir Sam Browne was to assemble at Peshawar. A small part of this had already gone to Jumrood, a fort at the entrance of the Khyber eight miles from Peshawar. I went to see this small force at the beginning of October and I found my old friend Shirres RA with his mountain battery and Lieutenants Dove and Talbot with the 3rd Company of Sappers.

My old chief Colonel Maunsell was appointed to command the engineers of the 1st Division at Peshawar. with Captain Lovett as Brigade Major. I had known the latter at Chatham some years before. I wrote to Colonel Maunsell to ask him, if I resigned my civil work on the canal, to post me to Campbell's company. I got a letter from him eventually to say he would do so, and that he would himself apply for me. He bade me apply through my regular superiors and said he thought there would be no difficulty about it.

Jacob had returned from leave by that time and so I applied through him. He said I had better not go without orders of some sort, to which I replied that of course I would not go without orders but if the military orders came first I would consider them sufficient authority.

The departmental authorities however did not immediately forward my application. They sent back to enquire why I wanted to go; it was evidently inconvenient to let me go just then, and the matter was in a state of abeyance till on Friday the 16th November I got a letter from Campbell saying the Colonel was writing to me to say that it was all right about my coming to him and bidding me join at once. A letter from the Colonel did also reach me to the same effect but owing to a delay in the post did not arrive till a few days afterwards. However this was quite sufficient authority for me and I wrote to Jacob saying I had got these letters and would hand over cash and books to him whenever he liked. He replied by two letters, one an offical one in which he said he would report me for disobedience of orders, the other a private letter jocular and chaffing saying he would come and take over from me and wish me joy of my military glory etc. I was rather in a fix. It was a very serious matter to be reported for disobedience, the gravest military crime, but then I thought from Maunsell's letter that my affair was settled and that probably the next post would bring intimation of it to Jacob, who indeed was evidently far from considering the action I proposed as a breach of discipline. So I resolved to brave the consequences and go.

I handed over to Jacob on the Saturday, spent Sunday in Mardan and rode in to Peshawar on the Monday. I met Lovett cantering down the Mall and was greeted joyously by him. I then went to report myself to the Colonel. 'Oh Moncrieff', says he 'I made a mistake, it wasn't you at all that was to be allowed to come, it was Glennie!' This was a nice bit of news! 'Well Sir', I replied, 'it is done now and we must make the best of it. I am certain to get a row in any case.' 'Oh I am not going to send you back now' he said.

The company to which I was now to be attached had already started for Jumrood where the whole division was to assemble, but Colonel Maunsell directed me to remain with him while I collected my campaigning kit etc to join the company next day. I dined that night (together with Colonel Maunsell and several other RE officers) with the officers of the 7th Native Infantry, a very good mess close to the part of Peshawar where the sappers were quartered. This regiment was under an old friend of my father's, a Colonel Stephenson who with his second-in-command, Colonel Worsley, had recognised me one day when dining at the mess with Campbell from my likeness to my parents. On this particular occasion however there was only one officer of the regiment among the eighteen or twenty who sat down to dinner that evening. Among the others were Brigadier General Macpherson, afterwards Sir Herbert Macpherson KCB who distinguished himself so much in this and in the following campaign - a jolly square Pickwick-like individual full of Scots humour.

Next day I started with Captain Lovett for Jumrood eight miles from Peshawar to join the division of the army assembled at the mouth of the Khyber. On the way we passed the Peshawar rifle ranges when Lovett jocularly remarked, "We have done with the grammar and now come the exercises." The road for four miles out of Peshawar is among fields and villages and was crowded with vehicles of all sorts, 'like going to the Derby' as one officer of hussars said, who was riding with us. After the fourth mile however there was only a rough stony plain as far as Jumrood, and long before we came in sight of the old fort there we had reached the tents of the army assembled for the advance next day.

I was soon greeted by many old friends at the sapper camp. most of my old Roorkee comrades were there all in great spirits of course. Campbell had been told that his company was to form part of the advanced guard of the attack and we were to remember the names of any of the men who distinguished themselves by any acts of courage. Our duty was to accompany the horse artillery and throw up breast works as far to the front as the guns could safely reach. This was the programme, but it was not carried out.

That afternoon a telegram was received by Sir Sam Browne from the Punjab Government telling him to order Lieutenant Scott Moncrieff. RE back to his duty on the Swat Canal at once. This telegram of course came to our Brigade Major who referred it to the CRE when he came into camp. Colonel Maunsell coolly refused to obey it. He said that he was not going to let me go back till the action was over and meantime he was going to telegraph Sir Andrew Clarke to beg him to allow me to stay. (Colonel Sir Andrew Clarke was the Public Works Minister). So I remained on, thankful that at all events I should come in for the action and hoping that events might so turn out that I should not eventually be required to go back at all. We were a very merry party in our mess tent that evening and we all turned in early as our hour of parade next morning was to be 5 am. No answer to the <u>ultimatum</u> arrived up to 12 midnight and so war was declared.

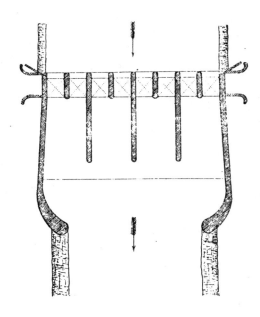

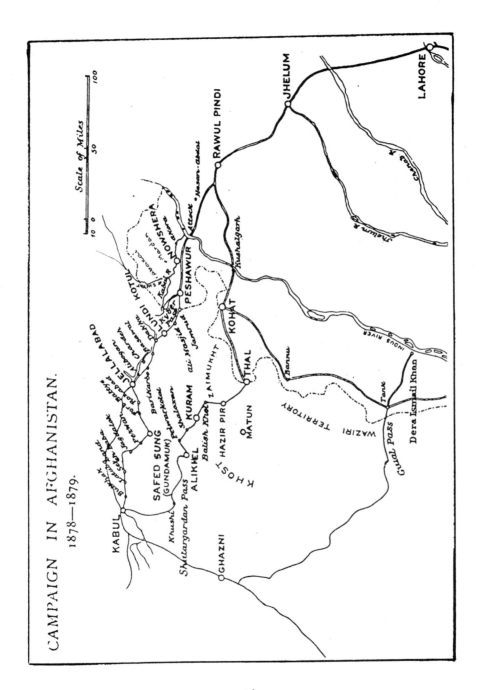

4
Ali Musjid

Although properly speaking we were not at war with the Amir of Afghanistan till the morning of the 21st November, two brigades of infantry under Generals Macpherson and Tytler were sent off from Jumrood on the previous evening to outflank the enemy. The distance they were supposed to travel was twelve miles, according to reconnaissances made by Colonel Stewart of the Guides. Actually it turned out to be twenty seven miles over very steep mountains and without water. Consequently instead of coming up in rear of the enemy by noon the following day they did not reach their goal till late in the evening when the frontal attack had been made and really repulsed.

The Guides infantry took part in this flanking movement and I saw Wigram Battye just starting off on it; he congratulated me much on being with the army. Brigadier General Tytler who commanded the 2nd Brigade was universally admitted to be the best general we had in the division. He was quiet and self possessed, always polite, always more anxious about the comfort of his men than about his own, brave and skilful in his dispositions, resolute in following up victory. He never spared himself and to this must be attributed his death from exposure in the second part of the war. As for Brigadier General Browne, he was so inefficient that he was deprived of his command before a month was over and he was sent back to his regiment in India. The cavalry brigade was under Brigadier General Charles Gough, a very fine soldier but disagreeable man. His brigade major was Captain Combe of the 10th Hussars, a very fine soldier, and perfect cavalry officer. The artillery was under Colonel Williams and the sappers under Colonel Maunsell, who shortly afterwards was promoted to be Major General and as such was second-in-command of the Division.

Sir Sam Browne who commanded the Division had been Colonel of the Guides for many years and had also commanded at Peshawar. He was a tall man with a grizzled beard and one arm; he had had the other cut off twenty years before in a cavalry fight in the Mutiny. Personally a brave man, he was by this time too old to be active and energetic and the whole campaign was spasmodic and wanting in push. His chief staff-officers were Colonels Smith and Sanford. The former was a man of no distinction, the latter was an RE and therefore looked upon with distrust by officers of other branches, who thought him a theorist, but he was unquestionably an able soldier.

The most influential man in the whole division however was the political officer Major Cavagnari. He was at that time probably the most rising man in India. Of a Corsican family, he had got into the Indian army when young, had rapidly pushed his way in frontier politics, had acquired a wonderful power over the tribes there and had learnt to rule them with sword and with presents in a way few men have done in modern times. He had a restless ambition and much personal energy but he played a hazardous game and as we shall see staked his life on a dangerous venture and lost it.

The morning of the 21st November was just dawning when we woke up. A clear starlit sky was overhead and the red streaks of day were just appearing in the east when we paraded. I had never seen my company before and could be of very little assistance to Campbell in getting the tools etc loaded on our mules. My Company Commander was a good deal excited and very wroth with the Regimental Sergeant Major who he said had taken away several of his best animals for other companies. However we got our men together at last and started for the rendezvous of the advanced guard. It was on the top of a low mound, and there clearly defined against the morning sky, I saw two horse artillery guns quite motionless, except the horses' heads tossing and champing at their bits. I confess to feeling my blood stirring in my veins a bit faster than usual for there was an air of business about the whole thing different from a common field day.

The advanced guard consisted of 250 men 14th Sikhs, 250 men 81st Foot, two guns RHA and the 2nd and 3rd Companies of Sappers, the former under Campbell and myself, the latter under Lieutenants Dove and the Hon MG Talbot. Campbell rode his famous charger 'Hotspur', but I was on foot as I think engineers should be when actually fighting.

We started very soon, and in the dim morning light I saw Sir Sam and his staff on the top of a low hill watching his force defile past him. Campbell had gone off to see about something so I was then in command. I pulled the men up to attention and saluted our general as we passed. I may here mention that our uniform was very different from that which we wear in peace time, the blade of my sword being almost the only thing common to both. We had drab coats and trousers, drab helmets, brown leather belts with revolvers and swords.

The road for the first two or three miles wound round low hills and it was sufficiently exciting as we got further and further into the pass expecting to see the enemy round every corner. After a while when we were fairly in the pass we could see some of the enemy's vedettes appearing on the tops of the hills. It was broad daylight now and the sun's bright rays warmed the sharp frosty air. The 14th Sikhs now got orders to extend and skirmish and it was a fine sight to see them with their yellow turbans spread out over the hills like a fan steadily advancing and driving back the outposts. Soon we came to a very rocky bit of the road but we sappers had our picks and crowbars out at once and cleared away a path which the horse artillery guns rattled over easily. Then up a little further into a wild rocky glen, when the Adjutant of the RA (Captain Rothe) came galloping up with 'Room for the guns please' and the horse artillery galloped by crashing over the stones. Ah! It makes my veins tingle still when I think of it though it is a good many years ago now. I felt we were in for the beginning of the fray and what soldier would not have been gladly there!

But there is many a slip etc. We were not destined to take the part we had been ordered and had expected. The programme of yesterday was not carried out. owing I suppose to indecision on the General's part. Lovett came riding up at that moment. 'Both sapper companies are to go back to that bad bit of road', says he, 'the artillery of the main body cannot pass it and you must do it thoroughly so as to allow every gun to pass without delay'. There was nothing for it but to return about half a mile and instead of going on with the guns and into action with them we had to blast rocks and clear away until a broad and level road was made, while we saw infantry, cavalry, artillery. and (unkindest cut of all) the other sapper companies pass us by and go up the pass. To this day I cannot understand why we were thus shunted. Campbell and Talbot were simply furious. Dove who commanded both companies was cool and quiet but he evidently felt it too.

By the time we had cleared the road we heard the first gun booming above us, it was then nearly noon and from that time until dark the artillery duel went on without ceasing. We had fondly hoped that as soon as the road on that particular place was cleared we might go on but our hopes were again destroyed. Lovett came back to tell us we were to improve some other places on the road, hold the pass until evening so as to guard against any attack by the tribesmen and then at night return to Jumrood and guard the baggage which had been left there. There was nothing for it but to obey.

Once I thought I was going to have a bit of a fight to myself. I had gone with some fifty men to improve a bit of road, when I observed a large body of tribesmen armed on a hill above me. I told the NCO under me to keep the mules under cover and if the tribesmen opened fire to take charge of them while I would myself lead the attack on the hill above. But they let us work on without molestation.

In the evening we went sadly back to Jumrood, placed our sentries round the baggage of the division and turned in to our tents. But before dark our men had captured four of the enemy, who had evidently deserted from Ali Musjid. They did not speak Pushtu, being western Afghans from Herat where Persian only is spoken. We did not get much information from them.

Early next morning we heard a single gun fired then shortly afterwards one or two fellows who had ridden out from Peshawar to see the fight the day before but had no official business there, came riding in and among them was Mr Archibald Forbes the celebrated war correspondent of the Daily News. Some wounded men came in also in litters.

Ali Musjid and the Khyber Pass

**   **   **   **   **

From these sources we learnt what had happened the day before. The two horse artillery guns had pushed on as we knew and had of course been the first to come into action. But wherever they came into sight of the enemy they were at once saluted by a round shot or shell from the enemy's artillery, for the latter knew the range of every piece of rising ground and therefore long before our men had found their range the enemy's guns were bowling them over. They had shifted their ground several times but always at the same disadvantage. Had the original programme been adhered to and the two sapper companies been there to throw up earthworks I think the gain would have been considerable. Then the general brought up his field artillery and his elephant batteries, but with all his guns he had fewer than the enemy and they knew every yard of the ground and he did not. Further, their guns were behind protecting works and were in positions difficult to hit; our guns were out on the open much exposed. Our cavalry were of course useless. Our infantry brigades were pushed forward among ravines etc, but kept without any sort of coherent plan while the artillery duel was going on at long ranges. The sappers were used as infantry to escort the guns I think.

This sort of thing went on all day until the evening came and then 'something must be done you know', more especially as the artillery ammunition was nearly expended. The enemy not only occupied the rocky fort of Ali Musjid but had also defensive works running up the ridges on either side of the valley. Against the southern ridge an attack was ordered and the 14th Sikhs and 27th Northern Infantry carried it out gallantly, but they were met with a furious fire which drove them back with great loss, two officers of the 27th were killed and one of the 14th badly wounded. They had to retire and darkness fell with the balance of victory so far on the Afghan side.

However just about that time the two brigades under Macpherson and Tytler turned up on the enemy's rear and this was more than he could stand. If he had held out and fought to the last we should have had a tremendous battle on the 22nd. That Sir Sam fully expected this is proved by the fact that we had to send from Jumrood during the night all the ammunition we could and I believe he ordered a general advance early in the morning. But a curious thing happened. Before dawn an adventurous spirit, Jack Chisholm of the 9th Lancers, thought he would like to see what the enemy was about and so went cautiously to the front, heard nothing, went on further till he got inside the enemy's works, saw nothing there and rode boldly into Ali Musjid where he found only a mule, and the enemy all gone! As the army was advancing to the attack, they beheld Master Jack riding quietly out of the fort with his mule! Inside the fort lay the slain, and all the baggage and food of the garrison but not a living creature.

The Guides told me afterwards that they had come upon the pass above Ali Musjid and during the night had heard bodies of men pass by, some on horse, some on foot. They had captured some and fought with others, but the darkness had favoured the majority and they escaped for the most part.

Thus ended the battle of Ali Musjid. It was not a great victory. We turned the enemy's position, it is true and captured all his guns, but in no very creditable fashion. There was much indecision and vacillation about our dispositions and the whole business was unsatisfactory. Perhaps I felt, and still feel, sore about the way my Company was used, but this I know, that a General who so little understood the use of technical troops (engineers) as to employ them solely as infantry in guarding baggage etc., would have been ridiculed in any European army.

We got orders to send forward the whole baggage of the army and to act as rear guard when it had all been despatched. For the whole of that day therefore camels were loaded and sent off in strings up the pass and it was not until evening that we were able to parade and go off ourselves. We marched all night, a very wretched march for we had to keep in rear of the interminable string of camels and accommodate our pace to their slow walk. Every time a load fell off, every five minutes or so, there was a halt till it was loaded again and so it was not till noon next day that we reached Ali Musjid very sleepy and hungry.

Beyond the glen where the two RHA guns had pushed to the front there was a very good road winding round the hill side. This had been made by Captain Mackeson in 1840 and though it had evidently not been repaired for thirty-eight years it was still in very good order. Up Mackeson's road the guns had travelled quite easily till at its summit they came upon a broad plateau about three miles from Ali Musjid whence the enemy's position could be seen quite well. It was a precipitous rock some 400 feet above the bottom of the valley, standing alone. but with rocky hills all round. A little fort was on the top of the rock wall armed with artillery, there was another battery of two guns halfway up the rock and at the bottom another gun to sweep the approach up the stream. On either side of the valley there were lines of stone breast works with guns at intervals. The whole position was strong and carefully planned. Some said it had been laid out by Russian engineers; this however I can hardly believe.

The main body of the army had pushed on through the Khyber Pass to Dakka, a fort at the Afghan end, where there was no resistance. Our two companies were ordered to remain at Ali Musjid, improve the roads and bring down the captured guns. These guns by the way were mostly old-fashioned brass smooth bores. They had been very gallantly served by the foe; I saw one dead man lying over his piece, who had evidently been wounded for his head was bandaged, but he had stuck to his post and fallen there like a hero. I do not think the enemy's losses were very great, at least I did not see more than a dozen bodies altogether, which were of course honourably buried.

Afghans with their old weapons

**   **   **   **   **

I remained at Ali Musjid four or five days working at the roads by day and not infrequently disturbed at night by attacks from the tribesmen who used to fire volleys into our camps, not doing much damage but giving us a good deal of annoyance. I had hoped I was going to be left with Campbell in peace but alas! I got a letter one day, to say that the Colonel's appeal to Sir A Clarke had been of no avail and that I must now return to the Swat Canal. It was a sad blow, but there was no help for it. I had therefore to retrace my steps and once more return to my work at Narrai.

There the storm burst on my devoted head. I had returned to my former duties for a very few days when I got a stern letter from the Punjab Government calling for a written explanation of my conduct. In reply to this I took the blame, as much as I could without bravado, on my own shoulders. I quoted Colonel Maunsell's letter but referred in other respects as little as possible to him, for I supposed that he would give an independent statement of the case to the Military Department. I could not shield myself behind him and did not attempt to do so. After one or two letters of this sort there followed a long and ominous silence. I had got into a very nice mess and what the upshot would be I could not tell.

Meantime I had a great deal of interesting work to keep me constantly employed and my mind from brooding over the disappointment I had had. The work was now extending daily and by this time I thoroughly understood it and had all the executive machinery fairly in my grasp. The weather too was remarkable. From September 1878 to the end of March 1879 there were unclouded days, not a drop of rain. At nights there was very hard frost and the mornings and evenings were bitterly cold but the middle of the day was sunny and bright invariably.

As the Guides had left Mardan their place was filled by various regiments moving up to the front, but I very rarely went to see them, partly because the very sight of eager warriors made me feel disgusted, partly because my work was all in the district now and repaid my attention, insomuch as the more I stuck to it the less trouble eventually I had with it.

Perhaps I was just as well there, for the 1st Division spent the winter in inactivity. Had I not been sent back I should have gone about with the 2nd Company of Sappers doing nothing but continual petty road work. My old friend Mason succeeded me, and as far as I know he and Campbell had really nothing of any engineering interest to do and no fighting at all. The war itself was confined to petty skirmishes with the marauding tribes. The Amir had fled from his capital and died in exile; the Government were now treating with his son Yakub Khan and meantime all the military operations stood still. Sir Sam Browne had advanced to the town of Jallalabad at the beginning of December and remained there till the middle of April.

So the winter passed away. I was in excellent health and really interested in my canal work. I had an occasional morning's shooting with my young friend, the son of the Afghan chief who was a first rate sportsman and very pleasant companion; but except this I never left the work at all. The Government of India did not go to Calcutta that year, they stayed at Lahore and I learnt afterwards that some of the authorities had taken a very serious view of my misconduct.

One Sunday morning in the beginning of April I got a very sad piece of news, Wigram Battye had been killed the day before charging at the head of his cavalry at the battle of Fatehabad. It was a fight with one of these combinations of tribes. Young Hamilton had been left in command of the squadron when his leader fell, and he fell upon the foe with such fury that unable to stand the shock they fled far and wide followed by the avenging horsemen who were wild with grief at the loss of their leader. Hamilton got the VC for this. To me it was a blow, I had quite looked upon Battye as a friend and liked him, as indeed everyone did, for his fine manly character.

ATTOCK, NEAR WHICH THE KABUL ENTERS THE INDUS.

5
Jallalabad

Very soon after this I was astounded one day by getting an order to rejoin the 1st Division at Jallalabad at once. I could not understand it until next day a letter came clearing up the mystery. Colonel Maunsell had written a very strong letter on my behalf early in the year. He said he heard that I had got into hot water, 'that "the youngster" behaved very well, he has never made any complaint about the matter, which is really my fault entirely and not his'. But this letter which cleared my character completely, was <u>wrongly addressed</u> and lay in the Dead Letter office for several months. The authorities meantime not hearing from Maunsell, concluded that he had nothing to say in my favour and that my conduct was as indefensible from his point of view as it was from theirs. When however this letter did appear it cleared my character completely and they did me the justice to reinstate me in the position I had been recalled from. I handed over my work at Narrai to a civil engineer named Sadler and again started for the front.

It was then about the middle of April, the cold weather had just passed away and though it was still quite cool at night it was pretty hot during the day. I found a good many changes at Jumrood and Ali Musjid. At the former place the headquarters of General Maude's division had been for the whole of the cold weather, and had left traces of their occupation in various huts and in the great improvement on the works of the old mud fort.

At Ali Musjid there was quite a civilised look. There were rows of low buildings to accommodate troops, arranged for defence as well as for health, and there were numbers of roads and paths about the place. Jacob and Cather were both here. Just beyond Ali Musjid was a wild and precipitous gorge, where the Madras Sappers were engaged in blasting a high level road, a work of much difficulty, from the perpendicular face of the cliff. Beyond this the pass widened out and went up by easy ascent to Landi Kotal, an encampment at the highest part of the pass, being a sort of plateau or upland valley with low hills all round. Here were the headquarters of the 2nd Division with Colonel Limond and his adjutant Lieutenant Bruce and several companies of the Madras Sappers, all commanded by men whom I had known at Chatham. One of these companies under Lieutenants Lindley and Macdonnell accompanied me for the next two stages.

Just then one of the wild independent tribes - the Mohmands - had crossed the Kabul river some ten miles from Landi Kotal with the view of attacking the road through the Khyber. A favourite method of harrassing us practised by these tribes was to lie in wait near the line of communication somewhere and if they came upon a weakly defended convoy, they would swoop upon it, cutting down camels and drivers and doing as much damage as possible. Then if they could not do this, they could at least cut down our telegraph-poles and make away with the wire; this was being constantly done, much to the inconvenience of everybody. But it was not often that they came at us in any large numbers, in such a way as to necessitate a force being sent against them. On this occasion we had word that they were coming in great force and we had therefore to travel with much caution. Our road lay down a rocky glen, something like Glencoe, where a road had been made by the Madras Sappers and other workmen under Major Blair and Lieutenant Rawson RE at the bottom of which a winding valley - bare and rocky - led to the western end of the pass, where is situated the Afghan fort of Dakka.

Our march that day was, owing to the precautions we had to take, slower than usual. When we reached Dakka, it was evening. A force was just being sent to a village some eight miles off called Kam Dakka, which had been friendly to us and which we feared would excite the wrath and vengeance of the Mohmands. The force we were then sending was the Mairwarra Battalion, a regiment of aboriginals from central India under a Major Creagh, a jolly Irishman. I thought of asking to accompany them, but did not. It was not until the following evening that we heard the story of their adventures. When they reached Kam Dakka it was nearly dark and they were preparing to occupy and defend the village when the headman promptly refused to have anything to do with them saying he would fire on them if they came nearer. Many a man would have returned to Dakka at once but Creagh, seeing that the Mohmands had not crossed the river and were not likely to cross till next morning, took up a position on the top of a low hill and spent the night in fortifying it to the best of his ability. He was right in his surmise for as soon as it was light the Mohmands began to cross the river in large numbers. Creagh sent a man off at once to Dakka for reinforcements and meantime awaited the attack of the tribesmen who presently came on in tremendous force. Creagh and his central Indians fought with great gallantry against very heavy odds, until a strong force of cavalry and artillery arrived from Dakka and routed the enemy completely. It was a very gallant piece of work and Creagh got the VC for it.

The next post after Dakka was a village called Basawal. Here I found the 9th Lancers in great luxury, the men turning out to do escort duty in all the pomp and glory of peace parades. Here also were my old friends the 2nd Goorkhas, and Colonel Sim RE who commanded the Madras Sappers. I dined with him and found he had been an old frontier engineer in former days, infected with that peculiar free-masonry which existed among all the Punjab Frontier Force.

Two marches more over bare and stony plains brought me to Jallalabad. This is the chief city of that part of Afghanistan and has I suppose about 10,000 inhabitants. The whole of the British force under Sir Sam Browne had been there for several months, but now the advanced portion had moved on some thirty-five miles to a place called Gandamak which lies at a greater height and is much cooler. Here arrangements had been made for the new Amir Yakub Khan, son of Sher Ali Khan to come and meet with the British and arrange for a treaty between the two countries.

The headquarters of the division left for Gandamak a few days after I arrived at Jallalabad. The greater part of the Engineers in the force were at Jallalabad for some little time after I got there, employed for the most part in doing nothing but drills and military exercises. A small detachment looked after the military telegraphs and signalling arrangements, and a big fort was being built, but the latter work was being actually constructed by civil labour raised in the neighbouring country. The remainder of the large number of RE officers did no technical work at all. With the advanced portion at Gandamak were Major Blair and Lieutenant Peacocke; two of the ablest men in the force, they were engaged building bridges and making roads with one company of Madras Sappers.

The fort at Jallalabad to which I have alluded was a large irregular work built round some big sheds for stores and was intended in the first place as a protection to these sheds only. Then as the weather became hot, it became advisable to shelter the sick and then the healthy in something more substantial than tents, so defensible barracks were built and other works necessary for a standing camp sprang up.

The direction of all these works was put under Lieutenant Glennie RE and I was directed to assist him. We had one or two sergeants to assist us and the work was interesting and gave one plenty to do. There was also the important question of water supply to see to. A small canal flowed past the fort. This was taken off the Kabul river some two miles above the city and we had to arrange with the people to continue a constant supply of water and also to see that no pollution was permitted.

For most of our fellows there however the life in camp was a pretty idle one. Some went in for sports of different kinds: polo, tent-pegging etc, some were great upon swordsmanship and revolver practice, others again studied the antiquities of the place, explored old Buddhist topes or mounds and collected coins, some of which were extremely interesting, going back to the times of Alexander the Great. The country near Jallalabad on the banks of the river was well watered and cultivated and we had many pleasant rides there. One place of favourite resort was the

Governor's palace, a picturesque pavilion in a terraced garden of orange groves and pomegranates where a little canal flowed placidly along, and it was a pleasant change from the heat and dust of the camp to go to this garden and find cool shade under the big plane trees and listen to the murmuring of the water and the voices of the birds among the orange trees.

A MOSQUE IN AFGHANISTAN.

* * * * * * * * * *

The weather however was getting uncomfortably hot and very soon the garrison of Jallalabad was reduced to two battalions infantry (Guides and 1st Sikhs), one squadron of the 11th Bengal Lancers, and two guns. The whole of the sapper companies left and went on to Gandamak leaving Glennie and me to finish the fort works with a few men and an immense quantity of stores. Glennie and I built ourselves a little hut of mud bricks where we were very fairly comfortable. We had a 'scratch' mess of doctors, commissariat officers, survey officers, transport officers, and any other casual individuals that might be about the place. This mess had its headquarters in a blockhouse in one of the sides of the fort.

During the month of May negotiations went on with the Amir and at last he consented to come to the British camp at Gandamak and arrange for a treaty. There was of course direct telegraphic communication to Simla and London, and the result of the deliberations was Lord Beaconsfield's famous Treaty of Gandamak. But this was not formally settled till the beginning of June.

I got a week's leave to go up to Gandamak about the middle of May. The first stage from Jallalabad was a fort called Rozabad in a cultivated and wooded country. This was the first private castle or stronghold, common among the Afghan chiefs, that I had yet seen. I was afterwards to become very familiar with the type at Kabul. Externally it was a large square block with walls about twenty to thirty feet high and at the four corners, towers of a greater height overlooking the interior and flanking the walls. One large gateway well guarded and furnished with a strong door admitted one to the interior. Inside there were rooms all round the walls, cool and comfortable, and in the interior space were quarters for servants or cattle. The gateway generally had rooms above it and on both sides. There are allusions to this arrangement in the Old Testament - in fact the whole country and its social arrangements reminded me constantly of the state of Palestine under the Judges and Kings! For supply, there were storehouses for grain and either a well in the centre, or in the case of Rozabad a little duct brought a stream of water cleverly into the interior and also worked a little <u>punkah</u> or fan for cooling one of the main rooms. Our forts on the Swat Canal at Narrai and other places were built much on the principle of these Afghan fortalices.

At Rozabad there was a small garrison. The Engineer in charge was Lieutenant Poulter RE whom I had known at Chatham, but who had since been employed in southern India. He was a man of much culture and refinement and of a very pleasant manner. He was also known to be sincere though not ostentatiously religious - a rare quality I regret to say among any of our fellows at that time and place. He had a curious theory with regard to heat. He thought that it affected one less if one wore thick clothes and he consequently used to wear the thickest winter clothes he could get in the sun. The result of this was that he got chills and rheumatic fever which eventually killed him.

Group of RE officers at Safed Sang (Gandamak), named from left to right: Dr Ongsbury; MG Talbot; HR Lea; C Blunt; Capt W North; AR McCrum; RV Philpotte; GW Bartram; SH Exham; WFH Stafford; JC Campbell; AH Mason; Subadar Hyder Shah; Maj.Gen. Maunsell; H Dove; Capt Stuart

The next stage beyond Rozabad was the village of Fatehabad near the spot where the battle had been fought. A small fort named Fort Battye after Wigram Battye has been erected there. Just beyond this my old company with Campbell and Mason were making a road and were encamped at a lovely spot called Minlah Bagh. It was a meadow with a little brook flowing past it and willow trees affording a pleasant shade. Behind it was a beautiful Afghan garden with poplars and willows, orange trees and pomegranates. Cattle were grazing on the sweet grass and the whole scene looked as fair and peaceful as anything at home. I was warmly welcomed by my old friends, both of whom I knew and liked very much. I stayed the night with them and slept in a doolie or litter, my bed being the sweet hay from the meadow, and the murmuring of the little stream quickly put me to sleep. It was indeed an oasis in a desert.

An old Afghan with whom I got into conversation there told me he had lived there all his life. He remembered the retreat from Kabul in 1842 well. He said, "I saw five sahibs riding across here towards Jallalabad. They had four horses only. Two were riding on one horse. They were going as fast as they could and were weary and wounded." History tells us that these were the five survivors of the flight from Kabul, that when they reached Fatehabad they were attacked again and four out of the five killed. The only survivor who reached Jallalabad was a Dr Bryden. This story has often been told.

The camp at Gandamak was about three miles beyond Minlah Bagh. It was pitched on a stony plateau on the east bank of a stream which flowed through a wide and strong water course. The cavalry brigade were encamped on the west bank and a substantial trestle bridge spanned the water course. The sappers had their camp close to the stream and took advantage of one or two trees under whose shade the mess tent was pitched. The usual idle life was going on – no work to be done. On the far bank of the stream in a grove of trees was the Amir's Camp. I did not see much of his people and did not see the great man himself at all; but his bodyguard were curiously dressed in a grotesque imitation of our Highland soldiers. They had regular doublets of red, and a kilt of a reddish colour, but baggy breeches underneath and buff coloured helmets instead of bonnets. They were armed with Enfield rifles.

On the Queen's birthday there was a parade of the whole force on one of the stony plateaux above mentioned. I was Orderly Officer to General Maunsell and so saw all the parade very well. I rode Selim, a white horse which I had bought from Dr R Pringle; he was a good looking horse and looked well on parade. My own uniform was drab coat and helmet, fawn coloured breeches and brown boots, brown leather belt with revolver and sword and steel spurs. I mention the last because our brigade Major Lovett never would wear spurs even when on a mounted parade. We REs were very slack in the way of dress, there was no uniformity and the orders on the subject were very vague. I hope they are better now.

The parade was a fine show. The cavalry and horse artillery as usual moved as well and looked as smart as they would have done at Lucknow or Ambala.

I left Gandamak next day and returned to Jallalabad. I found Glennie had been ordered up to headquarters so I was left as garrison engineer of Jallalabad. For some little time I was not much more than a forwarding agent, for the actual defensive work was done and all I had to do was to look after the stores and send anything to the Front that might be wanted.

The negotiations at Gandamak however soon came to an end and Major Cavagnari's secretary Mr Jenkins, BCS, rode through the camp one day on his way to Simla with the original treaty strapped on his back. He came back in a few days with it signed by the Viceroy. It provided 1) that a British envoy was to be stationed at Kabul, 2) that the British Frontier was to be extended to Kandahar, 3) that the Kuram Valley as far as Peiwar Kotal and the Khyber was to be ceded to England, 4) that in return for this the British Government was to defend the Amir from all foes. A few months more and this treaty was not worth the paper it was written upon.

6th Company Sappers & Miners at Safed Sang (Gandamak)

* *   * *   * *   * *   * *

Meantime orders were issued for the entire force to return to India. I got orders at Jellalabad to prepare rafts at once for the transport of all stores and for the sick and others by river to Dakka. I set to work at once preparing timber rafts, cask rafts, boat rafts. It was desperately hard work, but after two days of it Major Blair and a Captain Moir of the 17th Regiment came and took a great deal of it off my hands. The first cargo I sent off was a large flat bottomed boat full of telegraph stores whereby hangs a tale:- as soon as it was known that the war was over and no more honour and glory to be had, everybody who was not obliged to march down with troops and some who ought to have been with the troops but for selfish reasons, went on in front, pushed their way helter-skelter down, in a most unsoldierly fashion. A number of these warriors arrived in Jallalabad on the evening of the day that I had been loading up the barge with stores. It became known that a boat was going down early next day, and it was calculated would do the three marches in seven hours, so that one could reach Landi Kotal that evening and perhaps Peshawar next morning.

I was instantly besieged with applications to be allowed to go in this boat. I replied that there was no reason why they should not go, but of course they would travel at their own risk. I was sending a sergeant in charge of the stores and two natives to navigate the ship. Among others who sent for me and demanded a passage was Brigadier General A--- and his orderly officer, and of course I could not refuse them. Next morning was as usual very hot but there was a very strong wind blowing and the navigating natives said they would have some trouble in steering the boat. I told the officers who were passengers that no awning could be put up on account of the wind, but to my disgust I saw General A--- deliberately rig up an awning to shelter himself from the sun in spite of entreaties to the contrary.

They started off however and presently disappeared from view. Some hours afterwards we heard they had run aground on a sand bank some five miles off. We prepared and sent a light raft of inflated skins to take off the officers; a heavier raft was sent afterwards for the stores. But meantime A--- had sent his ADC through the river to the shore to ask for food and assistance. While the latter was away the light raft came to the rescue. All the officers begged General A--- to wait for the ADC who had gone on shore, but the General ordered the raft to start at once and left the young man to take his chance. Some hours afterwards the latter returned, saw the boat there but all the occupants gone. He went down the river to look for them and went on and on till night fell. He then had to make the best of his way weary and footsore to Dakka where he heard the truth. He reported the matter officially. General A--- was never employed again.

Cholera broke out among the troops about the beginning of June. It had originally started at Hardwar in April and had gradually spread through the Punjab and up the line of communication till it reached us just at our busiest time. It spared no rank or class but those who suffered most were the camp followers, men of poor physique, ill-clad and ill-fed. My faithful servant Kadir who had been with me from the first day I was at Roorkee was struck down with it one night and I never saw him again. A fine native officer of the sappers Haidar Shah by name also died of it and I was with him till very near his end. He begged that his necklaces (the badges of his rank) might be sent to his mother and that his body might be taken for burial to Kohat. This last however was forbidden by the medical authorities.

Meantime our work went on incessantly. At the river side there were two landing stages, at the upper of which Blair and Moir worked - at the lower I worked alone. Natives accustomed to the work rapidly made rafts of inflated skins and as soon as a raft was ready it was loaded up by a working party of soldiers and started on its journey. I do not now remember how many tons of stores, or how many sick men were thus sent off every day, but it was an enormous number. I myself was often up to my waist in water, there was a blazing sun overhead and the temperature in the coolest places was well over 100°, so the work was trying.

I began the raft work on the 30th May and continued it without ceasing, Sunday and week-day, till the 12th June, during which fortnight we shipped off an enormous quantity of stores. The 12th June was a day of supreme effort and of fearful heat. Late in the afternoon I was knocked over by sickness and giddiness. I staggered up to my hut and lay down on the little bedstead I had there, fearfully sick and in pain. I thought that the cholera had got hold of me too as it had taken many a better man - well, it seemed a little hard to die at that time, but still - just then Blair put his head into the hut to congratulate me on finishing up a stiff bit of work. Seeing I was ill he went out and came back with some wine in a tumbler. It was hospital wine which was going to be left behind with other stores and Blair had annexed a few bottles. I had not tasted any spirituous liquor for about three years, and the result was marvellous - I fell sound asleep and woke up late in the evening very weak but with the pain and sickness gone.

Next day about 9 o'clock we left Jallalabad - being about the last to depart from the place. We had a comfortable raft ready for us with an awning to keep off the fierce rays of the sun. General Maunsell, Blair, Moir, Hart VC, Jackson and myself, shared it with a queer old Afghan called Taimur Khan who, partly from attachment to Blair, partly from love of adventure, had come up to the front taking contracts of different sorts and making himself very useful.

We did the journey to Dakka, forty-two miles, in seven hours, winding down the wild picturesque gorges of the Kabul river, now floating on quiet pools and again dancing over swift rapids. Here and there the rays of the sun reflected off the bare rocks caused the heat to be terrific. In one place Blair pointed out an apt Scripture illustration. A great rock rose out of a barren plain, and in its shadow were lying motionless in their midday siesta a caravan of men and camels. Looking at this we understood the force of Christ being compared to the shadow of a great rock in a weary land.

We arrived at Dakka that afternoon finding Peacocke and Mason there, the latter in command of my old Company (the 2nd) of Bengal Sappers. The heat that afternoon was greater than anything I ever knew before and except on one occasion, since. The thermometer stood at 130° in the shade. Men were dying of apoplexy and cholera all round. The 10th Hussars marching from Busawal that morning had lost seventeen of their men who dropped out of their saddles on the one march. All day long we saw little groups of men crossing the plain to the little cemetery on the far side bearing the corpse of a comrade to add to the silent company whom we were there leaving behind.

We left Dakka during the night and marched to Landi Kotal, a march horrible for heat and flies and the continuous stench of dead camels which were lying rotting at every forty or fifty yards along the route. At Landi Kotal the heat was not quite so great and luxuries were procurable to mitigate it. But on the following morning I rose at 4 am and rode on my pony, Marco Polo, right into Peshawar thirty miles through the Khyber Pass in four-and-a-half hours arriving in time for breakfast. The ride was a fearful one. I passed several regiments on the march totally disorganised. British soldiers tottering along, their arms thrown into the nearest cart, their faces swollen and livid, their tongues hanging out of their mouths -not the semblance of military cohesion. At Ali Musjid I passed the headquarters of the Bengal Sappers. The sergeant major had just fallen out of the ranks with cholera and was dead, also a young corporal - not long since come from home.

During the week (June 1879) I spent in Peshawar the weather was still unmercifully hot and several deaths occurred, among them Lieutenant Poulter RE and Lieutenant Jacob's little son. About this time I also heard of the ambush in Zululand where an old Woolwich comrade of mine had perished - Prince Louis Napoleon of France.

My own affairs were still unsettled, but I spent the time squaring up the accounts of the campaign. I received news that I had been honourably mentioned in despatches, and finally, orders to return to the Swat Canal.

On June 20th I took my horse over the ferry on the Kabul river and rode into Mardan about sunrise. Major Swinton RE put me up for a week. We said farewell to three men who were to form part of Sir Louis

Cavagnari's embassy in Kabul: the secretary, Mr Jenkyns - Dr Kelly - and Lieutenant Hamilton VC. All three lost their lives in Kabul in August. (see M Bonthorp, The North West Frontier, pp 72f). 'Their fate is involved in a horrible obscurity', and led to the beginning of the second Afghan War.

On 29th June I started for a month's leave, to be spent with my cousins the Pringles at Mussoorie.

Bridge at Safed Sang (Gandamak) with Bengal Sappers

First portion of bridge on Kabul River

6
Abazai

I spent three weeks very happily among the clouds at Mussoorie with my cousins Dr and Mrs Pringle at Whytbank, an irregular house built on the top of a steep and irregular hill, surrounded by holm-oaks and rhododendron trees. I amused myself walking, riding, calling on friends, sketching, idling, recruiting health.

Then I went to Meerut and enjoyed myself for some more days at the house of Will and Susie Willcocks where also was Uncle Colin. He had been at home on three months' leave which he had taken after the conclusion of his very arduous work in the Mysore famine for which he had been made a CSI.

My return journey to Mardan was marked by one ludicrous incident. I stopped at Jhelum - the railway terminus - I there dined with my cousin Alick Samuells of the 32nd Pioneers (it was the last time I saw him, poor fellow) and started about 10 o'clock in a <u>dak ghari</u> for Rawal Pindi. About the middle of the night I was awakened by a crash and found myself lying with my heels much higher than my head though otherwise still comfortable inside my post chaise. I heard much violent Hindustani and a sleepy and 'H'-less English voice asking what the matter was. My vehicle had collided with another and we had got very much the worse of it, in fact the whole of the front part was completely smashed. I asked the occupant of the other vehicle, which had escaped without injury to send another for me from Jhelum from which we were now thirty miles distant and I composed myself to sleep again. When I woke it was broad daylight and I was still lying at the side of the road comfortably among the ruins of my post chaise. I looked out, it was pretty late, about 8 o'clock. I was at the side of the broad high road, in a rough hilly country, not a living creature was in sight, until I saw my bearer and the driver of the <u>ghari</u> curled up and asleep near a wall at the road side.

I sent off the latter to see if he could get a conveyance at the nearest changing post (horses were changed every ten miles or so) while I and my servant awaited whatever might turn up. I had about forty miles to go to Rawal Pindi and my leave expired next morning, at Mardan about 130 miles away still. I saw then no visible means of pushing on but in a short time the mail cart passed, a red box on wheels driven by a half naked native generally at a hand gallop. I made him stop, got up beside him with my dog, Jessie and so arrived at 'Pindi in due course about midday followed by my bearer in an ekka not many hours after. I reached Mardan all right next morning.

This was the last time I ever was at Mardan. I have often seen it in my dreams since but I believe the place is now very much altered for the better since the canal brought fertilising waters to it. The barren plain between it and Nowshera is fertile now with corn and trees and the wily Pathan who inhabits it is less of a freebooter and more of a peaceful agriculturist.

I was invited to dine with the Guides that night and I went. The news from the Embassy was good, they had gone via Kuram and had some good fishing in the Kuram River. I had given Kelly a tin box full of fishing tackle and he was enjoying it, poor fellow. How cheerful everything looked then, how gloomy it was not many weeks later!

Next day I rose early, rode out to Narrai where I put up, saw my great culvert now quite finished and looked at it with much pride. It was my first big work and I remember all the details of it to this day. Next day I rode on to Abazai where young Jacob was. He handed over the works, accounts etc to me, but for the next three or four days I was down with fever, for the first time. I was very fortunate having escaped this so far. Usually fever attacks young fellows before they have been many weeks on the frontier but here I had been in India for two years and a half and not had a touch of it. However, I soon got right again.

The life at Abazai and the duty there was very pleasant and interesting. I was in charge of about twelve miles of the canal, and had two large aqueducts, several large culverts, two super-passages (where mountain torrents flowed over the canal) a number of road bridges and the headworks to build, also a fort to guard those head works from the transfrontier tribes. My bungalow lately finished by Cather was in a bastion of the fort just overlooking the swift and clear Swat River where it issues from the hills. I had four horses and I had bought a light cart from Cather which I found useful when it was too hot to ride comfortably.

When I arrived there the weather was still very hot though a little rain had fallen and for the next two months there were few days without some rain, perhaps only a shower, perhaps a heavy pour for twenty-four hours. But my house was constructed so as to give the greatest protection from heat and take advantage of all the breeze available. The Swat River coming down from the snows and glaciers of the Hindu Kush was always cold and brought a cold current of air with it on the hottest nights. My house was so close that I could throw a stone from my roof into the river, but the elevation was such that no river mists ever rose to its level. I generally slept on the flat roof of the house, where too I had my tea in the evening, a delightfully cool place and with a beautiful view of the river and dark mountains beyond.

The work was hard but very interesting. Every morning I was up very early and in the saddle riding round my works, where perhaps recent rains had done damage freely. Back to breakfast about 10, after which I did office work and accounts till perhaps 2 or 3 in the afternoon. I then read or wrote private letters till 4, when I dined and after dinner it was cool enough to ride round the works again usually in another direction from the morning round. I returned about 7, had tea and to bed early.

There was society there too. When I reached Abazai first the Commandant was a Major Hoggan of the 7th Bengal Cavalry who lived there with a young daughter. His wife and another daughter were up at Murree where he and the younger girl shortly joined them travelling down the river one night on a small raft about forty miles to Nowshera, a very risky thing for a young and delicate girl I thought. Hoggan was succeeded by a Lieutenant Heath of the 11th Bengal Lancers (the crack regiment of the native army) a very smart fellow, formerly in the 10th Hussars and fresh from a distinguished part in the late Afghan war. With Heath I was soon on very friendly terms and we went about a great deal together. As he had very little to do he used often to accompany me on my rounds on the works. Heath was a brother-in-law of Lord Chelmsford who at that time was commanding in Zululand and of course we were intensely interested in all the news from that part of the world then.

There was besides a doctor called Jack, a Scotsman, son of a minister in Dumfriesshire. He was not a bad fellow but was not a favourite somehow, being rather awkward and dense.

I have said that Abazai was one of the Doaba outposts. The other two were Shabkadar and Michin. The Commandant of the former was a Colonel Fisher, a very young colonel, who had known my parents some eighteen years before. The Commandant of Michin was a Colonel Elton, a very good and kind man whom we all liked and respected very much. Michin was on the Kabul river and was only about ten miles from Peshawar. On Fridays Colonel Fisher used to invite us all to Shabkadar to spend the day and play lawn-tennis which was just then begun under its present rules (formerly it was played like rackets fifteen up). The road from Abazai to Shabkadar was a very pretty one under shady trees and I used to drive Heath over in my trap - very pleasant it was in the mornings and evenings in the fresh air in the beautiful scenery. The views about Shabkadar were very pretty and Fisher was always very cheery and hospitable. This was a very pleasant break in the week's work.

** ** ** ** **

Jacob left me pretty much to myself at that time. He was away at Murree a great deal with his wife and their one remaining child - a little girl about three years old. Occasionally he came to see how I was getting on and to give advice but he left me to make most of my arrangements for myself which was very pleasant and satisfactory. As far as one could see I was fairly settled at Abazai for the cold weather and I looked forward to completing some at least of the great works then in hand. I never saw them completed till twenty-two years later however, but a few photographs obtained many years after show me how they look like now they have been concluded under other superintendence than mine.

Although Abazai was my usual place of residence I had another residence at a place called Jinda. Here a large aqueduct was then being built over a stream which was in dry weather only a small rivulet not much bigger than a Scots burn, but in time of rain was a huge river quite impassable running between high banks about fifty yards apart and not infrequently seven or eight feet deep. A flood only two feet deep was quite sufficient to knock out of shape any temporary works that might be going on; and during the time I was in charge there were several floods, two of which were over five feet deep. The havoc they caused was very considerable and frequently necessitated my being on the spot for some days, so I used to spend the night at the Jinda rest house. There was a square fort on much the same plan as my old quarters at Narrai with a dwelling house at one corner, the whole built on the high ground overlooking the stream. The view from it was very fine, and when there was a flood in the stream it was very grand. The aqueduct itself was the first work of any size I ever designed in India. The idea of it and much of the details were given me by Jacob, but I drew all the plans and it was built according to those plans, so I naturally took much interest in it. The work cost some £30,000. The stone for it, and the lime was quarried from a hill quite close so material was cheap and easily obtained.

Sadler the civil engineer who had succeeded me at Narrai used sometimes to come and stay with me at Jinda and Abazai. He was a sociable sort of fellow and had spent a great deal of his Indian service in solitary places, so Abazai, with the few white faces there, was quite a change to him. He was not a very popular man, though I do not know why, for he was always very friendly and pleasant - his only somewhat disagreeable characteristic being a fondness for theological argument. He was a member of the <u>Irvingite</u> body (Catholic Apostolic Church) and was very fond of laying down the law about his own tenets in a way that people did not care about. Hoggan at Abazai was a firm believer in Spiritualism and his daughter was a medium, though she had suffered a good deal in health by it, and her father said he was not going to allow her to practise more. She married afterwards and I suppose gave up all that sort of thing. Elton, the Commandant of Fort Michin, was a very simple straightforward Christian whose blameless life won for him golden opinions from everybody, even from those who scoffed at his creed. So we had a variety of opinions when we all met at Abazai.

I have a very pleasant recollection of our Sundays there. In the morning of the blessed day of rest we generally all turned out to have a swim in the cool waters of the Swat river, than after breakfast we used to sit under the shady trees of the fort garden, situated on the banks of the river above the fort. When Elton was there he and I used to read the morning prayers and lessons together with any of the others who cared to join. Then after the sun got low we had a walk, the hot hours of the afternoon having been spent in reading or writing home letters. It was a perfect day of rest, very grateful change after the six days hard work.

I went in to Peshawar about the beginning of September with Elton for a day to buy a horse. I stayed with him at Michin on the way. We heard nothing but favourable news from the Embassy at Kabul then, while everything seemed to be going smoothly and well. What a change there was in a few days! The first tidings of disaster I heard were on the eighth. I had gone to Jinda to meet Jacob. He got a note from the Assistant Commissioner at Mardan saying, "There are ugly rumours of a serious rout at Kabul. I daresay there is nothing in it, but still one cannot help feeling anxious". Native news had, as usual, outstripped regular intelligence for two days afterwards we heard the whole fatal truth.

On the 5th September it appears a Kabulee regiment, which had not received their pay, mutinied and went to the Amir complaining. He is reported to have told them to go and ask the English Ambassador to remedy their grievance. He afterwards said he did not mean them to act upon his advice, but as a matter of fact they rushed off to the Residency in a body, a raging clamourous mob, shouting and furious. Cavagnari who knew nothing of their complaint when he saw the mob coming on, ordered his sentries to close the gates and fire on them. They dispersed, but only to get their weapons and call upon the other troops in the place to join them. The whole of the garrison seems to have risen and although the Amir and his Commander-in-Chief Daud Shah say they did their best to stop them it was too late. They attacked the Residency in great force and the result was that all the British officers were slain and all their escort, with the exception of a very few who escaped to the Kuram Valley, there told our troops the terrible tale.

There could of course be but one result, war had again burst out and the Treaty of Gandamak was worth no more than the paper it was written upon. I wrote off to Simla at once volunteering for active service and in a few days got a telegram, "Join General Roberts' force at once" from the Adjutant General. I was appointed an assistant Field Engineer to the army proceeding to Kabul. General Sir Fred Roberts was appointed to command that army. He himself was in Simla at the time that the news came but of course he started off at once for the Kuram Valley. The Officer-in-Command of the troops there was Brigadier General Massy, late of the 5th Lancers, a man who had a great reputation, since the Crimean days, but who lost that reputation very speedily by his indolence and want of energy. It took Roberts some time to reach Ali Khyel, where the advanced portion of the army then was and Massy allowed that precious time to be wasted, saying he could not move without more transport, more commissariat, etc etc. If he had been a man of energy he might have been into Kabul a few days after the disaster and punished the ringleaders before they had time to gather other troops together; as it was they pulled themselves together and in the four weeks that followed collected a strong force to resist the British.

I handed over my charge to Jacob on the 25th September and started next day for Peshawar to report myself to the military authorities and proceed once more on the war-path.

KABUL.

7

Kuram and Kabul

I started from Abazai on the 26th September 1879 to report myself at Peshawar and then push on to join General Roberts in the Kuram Valley. I had with me only my campaigning kit, which did not even include a tent at that time, for I had not time to get one. I did procure however a very small and light tent in Peshawar such as is used by native cavalry soldiers. I had ordered a regular officer's tent from the makers, but in the hurry and confusion of the campaign it never reached me, and went hopelessly astray.

I had two horses, Harkaway, a new purchase who turned out badly, and Marco Polo who was a right good one and did me good service. For a servant I had an Afghan called Majid, who had been in Kabul once before. He was a native of Mardan. I also had my faithful Jessie, who had already been with me in the former campaign, a white fox-terrier. On reporting myself to the military authorities at Peshawar I was told I might have to wait some days before they could give me transport, as all available animals had already been taken. This might mean a delay for several days, much to my disgust; so I resolved to see what I could do on my own account.

Fortunately an ally turned up in the shape of old Taimur Khan, a contractor who had reaped a golden harvest from the former campaign and was only too eager to get to the front again and get some adventure plus filthy lucre. I set him to work to get animals and he procured me some donkeys which were quite good enough for my purpose.

I spent Sunday the 28th September quietly at Peshawar in the Mission Station with my friends the missionaries; I received the Sacrament that morning and committed the care of myself, soul and body, to a merciful Creator.

Next morning I started for Kohat. The first day I marched to Matunni seventeen miles from Peshawar which I reached at sunset and put up in a little staging bungalow at the mouth of the Kohat Pass. I was up at dawn next morning, a bright red sunrise opening on a cloudless sky. The Kohat Pass is in Afghan territory. A tax is paid to the adjoining tribes to allow British officials to pass to and from Peshawar to the frontier station of Kohat, but one has to take an escort, as the tribesmen are not very particular about plunder even though they are subsidised. I had a longish march that day - twenty-two miles over rough ground, so was anxious to get my donkeys off early. The first sixteen miles or so of the way was a gradual ascent up a long valley passing walled Afghan villages here and there, some cultivated fields where the husbandman works his plough with his weapons by his side and barren rocky hills all round. Then on reaching the summit of the pass six miles from Kohat there is a fine view of the plains below and a steep descent by a zig-zag road till at length one is in British territory again and in the cantonment of Kohat. It is a small but pretty station well-wooded with flat-roofed bungalows mostly of the usual mud brick architecture, but in well-watered gardens. I put up in the bungalow of the Executive Engineer (Major Harvey) and was very comfortable.

Next day I started on my march for Thall, a frontier post eighty miles distant at the mouth of the Kuram Valley. It took me four days to get there for I could not do more with my donkeys and I did not want to get ahead of my baggage. The country was most picturesque, not at all unlike the Highlands of Scotland, clear rushing streams, a good deal of cultivated land where the harvest had just been gathered in, wooded valleys, rocky hills. The weather too was very pleasant, cold at night, bright and warm during the day. I was alone at first, but I fell in with a Dr Roe on the second day. He was going to join his old regiment the 92nd Highlanders and we journeyed together.

We reached Thall the frontier post in British territory on the 4th October. Here a number of troops of sorts had assembled waiting till they could go on in a good number. There were also some young subalterns going on to join their regiments. Dr Roe and I persuaded the commander of the post to let us all go on next day; I was to command the party much to my joy and I made all arrangements for the march, but at the last moment a Major Terry of the 25th turned up and of course took the command. His ideas were somewhat contrary to mine, but of course I had to acquiesce. The troops under our command were almost all cavalry, belonging to the 5th Punjab Cavalry, a very smart regiment with a somewhat striking uniform, dark green coat with scarlet tubans. The reason that we were only allowed to go on in strong bodies was that a few days before a young officer named Kinloch had gone up the valley with only two men as escort, had been attacked and killed. So orders were sent that only strong bodies were to proceed.

On Sunday the 6th October we started again over the Afghan frontier. The road lay among bare low hills and stony valleys, but the air was bright and fresh and the sunshine not too warm and I must confess to feeling very exhilarated at the idea of being off to the wars again. We passed the spot where poor Kinloch had been killed, his blood marks still fresh on the stony valley. Here the escort thought they had captured an enemy, but fortunately I knew the language and on cross-examination found he was the follower of a friendly chief and he was liberated accordingly.

During the next three or four days we continued our march up the Kuram Valley; the scenery, which at first was not very interesting, became afterwards very beautiful. On our left was the Kuram river, a clear and rapid stream with good fishing, in front were the mountains and the snowy range of the Safed Koh on our right. There were a few walled villages with some fine plane trees and cultivation round them. We overtook a large convoy of stores commanded by an old Woolwich comrade of mine, Lieutenant Builward RA. He had been attacked one day just before we came up, but had beaten off his assailants and pursued them with some slaughter.

On the 8th we arrived at Kuram, two walled forts or enclosures and a garrison of a native infantry regiment and the 13th Bengal Lancers under Colonel Low. The latter had orders to stop the first engineer officer that came up the valley to repair the magazines in the forts, which were falling to pieces; and as there were large quantities of warlike stores it was most necessary to keep them dry. I protested vigorously against being stopped, but Colonel Low's orders were most peremptory and so all I could do was to send a heliograph message on to the Front saying I was stopped and begging for orders to proceed. Meantime I had to collect such labour as I could procure locally and endeavour to repair the magazines. The 13th Bengal Lancers were very kind and I put up with them for a while though I changed my quarters soon to one of the forts so as to be near my work. These forts were in a very tumble-down condition, roofs leaking in every direction, and the ordnance department officer in charge - a smart artillery captain - was in despair. The only assistants I had to help me in the work were an old Scots soldier of the 92nd Highlanders - a native of Kirkcaldy - and a smart Afghan NCO of the 5th Punjab Cavalry. The latter collected the labourers for me and helped to pay them, the former supervised them under my directions, addressing them in a mixture of Hindustani and broad Scots, both of which languages were equally unknown to them! Meantime I myself was much troubled with severe intermittent fever and ague of the distressing sort so common on the Frontier, which came on every second day and pulled me down very much.

I remained at Kuram for a little more than a fortnight. Old Taimur Khan when he found that I was only doing repairs to the forts thought it was hardly good enough to stay with me and told me he would go back to Peshawar, and look out for Major Blair who he said would be sure to take him to Kabul. I offered him a present of some sort if he would stick to me (and I wish he had for it would have simplified my subsequent work very much) but he thought my star was on the wane and he left me. As it turned out I was in Kabul about four months before him and if he had stuck to me he would probably have made a pile of money. However he left me and we did not meet again for months. Poor old Taimur! Wild lawless 'cateran' though he was, there was much that I liked about him as indeed I liked many of the fierce energetic Afghans who worked with me then and afterwards. They had a rough loyalty of their own and their chief faults were due to their fierce and fanatical creed.

About ten days after I had arrived at Kuram the 9th Lancers turned up in all their pomp and pride, Colonel Cleland commanding, quite the same exquisite dandy that he had been in the days of the voyage out. His tent and furniture etc were on the most lavish scale, his clothes were a wonder to everybody! He regarded everybody but cavalry with a lofty contempt and considered the Afghans as a very poor sort of foe. Two months afterwards he was mortally wounded.

About the same time Major WV Holmes RE turned up to be CRE of the Kuram Division. I had just met him once before but could hardly say I knew him. This was the beginning of a very pleasant friendship with him which lasted till his sudden death in 1882. He was a hearty, cheery fellow, a very good practical engineer and scientific withal, and a man of the soundest judgment and common sense.

The headquarters of the Kuram Division were at a place called Ali Khyel one march beyond the Peiwar Kotal and three marches from Kuram.

Holmes went on there on the 23rd October and on the afternoon of the same day I got orders, to my intense joy, to go on to Kabul at once. I lost no time in packing up and marching off and that night I reached Shalozan ten miles off, the site of the proposed new cantonment where my old friend Captain Miller was quartered. I put up with him that night and started early the next morning for Peiwar Kotal. Miller had a very comfortable little hut at Shalozan, and had settled down into peace routine in wonderful fashion. He gave me a most excellent dinner, in fact it was difficult to realise one was on active service and in an enemy's country.

The march from Shalozan to Peiwar was a very interesting one. In front and on either side were lofty pine clad hills, and in the valleys were many trees unknown in India but familiar to European eyes, also birds such as magpies and wood pigeons which reminded one of home. The ascent of the pass was by a long winding road of recent construction, one of Colonel Perkins' and Lieutenant Bagot's engineering triumphs. At the top of the pass, the scene of the battle of 2nd December 1878 was the little post of Peiwar Kotal, garrisoned by the 8th Regiment who lived in little log huts like those one sees in pictures of Canadian backwoods. All round these huts was a forest of splendid deodar pines, such as one afterwards became familiar with in the hills round Simla. The climate of course was cold and bracing and the soldiers all looked rosy and healthy. The Government of India had sent an officer of the forest department to report upon the timber supply there and to superintend the felling of trees

for engineering uses, and with this gentleman (a Mr Bagshawe) I had breakfast and spent a few hours.
My baggage animals (camels) had been much exhausted by the steep pull up the pass, so I was uncertain whether to proceed to Ali Khyel that afternoon. I telegraphed for orders to Ali Khyel therefore and got a reply to come on at once. I left my baggage to follow next day and taking in my holsters and wallets, what I needed for myself and my steed for one night I pushed on at once. The ride was a very pleasant one. It was a lovely afternoon and the scenery was very beautiful. At first the road lay in a narrow valley with pine clad hills on either side then it opened out into a sort of plateau and wound among low wooded hills and past thriving villages. The trees had on their gay autumn tints just as at home, the harvest of maize had been gathered in and the flat housetops had in many cases been utilised for drying the ripe golden grain. It was a lovely evening as I rode by, and I enjoyed the scenery and the ride very much. I arrived at Ali Khyel about 7 o'clock and reported myself to the Commander of the Kuram Division, Brigadier-General Gordon who kindly asked me to dine with him.

A few days before this there had been a very determined attack on Ali Khyel. The post occupied by our troops was on a somewhat exposed plateau partially fortified. The troops there were very largely composed of scattered bodies of men and officers of all sorts going on to join their corps at the front. Thus the cavalry was composed of a number of troopers of different regiments commanded by two subalterns of the 10th Hussars (on transport duty) and a doctor who had once served in a dragoon regiment as a private soldier! In the cavalry combat that took place this doctor, it was said, wielded his sabre with great effect, though whether he afterwards dressed the wounds he caused I cannot say.

I slept that night in Holmes' tent, my saddle serving me as a pillow for though I could get shelter from the cold night air, nobody could spare a bed. My baggage turned up next day. I might just as well have stayed at Peiwar Kotal and come on with it, as it turned out, for we did not start for Kabul till next day.

KHELAT.

**   **   **   **   **

We started at 6 am next morning (26th October). There were a few officers of the 92nd Highlanders (the Honourable 'Jock' Napier, son of Uncle D Pringle's friend Lord Napier and Ettrick; my kinsman Henry Dick-Cunningham, Macgregor, and Dr Roe) whom I used to see a good deal of on the march and fraternised with generally. Then there was an old schoolfellow of mine, Robertson of the 8th Kings, an Oxford man, who was attached to the transport and was also correspondent of the Daily Telegraph - he wrote a book about the campaign afterwards called 'Kuram, Kabul and Kandahar', and subsequently left the country and took to literature.

The first march was a long tedious pull up the bed of a stream with pine-clad hills on either side for about eighteen miles. We marched very slowly, for all precautions of examining the flanks and crowning the heights had to be taken, so that it was not till dusk that we arrived at our halting place in a valley called the Hazar Daraklet (Thousand Trees) defile. It was bitterly cold, I suppose we were about 8,000 feet above sea level.

We were up at 5.30 next morning and marched at once to Shutargarden (Camel's Neck) the summit of the Pass leading to Kabul. From this high pass there is a rapid descent into the vale country near Kabul and the view looking over the plains was most extensive. I found my old friend Shirres of the Artillery here, looking very hale and rosy, in great spirits about some fighting which they had had recently when his guns seem to have played a distinguished part. While we halted for a few hours at the summit of the Pass (where I forgot to mention was a small entrenched camp occupied by a Sikh regiment, Shirres' two guns and some signallers) I made the acquaintance of Sir Hugh Gough VC under somewhat ludicrous circumstances.

Shirres had asked me to breakfast with him shortly after arrival, but as I felt my usual attack of fever coming on I went to the pass-road to see if my baggage was coming up in order to get a warm coat to protect me from the shivers. I happened to be standing beside some boxes which I knew by experience to be explosives and also knew to my amusement that these had been placed under the charge of a young artillery officer who was dreadfully afraid of them. I daresay as I stood there with hands in pockets, unshaven chin and not very smart clothes, I looked a mean creature - I felt myself such - but I did not know that I resembled a private soldier, yet such did Sir Hugh Gough eventually take me for!

I heard a voice say, "What's in those boxes?" to which I briefly replied with a glance towards the speaker, "Guncotton I believe". "Take your hands out of your pockets, sir, when you speak to *me*" said the voice and turning round and I beheld a very red face blazing with wrath. I was so very miserable that I had not even the pluck to uphold my dignity and meekly begged the pardon of the worthy man, whom I did not know from Adam. Some little time afterwards, when I had to march on I went to see Colonel Gordon and bid him goodbye. I was very kindly welcomed by him in a tent where he was sitting with the owner of the red face to whom he introduced me. The red face grinned when I said we had already met, and from that day forward Sir Hugh Gough and I were on the best of terms.

From the summit of the Shutargarden Pass we descended that afternoon some eleven or twelve miles to a place called Khushi (Delight), whence the name it would be hard to say, a dreary looking spot, but not nearly so cold as the previous halting place. Here we halted for two days which I spent very inactively for I was very weak with fever. We were then only about forty miles from Kabul. The country between seemed to be a series of bare plateaux and stretches of sandy desert with valleys occurring in an unexpected fashion here and there, which valleys were as a rule beautifully fertile and well wooded. But the crossing the bare plateaux was very weary work and often I used to dismount and sit in the shade of my horse on the ground to get away from the perpetual glare of the sun!

One day riding at the head of the column with Macgregor of the 92nd we had a bit of excitement. We saw a band of Afghan horsemen in the distance and simultaneously we went racing after them. However they had the advantage both of start and knowing the country, and disappeared in some broken ground; before we could follow them an officer came from the commander of the convoy tearing after us to forbid such zealous chasing of our country's foes.

However on the 1st November we reached early in the day Charasia, the scene of a battle four weeks previously, and only eight miles from Kabul. Shortly afterwards we reached the Bala Hissar or citadel of the city of Kabul, a large fortified enclosure of irregular shape divided into the Lower and Upper Bala Hissar. The latter, contained within the former, was a sort of castle containing magazines and barracks, the lower Bala Hissar containing the palaces of the nobles, the Amir's gardens and Halls of Justice, and a large number of smaller dwellings. It was surrounded by a thick and high wall, a stagnant moat and pierced by one or two gates.

From the Bala Hissar in a northerly direction was a fine road or avenue of trees for about two miles reaching to the walls of the Sherpur Cantonment. This consisted mainly of mud-brick barracks surrounding three sides of an inner space, where were houses, orchards, mosques and wells. One of these houses was occupied by engineer officers and was known as the RE Castle. On the fourth side stretched two long, low, flat-topped hills, the Bemaru Heights - so named from the village of Bemar at their eastern end.

The whole energy of the corps - which means a good deal - was at this time directed as far as I could see on turning the Sherpur Cantonment into comfortable winter quarters for the British Army, which then numbered nine regiments of infantry, three regiments of cavalry, four batteries and one company of sappers. Nothing was being done to the defences. There were gaps at the ends of the Bemaru Heights by which an enemy could easily enter our position, and the Heights themselves were not fortified in any way. Nothing was being done to remedy these defects or even to clear the front of our position of the thick mud walls that separated the fields, or of any other cover which an assailant might have.

I was introduced by Cather, after duly reporting myself, to the CRE whom I found a comparatively young, tall and handsome man, but whose manner and language to his servants were not calculated to leave a pleasant impression. He told me at once that I was placed under Captain Nicholson, who with Lieutenant Talbot had gone with an infantry brigade towards the Khyber line to establish communication with India; that if I had arrived a day or two sooner I should have gone too; that I was to be employed making the road towards India for the first twenty miles or so; that my headquarters would be a place called Butkhak about ten miles off, that the road would have certain gradients and certain widths (with rapid sketches of engineering details) that he could give me no assistance in the way of NCO's or sappers, nor even tools, but that I would receive authority to purchase and hire anything I liked and he would leave me to make my own arrangements for everything until Captain Nicholson returned when I should be guided by his orders. This was a pretty big programme for a junior subaltern, but it meant a free hand and I rejoiced accordingly. It was much the sort of work that my training on the Swat Canal had been, and so I did not feel strange to it.

The Colonel then took me to the General. At a little tent with a flag before it we stopped and he asked, "May I come in sir?" to which a pleasant voice replied, "Come in". Perkins raised the flap of the tent, and in front, facing us, a little grey-bearded man sat writing. "Moncrieff, let me introduce you to Sir Frederick Roberts", said the CRE. I stood in the doorway and saluted, but the General rose with a frank smile on his pleasant face and greeted me with a very hearty shake of the hand. When the CRE said he was going to send me to Butkhak the General said "Yes, very necessary, the road should be pushed on at once. Macgregor!" "Yes" said a deep voice from the next tent. "Come in here a minute, will you?" Presently Colonel Macgregor, the Chief of Staff, came in looking gruff and fierce. I was introduced. "Let this officer have transport, escort and money, as much as he requires, and as soon as possible go out to Butkhak." Colonel Macgregor asked me what I required, so I said I would let him know as soon as possible, but would not be able to start for a day or two as I would have to purchase stores and tools. "All right", said he, "the sooner you go the better, meanwhile I'll give orders for transport to be given to you whenever you wish it."

During the next few days I used to go daily with my servant Majid who had been in Kabul before, into the city to purchase such tools as I could get. There was a certain part of the city where workers in iron lived and there I procured a quantity of picks and shovels, axes and hammers, also some English-made tools such as saws which were of immense use afterwards. I took a few mules with me which I loaded up with these tools and paid for on the spot. The city of Kabul was then very large, with very narrow streets, noisome and foul and with houses of two storeys as a rule, built of mud (ie sun-dried) bricks. It had one or two main bazaars, wider than the rest and roofed in, with little squares or open places at intervals.

The merchandise to be obtained was very varied. Fruit was abundant and very good, also wonderfully cheap, eg a donkey load of grapes cost about 6d. Then there were furs of all sorts from Central Asia and Siberia, with <u>poshteens</u> (sheep skins, made into coats and boots, with the wool on and the underside of the leather cured) of all sorts and beautifully ornamented in some cases; china also chiefly from Russia, also hardware of different sorts and quaint leatherwork. There were also sweetmeat shops which were much patronised, and refreshment rooms (!) where kabobs and new bread could be bought. I bought some furs, a big <u>poshteen</u> coat and boots, also a Russian teapot and some other small articles for my own use.

The coinage we had in circulation was as varied as the merchandise. Of course there was the British rupee, in limited numbers. There were Kabul rupees, rude thick silver coins as a rule, but some of them were what were called 'Kalimah' rupees, which were coins with the Amir's name and date on one side and the 'Kalimah' or Muslim creed on the other, beautifully stamped. Then there were Bokhara 'tillahs', beautiful thin gold coins supposed to be worth $7\frac{1}{2}$ rupees and current at that value. Some knowing fellows however suspected that they were really worth more and bought up as many as they could and sent them to Bombay where they fetched over 9 rupees each for their weight in gold. One officer I heard made a lot of money in this way. Lastly there was a quantity of Russian gold pieces, 6 roubles I think, which by a curious irony of fate fell into our hands and thus it literally came to pass that British soldiers received their pay in Russian gold. I am very sorry I did not keep specimens of these coins which continually passed through my hands.

There were a number of excellent horses for sale at wonderfully cheap rates until the 9th Lancers spoiled the market by paying absurd prices. Cather bought one weight-carrying pony about 14 hands for 50 rupees, I bought a 13.1 mare for 54 Kabulee rupees that I afterwards could have sold at Simla easily for 200. I had that pony for nearly three years, but she got navicular disease. I sold her by public auction for what she would fetch at Simla and got 80 rupees for her, so it was a good bargain.

I found my knowledge of Pushtu of the greatest possible use, though Persian was the language usually spoken. In a certain quarter of the town resided a people known as Kizilbashis, Persians by descent, aristocratic in appearance and manners, and Shiahs by religion. (The Shiahs are a large and important sect of Muslims). These were quite different from the pure Afghan or Pathan, and also from the Hazaras, a race inhabiting western Afghanistan, men of Mongolian blood, with squat figures, small eyes, high cheekbones, and hairless faces. The Afghan proper is essentially Jewish in appearance. Certainly the variety of race and face to be seen in the crowded streets of Kabul was remarkable: besides the races above mentioned there were the soldiers of the British Army, Tommy Atkins with his cockney voice, the Highlanders of the 72nd and 92nd in their tartan kilts and trews, tall Sikhs with huge turbans and great whiskers, little Goorkhas ugly and merry. There were women too, covered with a white (or what may be called so by courtesy) veil, that covered the whole body, and green slippers, and Persians with the conical sheepskin hat of that country.

In the curious scene however one could not help imagining what must have happened so shortly before, the barbaric insults that had been offered there publicly to the bodies of our deceased comrades of Cavagnari's Mission. No trace of these could ever be found. A commission was then sitting to investigate the circumstances, and woe be to any wretch with whom was found any property that had belonged to any of the Mission. His trial was brief and the gallows was the end of it. Yakub Khan was then a prisoner, and many officers openly declared he was the first who should have been hung. However the case against him was 'not proven' and he was shortly afterwards deported to India.

After a few days I got everything ready and applied for an escort and transport to take me to Butkhak. These were promised to me at a certain hour, but they did not turn up. After waiting a little while I went straight to the Chief of Staff and told him of the delay. Macgregor sent off some peremptory orders and the result was that I got them speedily and started off for Butkhak.

Amir Yakub Khan

* *   * *   * *   * *   * *

For the first three miles or so, the road led over a bare stony plateau called Siah Sang (Black Stone), then descended to the Loghar River, a stream about thirty yards wide and about six feet deep. This was crossed by a strong masonry bridge. For the next two miles the track lay over a swamp in which there was then a considerable quantity of water. I had orders to make a raised road over this swamp, as it was said there was about four feet of water over the track in the winter months. Then for about six miles more the track lay over easy ground till it reached the village of Butkhak which was at the mouth of the Kurd Kabul gorge, the first scene of the fighting and massacre in '42. To the south of the road from the Loghar River to the Kurd Kabul there was a high range of mountains running east and west. To the north lay the Kabul River into which the Loghar flowed. It was then running deep and unfordable except at one point. In the summer time there was barely enough water for a horse to drink!

Butkhak means the dust of idols, the story being that one of the ancient Mughals found an idol temple there and smashed up the idols to dust. In 1879 it was a village with some 800 inhabitants, of an irregular shape, with a wall running round it. Just outside the village were two square forts of the regular Afghan type, and in one of these I took up my quarters with the ten troopers who formed my escort.

The head man of the village, one Taimur Khan, was a very curious-looking old chap. He had an enormous purple nose, the biggest I ever saw I think, which was by far the most <u>assertive</u> feature in his face, making one forget the rest of his expression. His eyes were small and cunning, his mouth generally wore a servile smile and his thin lips, when he spoke to me disclosed his toothless jaws. His thin beard would have been white had he not dyed it red after the fashion of the Afghans. He was about seventy years of age and had lived at Butkhak all his life. During the massacre in January '42 he had found a little English boy crying by the then dead body of his mother; he had taken him to Butkhak and had looked after him kindly, so when Sir George Pollock's avenging army arrived, Taimur restored the child to the English, and thereby got a handsome reward and several letters, which he showed to me. It may be imagined with what feelings of interest I read these letters relating to the events of forty years before. Strange to think that this bulbous-nosed old chap had been living on there in that same place during the momentous interval of British history between 1842-79.

There were two men also in Butkhak who served me right loyally, one was the heir to old Taimur, his name was Khajar Khan, a thoroughly honest man as I found and very willing to give me all the help in his power. The name of the other I have forgotten, he was not in such a good

72

position as the others, but he did me excellent service in getting both materials and labour.

About the latter however there was no great difficulty. There is a Mongolian people inhabiting western Afghanistan called Hazaras totally unlike the Pathans (or ruling class of Afghans) in creed, in fact, in language and in sentiment. They hate the Pathans and lose no opportunity of showing their ill will. These Hazaras are hard working, enduring and independent, and go in search of employment in large numbers to north-west India, but their home is among the mountains to the west of Ghazi. Large numbers of them came asking for work to the RE at Kabul, and the only limit to the employment was the question of tools, food and quarters. I soon had about 1000 or more working under me, whom I had to house and feed, but who did their work very expeditiously and well, and being of a cheery disposition accepted most of the hardships of the winter with very little murmuring.

More difficult however was the question of material. A road is not much use without bridges, and for military bridges, timber is the first requisite. Besides I had orders to put one of the small forts at Butkhak in a thorough state of defence as well as make it into decent winter quarters, so here again timber was an absolute necessity. So I set to work to see what I could raise from the surrounding country. The only trees were the few poplar and willow trees near the walled villages and perhaps some fruit trees and walnuts. The latter of course one desired to spare, but I endeavoured to bargain for the fair purchase of the former. With two troopers as escort I used to ride all over the country visiting the headmen of the various villages and conferring with them. Sometimes they sold me timber very readily, but in some cases I met with flat refusal. However I managed to get enough for my needs, for the most part green wood of a very weak order which no civil surveyor would ever dream of specifying, but it had to be made into bridges for elephants and heavy siege artillery, and it served its purpose too. I often wonder whether the Afghans have renewed these bridges in later years!

What between laying out these twenty miles of road, measuring work done, paying the labour, surveying, and fortifying Butkhak and the bridge-heads at the Loghar Bridge my time was about as fully occupied as any man's could be. Of course it was a big job, and I really did not finish it properly till the following March.

I was not at all well, however, and but for the responsible nature of the task which kept up my spirits in spite of the ailments of the flesh, would have gone on the sick list. I never really got properly well till the spring, and then only for a few weeks, for residence in the pestilential Bala Hissar brought on fever again. But this is going on too far, and I must tell what happened in the early days of winter.

At first I was alone at Butkhak with only a few troopers but shortly after I reached that place General Sir Herbert Macpherson and the 1st Brigade marched in. With him was Captain Nicholson and my old friend Talbot.

The 1st Brigade soon moved back to Kabul, leaving one company of infantry and three squadrons of cavalry. Captain Nicholson and Lieutenant Talbot moved to Lataband, a small fortified camp at the foot of the Lataband Pass where they had to make a road.

Between Kabul and Gandamak there are four routes or passes. The first (nearest to Butkhak) is the Jospari Pass, a name meaning sheep; it is evidently just a track for the passage of flocks. I had explored it one day with the CRE and found it very steep and stony. Next came the Kurd Kabul and Chenar Passes, also narrow and steep. Lastly, the Lataband Pass was highest of all, but open ground where ambuscade would be difficult.

In the Chenar Pass I had once a somewhat unpleasant adventure one day in November. The CRE was at Lataband - where I had never been - and he sent me an order one morning to come at once and meet him to lay out a road over a small pass called the Surkh Kotal about three miles from Lataband and nine from Butkhak. Between Butkhak and this Surkh Kotal was a great stony plain cut up by a number of ravines and crossed by many paths. I sent my baggage and servants off immediately on receipt of the CRE's order, despatched some necessary business, which delayed me longer than I had expected, and then started off to ride alone. My escort I had sent on with the baggage as I expected I would catch them up before they got very far on the road. However, owing to the delay, I did not overtake them, and - I missed my way. I followed one of the many paths or camel tracks, the most important as I thought, but instead of going to the Lataband Pass it took me off to the Chenar Pass, the very existence of which I then did not know. It was getting late in the afternoon, a dull cold day, and I rode on and on further up a wild and desolate valley, where there was not a sign of any life, not a tree nor a shrub to say nothing of tents or human habitation.

At last I met a band of men of the Ghilzai tribe, the wildest and most independent of the Afghans, whose business in life is plunder and fighting. I asked them if this was the way to Lataband, and received a shout of scornful laughter in reply which roused my ire considerably. One of them pointed to the rocks on the side of the pass and said it was miles away in that direction, which the others considered a great joke. Knowing the avaricious nature of the Afghan I said to one of them, "Come this way and have a talk with me." He stepped aside and I then told him I would give him a reward if he showed me the way. "How much will you give?" he said. I produced a coin, it was only a small one, but all that I chanced to have in my pocket. He again laughed in scorn, so I quietly intimated to him by tapping the hilt of my revolver that if he didn't tell me the way quickly it would be the worse for him. Instantly the man's manner changed. 'Follow that path' he said, 'it will take you there all right.' Away I went, fully expecting to hear a jezail (matchlock) bullet whistling after me, but these weapons take some time to come into action and I was round a shoulder of a hill before they had time to send a parting salute after me. When I arrived at Lataband I found the Colonel had gone to meet me at the pass before-mentioned and not finding me there had gone on to Butkhak, so we missed one another.

Nicholson and Talbot with men of the 23rd Pioneers meantime were tackling the big road over the Lataband Pass. It involved much heavy rock cutting. I was their agent for supplies of most sorts, in addition to my other duties, and it turned out to be a fortunate circumstance that I was, for when the fighting broke out in December I had a number of baggage animals at my disposal, generally used for sending stores of all sorts on to Nicholson.

On the 1st December the ex-Amir Yakub Khan was sent from Kabul by stages to India. He came to Butkhak under an escort of the 9th Lancers. Whether Yakub was implicated or not in the massacre probably no-one will ever know. But the general opinion was that he should either have been hanged as guilty, or honourably acquitted. As it was the Government took the middle course of making him a political prisoner, giving him a comfortable house at Dehra Dun where he amused himself with sport and ruined the shooting in that district utterly.

On Monday 8th December I rode into Kabul to buy tools and other materials for my work. It was a bright clear frosty day, very cold, and the little Kabulee boys were making slides on the gutters just as little boys do at home. The city presented its usual busy appearance. While I was negotiating for my purchases, a respectable Kabulee citizen, who was employed as a contractor in partnership with another man, on the big works we had going on, came up close to my horse and whispered, "Be careful about going about now, sahib, the whole country is up." I asked him what he meant. He said, "There are thousands of men coming to attack the English from all parts of the country, soon the whole country will be swarming with them." I thanked him, but laughed at the idea, which I attributed to exaggerated rumours. I heard that day that General Macpherson and his brigade were going to march out to disperse a supposed small gathering in the Chardah Valley, but none of us attached much importance to it. General Sir Michael Kennedy, the Director of Transport had just arrived at Sherpur and so little did any of us think of serious business that there was a review - in the usual pomp and circumstance of peace parade - to show him the troops.

Two days afterwards however we heard the unmistakable thunder of Macpherson's artillery, more or less all morning, and the heliographs kept flashing messages from the west which made us prick up our ears. Our garrison at Butkhak consisted then of one company of the 67th and three squadrons of the 12th Bengal Cavalry. The former were commanded by Lieutenant Atkinson, the latter by Major Green. The infantry were inside the fort and very fairly secure and safe, but the cavalry were outside with very little artificial protection and in event of a night attack might have been thrown into confusion. It was not however until the 11th that we had any reason to apprehend attack. On that day we learned that the cavalry and horse artillery under Macpherson had met with a very serious reverse, that the 9th Lancers had suffered severely and the Horse Artillery had lost four guns. We could see large bodies of men collecting about the hills near the Kurd Kabul, so at night we had strong pickets out, patrolling all round.

Colonel Perkins was at Lataband when this fighting took place but he arrived at Butkhak en route for Kabul on the morning of the 12th. He was much dissatisfied with the state of the defences, and gave me a very severe reprimand on the subject, as I still think, unjustly. It had the effect of making me work at these defences day and night for the next two days, and they were no sooner finished than we had to abandon the fort altogether. On the 11th, 12th and 13th there was steady fighting every day, but at Butkhak we could take no share in it. Our force being chiefly cavalry was of no use in the hills, where there were large masses of the enemy. In the open plain two miles wide, which separated us from the hills, our horsemen had it all their own way, but the enemy rarely gave them a chance. On this occasion the Afghan had clearly the best of it.

That night the 12th Bengal Cavalry captured eight prisoners. We wired to the Chief of Staff for instructions. I grieve to say we got orders to shoot them all. And murdered they were by lamp light about 9 pm. It was most brutal and revolting. I do not know who was responsible for this infamous order but I may say that nothing in all my career as a soldier has ever caused me such shame and disgust. Poor Atkinson who had the order to execute, and was a brave and honourable man, turned pale with anger and shame when it was given to him.

The next day (Sunday 14th December) the enemy were so far successful all round at Kabul as to drive us back from the city, the Bala Hissar and the neighbouring heights, and force General Roberts to retire into Sherpur and there assume the defensive only. At Butkhak we were working at the defences all day long. About 6 o'clock orders came that we were to parade as soon as it was dark and make the best of our way into Sherpur. Then followed a night march, which was one of the most exciting episodes to me, of the whole campaign.

Our little garrison at Butkhak had been increased by two officers (Lieutenants Cooke-Collis and Daly) and about 150 men of the Guides (chiefly cavalry) and all the baggage of that corps, which had marched to Kabul two days before having performed the feat of marching about thirty-six miles in one day. Our orders therefore were to parade at

8 o'clock and march in the following order:- I was to go first with Atkinson and his company of white soldiers, then the baggage of the infantry, then a squadron of the 12th Bengal Cavalry, then the whole of the rest of the baggage, then the Guides and another squadron of the 12th and finally a rearguard of the 12th. The whole force was under command of Major Green of the 12th, a brave cavalry leader and a good man across country, a qualification which now served us well, for he had observed to some purpose the lie of the land.

The road for the first four or five miles lay over an open country, then we came to the great swamp, over which my road was now sufficiently far on to enable one to have no anxiety as to that point. Just beyond this was the Loghar Bridge, a solid structure of brick, with however a very narrow roadway. Beyond this was a low pass in the hills called the Siah Sang, or Black Stone, and a few miles beyond this was the Bala Hissar, up to the very gates of which the road led and then turned off sharp to the right to go to Sherpur, two miles further.

The crucial point of the whole therefore was the bridge. Once past that and we were all right. But an enemy with his wits about him would certainly seize that point, and like other famous bridges it was a place where 'a thousand may well be stopped by three'.

We paraded quietly in the dark at 8 o'clock. I had a lot of transport animals for sending stores up to Nicholson; these I gave to the 67th. The cavalry had their own carriage. No sooner had we started than we found that some of the Guides had gone on or tried to go on, ahead. Their officer either through wilfulness or ignorance had not waited to move off in his regular turn. This was very trying for Major Green's temper - and I think he used some pretty plain language to the officer in question. The blunder was the more annoying because the Guides - who did not know their way - went astray and we lost valuable time in putting them right again. Eventually we got off all right. It was a very dark night, bitterly cold, and frosty. I trudged along on foot beside Atkinson at the head of the column. We sent a few troopers in front to feel the way. I kept wondering whether the enemy would have the sense to hold the bridge, and if he was doing so, how we would turn him out. There was only one way I could see, and that was to fix bayonets and try and carry it with a rush. I had also the uneasy consciousness of having, not long before, built a bridge head or fortified post to defend the bridge. If they had discovered this, it might give us trouble.

We marched along in silence, broken only by the brayings of some misguided brute of a mule, until we came to the swamp and there we were half way across when a trooper rode back to me to report the enemy was in front. My heart gave a leap as I asked him if they were on the bridge. "No" he said, "on the other side, at the Kotal (or pass above mentioned)." I rode back to Major Green and reported this. He was incredulous at first but he pushed a squadron forward under his own command and it was with intense relief that I heard him clatter over the hard masonry bridge, now not far in front of us. We followed after as quickly as possible, and not long after found Green and his squadron had halted in open ground beyond the bridge. He said it was quite true that the enemy were there, we could see their watch fires in fact. To fight with them would be madness, indeed our object was to avoid a collision as far as possible. To do this we must leave the road and work off over the open country to our right, gradually feeling our way till we got near Sherpur.

As soon therefore as we got across the bridge we left the road and struck country, Green leading the way. It was very rough going and the horses stumbled and floundered on their noses in the dark continually. However we reached the Kabul river eventually at a point midway between Sherpur and the enemy and we crossed in safety. Just about that time we heard the sound of heavy firing at the Bala Hissar and discovered that our rearguard in the darkness had failed to keep touch with our main body, had not noticed that we had left the road, had gone unsuspecting straight on and thus walked straight up to the enemy! In the wild fighting that ensued very little damage was done, the only casualty being a mule, and as he, poor beast, was carrying all the officers' mess gear of the 12th Bengal Cavalry his loss was very severely felt. One or two men were slightly wounded.

After waiting a long time outside the walls of Sherpur we were admitted about 3 am. I went to the RE quarters, found a vacant room and bed, and was soon sleeping the slumbers of the weary. Thus ended our night march.

When I awoke the sun was high in the heavens and I saw Onslow standing by my bedside. He told me they had never expected to see us again, also he informed me of all that had happened in the past few days, how Macpherson had first gone out and that Massy with the cavalry brigade and four RHA guns had gone with orders to occupy a certain point, but having gone past this point had been caught in difficult ground by the enemy; how the 9th Lancers had charged brilliantly but with little effect and great loss, including their colonel - Cleland, who was mortally wounded; how the major of the RHA had got in a funk, had ordered his men to cut the traces and ride for their lives, how all had done so except our old comrade Hardy who was last seen standing over a wounded comrade and fighting to the last, how MacGregor had afterwards recovered the guns, how the 72nd and 92nd and the 5th Goorkhas had fought on the hills round the city, how Spens of the 72nd and young Guisford and Forbes of the 92nd, and Butson of the 9th Lancers, and John Cook of the Goorkhas had all been killed, how Dick-Cunningham of the 92nd and Vousden of the 5th PC had both behaved with great valour, also Hammond of the Guides and Padre Adams. And so on with a very thrilling tale, listening also with interest to hear my yarns. The 9th Lancers had lost a terrible number of officers in proportion to their numbers and the regiment was at that time commanded by the junior captain.

I was not long in getting some breakfast and then I went to report myself for orders to the CRE. On the way I met Sir Hugh Gough who shook me warmly by the hand and expressed thankfulness at seeing me again, alive. It seemed to be the prevalent idea with regard to the Butkhak garrison that the previous night's march was a sort of forlorn hope. The credit due to Green for the safety of the force is all the greater.

5th Company Sappers Bridge over Kabul River

Another 5th Company bridge over the Kabul

8
Butkhak and Sherpur

Sherpur was defended in four parts, the third part under Brigadier General Hills, being along the Bemaru Heights. This troops were Sikhs, Goorkhas and Punjab Infantry, with some working parties from the 72nd Highlanders.

Each evening I consulted with the Brigadier as to work to be done the next day, and the number of men needed. Then I asked the RE Adjutant for the necessary tools. The requirements of all four brigades were then reported to the CRE who could alter or modify any of the plans.

The Bemaru Heights consisted of two flat-topped low hills, each about half a mile long. So the siege went on for about ten days. There was plenty of excitement, and occupation for mind and body, but among the vast majority of us there never was any misgiving as to the ultimate result. It was a very easy sort of warfare in one way, viz:- we always had our nights quiet. The enemy in that respect behaved like gentlemen, they invariably stopped fighting at dusk and did not open the ball again till we had breakfast comfortably next day. Had we been fighting a 'civilised' foe we should have had no peace night or day.

I had my meals, breakfast and dinner at least, pretty much as usual in the RE castle, where in the evenings Dundas, Burn-Murdoch, Onslow and I used to gather round the fire and joke and chat merrily till about 10 pm when we all had to go off to our respective stations. My place was at the top of the west end of the Bemaru Ridge where I bivouacked at first but subsequently owing to snow was permitted to sleep inside a small tent. General Hills and Joey Deane had a tent between them of the usual 80lb 'Kabul' pattern which I also shared one very snowy night. I had been round all the sentries and was preparing to bivouac in the snow when General Hills invited me to take what shelter I could inside. I found I had only room to lie across the door of the tent and, as the wind was drifting the snow I awoke in the morning covered to the depth of several inches with it; I was however quite warm and comfortable in spite of it.

During the day the actual amount of work that I got done on the defences was often very little. As soon as an attack appeared to be threatened on any point 'the alert' sounded and men laid down their tools and stood to their weapons of offence. Often this would sound shortly after we had begun work, the fighting would be confined to a few straggling shots at irregular intervals and long shots on our part from our guns.

On one day only did the fighting forces of the enemy show in any force. I think they showed themselves then to try and overawe our soldiery. They collected in immense crowds with their banners on the top of a flat table land some two miles in front of our position. I cannot say how many men were there, but there appeared to be about 20,000. We could see them very clearly through our field glasses. They were rather too far off for our guns to reach.

There were many incidents of a more or less exciting nature which fell to the share of us all. One day in the early part of the siege I heard the General and Colonel Perkins discussing the distance from our line of a certain low hill whence the enemy could harass us with advantage. There seemed to be no range-finder available and the CRE proposed to pace it. This the General would not permit, so I stepped forward and asked leave to do so, which was granted and away I went, taking one or two men with me. When I got to the top of the hill the distance being about 1000 paces I got a grand view of the enemy's position which was certainly an excellent one for attack, but which they did not by any means utilise as they might have done. As a matter of fact I walked back without having a shot fired at me.

Some days afterwards I was working with a party of Goorkhas just outside our walls in much the same direction when I found that I was the object of much attention from a man concealed behind a low wall or tower some 400 yards off. After a few shots fired 'into the brown' of my party he began to take pot shots at me just as a good sportsman picks out an old bird from a covey of grouse. I shifted my position several times and each time got a bullet close past me. The Goorkhas began to get very angry; they would not work and begged me to lead them in attack against him, but I had no orders for this and as I saw they would not work quietly under fire I ordered them to fall in and march back. After they had gone I retired too, waving adieu to the disappointed sportsman. My syce (native groom) was holding my pony some distance in rear and I found him in great excitement, as he said a bullet had passed between him and the pony without doing damage to either.

Our demolition work was especially risky and unsatisfactory on account of the defective material we had to deal with. The only explosive we had was gunpowder from the magazines which we had found at the Bala Hissar when first we marched into Kabul. There were tons and tons of this lying about and the CRE detailed Nugent to take away and store about a ton for our own use and destroy the remainder. This somewhat hazardous operation had been completed some little time before the siege began. Then the fuse which was supplied to us by the Ordnance Department had been lying in the open for months at Kuram and was quite useless and unreliable, so that we never knew when we lighted a fuse whether it would burn or not. Blowing up walls etc was therefore a most uncertain task.

One day Nugent and I were hard at work demolishing the tough mud walls of a village when the CRE came by and set to work to assist us. The fuses were Nugent's own manufacture, they were simply twisted lengths of cotton which had been steeped in saltpetre and gunpowder and allowed to dry. They burned very reliably and well in the open but as soon as any earth (technically called tamping) was piled over the charge to increase the explosive effect the pressure of the damp earth on the fuse extinguished it.

After some unsuccessful attempts we tried the plan of wrapping the fuse in straw which to a certain extent protected it. But we nearly blew ourselves up in doing so.

We had a series of large charges to be lighted simultaneously; the colonel and Nugent lighted while I gave the word. Soon the fuses were sputtering away and we scrambled off on the top of a roof where in a few seconds we heard the mighty crash almost at our feet. We all lay down on our faces while bricks, beams and rubbish of all kinds kept falling round us and we were enveloped in thick clouds of dust. "Are you both there?" said the CRE and then having got satisfactory replies from us both he remarked that he did not think the native powder we had been using would be so strong. The experience we had then however led Nugent to order some tin tubes through which the fuse would pass without being affected by the earth pressure, and alas! there can be little doubt that these tubes were the cause of his death a few days afterwards.

Long before the end of the siege we had got all the defences quite sufficiently strong and the work of improving the trenches and putting obstacles in front went on very languidly after about the 20th. On the 22nd however we heard that the enemy were going to attack us in force next morning before dawn and that the signal was to be a beacon fire on the Azmai Heights. I think we only half believed the tale, as we had had previously many false alarms. Dundas, Burn-Murdoch, Onslow and I dined together as usual, for the last time as it happened, on the night of the 24th and we thought that Gough's brigade would probably appear next day and the enemy would all vanish. We dispersed for the night, without thinking much of a chance of a fight next day.

Dundas had kindly lent me a cork mattress which my Pathan servant, Majid, used to take up to the top of the Bemaru hill every evening and lay it on the ground for me to sleep under a very small tent. There I went that evening and was comfortably slumbering when I was awakened by voices talking and men running about for their rifles. It was about 6 am and just beginning to be light. On the highest top of Azmai a great beacon fire was blazing, lighted as we afterwards heard by old Mushki Alim the <u>mullah</u> who had preached war against us. It was immediately followed by heavy firing to the east and south of our position, then two light or star shells were fired (as I afterwards heard, by my old friend Jock Shirres who was commanding two guns at the northeast corner) which illuminated the whole foreground and showed us hundreds of the enemy rushing forward to the attack.

For the next half hour the noise was incessant. Along the whole front of attack the 28th NI and the Guides kept up a continuous independent fire, quite uncontrolled, I should think, by their officers, and every now and then Shirres' guns kept booming away. As it got light we saw the enemy had retired from that part of the field leaving many killed and were preparing to go for us in some other part. Bodies of them went rapidly from one small enclosure to another till we could see a good many had come round to the north-west side (where my post was) as if meditating attack there. We had one gun on the top of the hill blazing away at Azmai about 2000 yards off, and another gun half way down firing at the gardens near the river.

General Hills however sent me down to fetch that gun up to fire due west towards the enemy working round them and I rode off accordingly. My friend Cowan was commanding the gun and sang out cheerily to me "This is a great battle, Scotty, isn't it?" We rode up the hill with the gun under a very heavy fire. It seemed to me as if the bullets were hopping off the guns and wagons like hailstones. I thought my little mare was shot, for a bullet passed under her knocking up the gravel and making her scramble. One of the gunners said to me, "Your horse is shot, sir," but I found she was not, although evidently it was a pretty near thing.

A few well directed shots from Cowan soon made the enemy clear back and all danger of attack there passed away. The CRE rode round shortly after this and ordered me to go on with preparations for defence so I went down to the Park to look after tools etc. There I saw Cather, and Nugent with some tin tubes in his hand saying "I think these ought to answer the purpose." He meant that by putting the extemporised fuses through these tubes we would be able to overcome the difficulty of the tamping extinguishing the flame. I never saw him in life again.

I had to go into the RE Castle for something and there to my amusement I found my poor little dog Jessie sitting in the middle of a room howling! She heard all the noise of battle outside and thought she was missing all the fun! However I was afraid she might be shot so I let her stay.

For the rest of that afternoon I had to stay at my post, completing the defences. We could see that the enemy were being beaten back from point to point, and each abandoned post was marked by volumes of smoke as our troops set fire to it. By and by the evening drew near and in the dull raw winter twilight the aspect was gloomy and weird, with smoke of burning villages, of artillery and musketry, bodies of troops rushing to the fight and the dead and wounded strewing the field.

Just then General Hills rode up to us - his staff - from whom he had been temporarily separated and said, "You may go, gentlemen, the fight is over and we have beaten them at all points". We saluted and were riding away when he called to me and said, "I have bad news for you, one or two of your fellows have been killed." I asked with a choking voice who they were and when he said he did not remember the names I went over our little list. "Dundas?" "Yes", "Burn-Murdoch?" "No, but he is wounded", "Onslow?" "No", "Nugent?" "Yes". I hurried off to the RE Park and there found Cather who confirmed the sad news. Dundas was in command of the north-east party. We were ordered to blow down a tower and he and Nugent laid two mines arranging to light them together. They had done so but had hardly got away when the mines exploded leaving them in the debris. When others rushed forward and found their bodies, life was extinct. I saw their bodies afterwards. They were not much disfigured. That night Onslow and I dined alone together, with but few words, for it was impossible to forget the kind genial brother officer who had been with us twenty-four hours before and now was lying cold and dead.

Next morning broke cheerlessly enough as regards weather, a dull snowy day with showers of sleet and a leaden sky. There was no fighting - all the enemy had gone. Supplies once more began to come in to us, and the siege of Sherpur was now a thing of the past.

Gough's brigade marched in that day from Butkhak. They had had no opposition at all on the journey; at Lataband they had joined with the small garrison that had been keeping guard there under Major Hudson 28th NI. (He was afterwards General Sir John Hudson, KCB Commander-in-Chief of the Bombay Army) whose right hand man was my Captain - Nicholson. The Lataband garrison had had a very quiet time, and I really believe we could have stayed on at Butkhak too, without danger.

The Lataband garrison had been reinforced a few days before by the Bengal Cavalry under Major Green. They had slipped out of Sherpur one snowy night, had swum their horses across the Loghar river and arrived at Butkhak about midnight. There they were greeted with a volley of musketry which emptied some saddles and made their CO pretty wild with rage. He rode on twelve miles to Lataband, which he reached amid a heavy snow-storm before dawn. He ordered his men to picket their horses and lie down to take such rest as they could. When the day broke Major Hudson was surprised to find two squadrons of cavalry more or less buried in the snow close to his camp. Christmas Day broke bright and clear, perfectly calm and still. The snow was lying pure and white all over the ground, the sky was cloudless and everything looked so quiet and peaceful that we could hardly realise that but two days before we had been fighting hard. Burn-Murdoch and I went to the General's quarters where the sweet familiar service for Christmas Day was read by Padre Adams. We had the Communion Service afterwards and nearly everyone present partook. There were a large number present, and I think that all there felt humbly grateful to God for His deliverance. Several of us went to wish the CRE a happy Christmas. He was very pleasant and cordial.

That afternoon Dundas and Nugent were buried. I never saw a more striking funeral. The hastily made coffins were of course borne on gun carriages and covered by Union Jacks as usual, but the great cortege of officers were all in their fighting uniform, not in the usual bright display of peace. The firing party for Dundas was from the 92nd Highlanders, commanded by Captain Singleton (afterwards killed at Majuba Hill) and the tartan kilts and scarlet coats of the men stood vividly out against the bright pure snow. The 67th Regiment furnished the firing party for Nugent. The procession wound slowly past the scene of much fighting two days before, the sad wail of the pipes alternating with the rich music of the Dead March in 'Saul'. At the little cemetery Padre Adams met us with the beautiful words of the Burial Service. Soon the volleys were fired and we laid our comrades to rest, far from their native land.

Kandahar

**   **   **   **   **

After the fighting was over we settled down to work again at defences, and roads and other such matters. Childers was sent out to Lataband with the 23rd Pioneers to make the road over the pass, sorely against his will; and my bit of the road near Butkhak was left unfinished pro tem. I was given a section of the defences of Sherpur to work at, and very busy I was, pulling down the walls and villages which had afforded cover to the enemy in the recent fighting.

One day while making my way through the snow I came across my old friend Mr Gilson Gregson, the great apostle of temperance. I was intensely suprised to see one, who, I imagined, was miles away in India. He had, it seems, been at Peshawar on one of his temperance tours, when he was invited to go a little bit up the Khyber to see some regiments there. Then he was invited further and further until he reached Kabul itself just before the fighting began. He was through the whole siege at Sherpur, staying with the 72nd Highlanders, and he did not relish it at all! He was very well and hearty, and I was very glad to see him. We had a little prayer meeting on the last night of the year, he and I and several others. Gregson returned to India with one of the early convoys.

During January I was backwards and forwards between Butkhak and Kabul. At the former place I built myself a little house, and was very comfortable. It was in one of the forts which we had not formerly occupied. Another was occupied by a squadron of native cavalry, whose officer and I had our frugal meals together. My lot was certainly a happier one than his, for while he had to pass the time in idleness, I always had more than enough work to occupy me on the road. At Kabul I had still a good deal to do on the defences. The CRE had been very unwell after our Christmas dinner (on which occasion we had sat down seventeen to dinner, ie fifteen REs, a signalling officer, poor Straton, afterwards killed at the battle of Kandahar, and Martin of the survey) and had not formally relieved me of my charge there. The work was not particularly interesting.

Numbers of labourers were employed on odd jobs about the place, and in the evening they all paraded for payment. The orderly RE officer was present, and one British soldier with a bag of money. A head man of the coolies also attended. As we had no small change, and had usually to pay the men in gold coins, of which one went to pay thirty men, the following would be the procedure. The men squatted on the ground and thirty would be carefully counted by the soldier. The head man then said 'Shemna si nafar, bigarash' (You thirty men, catch hold of it) and gave the coin to the thirtieth man, who generally seized it and bolted as hard as he could go, followed by the remaining twenty-nine in hot pursuit!

The soldier who worked with me was a cheery excellent fellow named Rutherford, a private in the 72nd who had been a shepherd lad in the hills near Blairgowrie in the days of his youth. Among other items of news that he gave me were the tidings of the disaster to the Tay Bridge. I think he told me of this the day after it happened so it shows how quick we were in hearing news.

Before very long, however, fresh officers having turned up from India, I handed over my work in Kabul and returned to my beloved road, which I soon had in good order.

I lived partly at Butkhak, occasionally at Lataband, for the early months of the year, occupied daily with the construction of the road. I see from my diary that February was a month of intense cold, snow falling nearly every day, and keen frost at night. The sun's rays, however, were always strong enough to melt partially any ice that formed during the night, so that although we very frequently skated on some little ponds at Butkhak we were only able to do so for a few hours in the forenoon.

The two most difficult parts of my work lay in opposite directions; one was the crossing of the swamp near the Loghar River, the other the crossing of a pass near Lataband, the road for some two miles there being on very steep hilly ground. I had frequently to visit these places and was in the saddle often for many hours. I have a vivid recollection of the bitterly cold winds from the north that seemed to penetrate through the very thickest clothing, and be far more severe than anything I had ever experienced. I was however very comfortable inside my little house at Butkhak, when my day's work was over, and many a time was able to offer shelter and hospitality to some passing officer, who half frozen with a long cold march, was delighted to find a snug haven of rest.

In March the spring began, the snow gradually melted, and the weather became genial and pleasant. The heavy guns with their teams of elephants and bullocks turned up at Lataband on the 3rd of April, and on the following day I accompanied them over my road, with a small party of native sappers ready to give assistance where necessary. The major and the captain of this battery were neither of them men of any nerve; fussy and excitable, they made a great fuss whenever the road appeared the least difficult. The only officer in the battery who apparently knew his business was Beauchamp Duff, then senior subaltern, an old Woolwich comrade of mine, and friend of my family. For me it was a somewhat anxious day. I had a considerable number of bridges, built of wood in a very haphazard fashion, on the road, and it was with trepidation that I watched the first elephants slowly come on to them. My relief when all of them were successfully passed was very great.

I have often thought since that it was a great responsibility for so young an officer as I then was, to have the entire designing and execution of twenty miles of roads and bridges. The CRE, it is true, gave me general instructions, but I never sent in any sketch of any of the works that I carried out, nor was I apparently expected to do so. I believe that the general was pleased, and he sent a general report of good work done by me to the Commander-in-Chief, who wrote an appreciative reply. I was also 'mentioned in despatches' for good work at the defences of Sherpur, the fact being that we REs were all doing more work than we could properly manage and the general took that form of thanking us, otherwise I am not aware that I did anything worthy of mention.

It was a very healthy happy life that at Butkhak, and it is a part of my career that I look back upon with much pleasure. The experience I gained of road construction was considerable, and the satisfaction with which I saw an officer driving a dog-cart, which he had brought from Peshawar, along my road was one which engineers only would sympathise with. I had completely shaken off my ill health, and even the kind general recognised that I was quite a different person from the fever-stricken lad that had turned up at Kabul the previous autumn.

A halt in the shade of a Minar at Kabul

* *   * *   * *   * *   * *

On 13th April, having finished all my work on the road, I was ordered to Kabul, where the force had been organised in three divisions. I was posted to the second, whose headquarters were in the Bala Hissar.

Much work had been done to make this citadel both defensible and habitable. Old houses had been cleared away by the score, defences had been built up and armed, and it was both a strong and a comfortable place by the time I found myself there.

Yet it had one fatal drawback. All round it lay an irregular broad moat or ditch, full of stagnant water in places, and everywhere foul and insanitary. Troops were only allowed to remain in the Bala Hissar for a limited time. But we engineers and the artillery remained there without change. When the weather got hot malarial fever broke out. From midday until I left in July I had constant attacks of intermittent fever, which undid much of the good effected by the fresh, active life at Butkhak.

In many respects the life was cheerful enough. There were about a dozen of us REs who lived in a little defensible square, two sides of which were simply walls loopholed etc, the other two sides having comfortable rooms, with a flat roof and loopholed parapet. It was great luxury, and as the necessities and even luxuries of life were easily procurable we lived very comfortably. Of work there was very little to do. I had a hospital to build, and we had odd jobs to do in the way of surveys, water supply schemes, and miscellaneous duties, but the work was very light and we chiefly spent our time in amusement. There was any amount of cricket and lawn-tennis, there was a pack of hounds which used to give us capital runs after a drag, there were many beautiful rides in the surrounding country, which with the fresh spring foliage was exceedingly pretty. Sherpur being two miles off, with a club (!) to which we all belonged, made a pleasant object for a quiet ride or even walk when we were not in the mood for more extended exercise. The country was as quiet as it would be in the neighbourhood of London, and the idea of our being on active service was often treated as an excellent joke.

I made the acquaintance of many officers of other branches of the service, of course, but among others too, like-minded with myself in religious matters, Acklom of the Connaught Rangers, a senior captain, and Hay of the Artillery, a subaltern somewhat junior to myself. With these two excellent fellows I became great friends, and we enjoyed many long rides together.

Among many interesting men whom I met at Kabul, there was one, Yahiya Khan by name, a native of Istalif, a town some forty miles to the north of Kabul, whose history was a most interesting one. Intended as a

Muslim cleric, he was sent to learn at the chief mosques in Kabul when he was young. He was much dissatisfied with the formality and hypocrisy that was everywhere prevalent in these religious institutions, and he went off successively to Jallalabad, Swat and finally Peshawar to seek peace of conscience, without success until he came in contact with the Christian missionaries at Peshawar, by whose influence he embraced Christianity and was baptised. This was in 1864. The missionaries had given him a copy of the New Testament in Persian, and had bidden him return to his own country and make known to his fellow countrymen the truth it revealed. After many adventures and much persecution he regained his native village and there he seems to have lived all those sixteen years the life of a consistent Christian, studying his Testament and teaching the truth to his family. He was anxious that his wife and family should be baptised, and when Sir L Cavagnari was in Kabul, he tried to gain access to him to ask his help. But the massacre followed and then the fighting, so it was not till everything had settled quietly down that he ventured to come to the British camp and ask to be allowed to proceed to Peshawar with his family. He went first to the chaplain to the troops, Padre Adams, who not knowing his language, and knowing that I spoke the languages of the country, sent him on to me. He was in no hurry to go to Peshawar and as I wanted to see more of the man, I engaged him to come and read Persian with me every day for an hour. Our lesson book was the New Testament, which he had kept so well all those years, and which I found he knew very thoroughly. He eventually went to Peshawar with his wife and children, who were baptised by Mr Hughes. He subsequently returned to Kabul, after we left, and I heard of him no more.

The Amir's Hall of Justice was, during our occupancy of the Bala Hissar, used by day as a carpenters' workshop for British troops. There too in the evenings, some godly soldiers of the 67th Regiment used to meet to read, pray and sing hymns. I often went to these humble meetings and realised how strange it was that the walls of a building erected by fierce Muslims should echo the simple hymns and praises of Christian soldiers. On Sunday evenings the chaplain of the 92nd Highlanders held, in the lines of that regiment at Sherpur, an evening meeting conducted in the Scottish Presbyterian fashion. I frequently went there, accompanied by Colonel Battye of the 2nd Goorkhas. The meeting was invariably well-attended, by quiet sober Scots in the 92nd. One of them was precentor, who raised the tune from a well known tuning fork. To hear the old fashioned psalm tunes sung to the metrical version of the Psalms, in a strange land, brought tears to my eyes and a lump in my throat. One can faintly imagine the feelings of the Babylonian exiles.

Towards the end of July, when arrangements were well advanced for handling over Kabul to the Amir Abdurrahman, there came ugly rumours of disaster at Kandahar. And before long the fatal news of the defeat at Maiwand and the siege of Kandahar came to us in all its verity. At once there was a change in the quiet humdrum life at Kabul, when it became known that a division 10,000 strong, of picked troops was to go off under Sir Fred Roberts.

Colonel Perkins was to be CRE and required about twelve other RE officers, but they were all chosen from among the senior subalterns and I was too junior to get the chance.

On a beautiful Sunday evening in August I saw the last of the Kandahar column set off under its gallant commander. The soldiers made a short march out to Beni Hissar, some four miles, and were encamped in fields beside running brooks and shady trees. I happened to be on some duty at the Bala Hissar, when I saw a cavalcade riding out, among whom I recognised Sir D Stewart and Sir F Roberts and others. My duty was practically over so I mounted my steed and galloped after them, overtaking them before they arrived at the camp. It was a lovely calm evening, the scenery was most beautiful all round, and the men were lying about on the grass, or bathing in pools in the streams.

When the little cavalcade rode up, the news seemed to spread like wildfire that Sir F Roberts had arrived to take over command, and all 10,000 men seemed to spring to their feet; they cheered again and again till they were hoarse. The General himself looked very pleased, as well he might. I could realise that such a spirit was the sure precursor of victory.

I bade goodbye then to Sir F Roberts and to Colonel Perkins. They both shook me warmly by the hand and said they were very sorry I was not coming with them. So was I. Years passed before I saw either of them again.

We stayed on at Kabul for about three days after the Kandahar column had started. I was employed on staff duties during that time. The weather was most beautiful, and I thought I had never seen the country to such advantage.

I was attached to General Daunt's staff. As he had little engineer work for me to do, he made me do assistant quartermaster general and baggage master. As such I had to marshal all the baggage at the beginning of a march and see it off, then ride on ahead and lay out the camp at the next halting place, mount guards over the drinking places, see that the ground was clear and fit for camps etc. It was very pleasant work and good experience.

On the 11th August we finally marched away from Kabul. The new Amir Abdurrahman and his staff took over the city from the British under Sir Donald Stewart, and a meeting of the principal actors in this transaction took place in a tent or canopy pitched outside the walls of Sherpur. As British officers were permitted to be present, if not actually required for duty with the troops I took advantage of the opportunity.

The new Amir was received by Sir Donald Stewart and Mr (afterwards Sir Lepel) Griffin by whom he was conducted to the tent of meeting. He was a big burly black-bearded man dressed in a mauve coloured coat with gold lace, black lambswool cap, and Russian boots. The conversation was at first interpreted by Mr Griffin, then by one of his staff who was better acquainted than he was, with colloquial Persian. Of the conversation I now remember but little. One remark the new Amir made was this:- 'My present prevailing sentiment is that of gratitude to the British Government'. Most of the leading British officers were then presented to the Amir, and then we took leave, mounted our horses and at last bade farewell to Kabul. I was one of the last to leave.

We encamped that evening at Butkhak and proceeded by regular marches to Peshawar, halting at Gandamak and at one or two other places. The weather was very hot, and we were much exposed. I find from my diary that we generally rose at 3 or 4 am and were often out till 4 or 5 in the evening, but this was inevitable seeing that the long column of about 10,000 fighting men and baggage, with about 10,000 followers at least, had to march along one narrow road. General Daunt on whose staff I was, was Colonel of one of the battalions of the Norfolk Regiment, a battalion that I had known pretty well during the campaign. He was a very pleasant man, and the other members of his staff were all of a very friendly disposition and we got on excellently.

At Jallalabad we halted for three days. I little thought when I left it some fifteen months before that I should come back again, and from the west. Everything was much as we had left it; the year before, and in the pleasant autumn weather the country looked very fair and beautiful.

Down the Kabul river fifteen months before I had travelled on a raft for four marches; we marched by short stages, through wild picturesque gorges, and bare stony valleys. Nothing of any importance occurred on the march. The tribes on the north side of the river were at war with each other and therefore occupied with their own affairs. Those in our rear never molested us, though, as our rearguard marched out of each camping ground for the last time, they generally swooped down like vultures to try and find anything of value that we might have left, and frequently quarrels thus arose over their booty.

I arrived at Peshawar on the 2nd September after a campaign of nearly a year. I stayed with my hospitable friends the missionaries, whose kindness to me I shall ever gratefully remember, and it was with much humble thankfulness that I once more worshipped in the church at Peshawar where a year before I had committed myself to the merciful keeping of Almighty God, who had now brought me safely through all the perils and dangers of an arduous campaign.

9
Hill Station Life, 1879-82

At Peshawar I received orders to report myself to the Superintending Engineer, Sirhind and Lahore Command, Military Works, for employment in the hill division of Kasauli.

During the campaign, a change had taken place in the policy of the Indian Government which affected the whole of my future career. Hitherto RE officers were eligible for all branches of the Public Works Department, and civil engineers also were liable to be appointed to the Military Works branch as well as to any other. Owing, however, to the views of the Public Works Member of Council (I believe) it was decided that civil engineers should be withdrawn from the Military Works branch, and REs transferred to it from the Irrigation, Civil, Roads and Railway Branches. Those RE officers who had attained position and experience in any of the latter branches were not disturbed in their appointments, and a few juniors were still allowed to remain in railways, but the bulk of us who had been on active service were transferred en bloc to the Military Works branch, very much to our indignation.

I was very sorry to leave the Irrigation work. Most engineers who have served on it become fascinated with the interest of the work, and had I not been transferred I should probably have stuck to it for the whole of my career, like my Uncle Colin.

As it was, I can now see that the transfer did me good. It gave me a far wider experience of engineering than I should have had if I had remained always on canals, and it took me away from the Department when a stagnation of promotion was just coming on.

I re-visited the Swat River Canal for a few days chiefly for the purpose of collecting my belongings, which I had left at Abazai during the campaign. I was the guest, while at Abazai, of Mr Lindsay Heath, the new executive engineer, a very nice fellow. With him I visited many of the works in progress, which I had either begun or helped on. It was very interesting to see them again. I left the place with much regret, for the work there in its freedom of action and direct responsibility was just the sort of thing I delighted in. To carry out scientific engineering in such an out-of-the-way place and with such poor materials and labour was a task calling forth one's best energies, and proportionately of absorbing interest.

The weather was very rainy and during that visit we had some big floods. On the other hand, between the showers, the country looked lovely, with its fresh green crops, and wooded villages and background of mountains in beautiful tints of light and shade.

It was a great pleasure to see again old friends at the Doaba outposts of Michin and Shabkader, Colonel and Mrs Fisher, Colonel Elton and others.

I have often wished I could re-visit those scenes. I am told the canal is paying now such a handsome revenue that the Government are only sorry they did not make it much bigger, and proposals are now on foot to enlarge it and take it to further arid wastes beyond Mardan. At that time it was thought that it could never pay a decent percentage on the capital outlay, but that indirectly it would pay as a pacificator of warlike people. It has done far more than that, and I feel proud of the small share I had in so excellent a result.

I left Peshawar on the 11th September. I re-visited it some six weeks later when I went up for my exam in Pushtu (I passed with flying colours and got the government reward of 1000 rupees. I did not need money just then so I sent it home to my sisters, and it gave them a nice tour in France and Italy where I met them).

The railway which now connects Peshawar with Lahore and the rest of India was then not completed further than Ratiyal a small station between Jhelum and Rawal Pindi, some 150 miles from Peshawar. I had therefore to travel by road (dak ghari) as far as this terminus (the line was opened to 'Pindi a very short time afterwards). The usual bridge of boats at Attock was at that time not in use, as the floods and rains had swollen the Indus to such an extent as to render such a form of bridge impracticable. I had therefore to cross the river in a large barge and had ample time to admire the rocky picturesque gorge which has been the chief site for the passage of armies since the days of Alexander the Great. Many troops were crossing in barges at the same time as I was and the scene, in the early morning, as viewed from the dak bungalow on the rocky heights above the stream, was most picturesque.

At Ratiyal I found most of my horses and servants waiting for me, also a goodly contingent of returning warriors going my way. There was therefore a big party of us in the railway journey to Lahore. At this place I spent a day, reported myself at the headquarters of my command, and then pursued my railway journey to Ambala, the nearest railway station at that time to Simla and all the hill garrisons in the vicinity, Kasauli, Dagshai, Sabathu, Solon and Jutogh. From Ambala one had then to travel by dak ghari to Kalka about forty miles off, at the foot of the hills. Those who were going to Simla had to change at Kalka into a <u>tonga</u> or hill cart. Those for Kasauli had either to ride or be carried up the steep hill road to the station, as the road to it was not fit for wheeled traffic.

Kasauli is an extremely pretty station built on the top of a ridge some 6000 feet above sea level, and directly above the plains. The top of the ridge is covered with pine trees (the chirpine - p. <u>longifolia</u>) very like Scots firs. The houses of the residents are scattered about among the pine woods. There is a remarkably pretty English church, built of grey stone, with a square tower such as one would see in an English village, and the barracks for the troops, surrounding a tiny parade ground are like English cottages, built in Elizabethan style with square mullioned windows and diamond panes. The garrison was small, consisting only of a few companies of men of various regiments sent there for their health; but the place was the summer headquarters of the general commanding the Sirhind Division, and there were schools of signalling and garrison instruction permanently located there. It was also the headquarters of the Civil Government of the district, and of one or two government departments. Thus there was a considerable European society of a miscellaneous order.

The climate and scenery were simply charming. The air was cool and delicious and the views in all directions superb. I put up for the first few weeks in a very comfortable hotel, where I lived <u>en pension</u>. I had a nice large sitting room with a bedroom and bathroom opening off it, and I had from my windows a splendid view of the snowy range in the far distance. In the immediate foreground there was a deep valley going down thousands of feet, and in the middle distance range upon range of lower hills, with the wooded ridge of Simla forty miles away. On the other side of the station one could look over the plains of the Punjab for miles and miles till at last they melted away in the distance. After living at the hotel I was offered a house, which I occupied with a Captain Yaldwyn of the Commissariat Department - this house was at the very top of the ridge and from it we could see both ways - on the one hand to the plains, on the other to the eternal snows.

** ** ** ** **

My work at Kasauli was new, and not quite to my liking. In the Military Works Department my Executive Engineer was a somewhat elderly Major Beckett, originally a civil engineer, who had got his commission just after the Mutiny. Personally he was courteous and kind, and yet, somehow, not popular. He was a <u>very</u> exclusive Plymouth Brother, and I think the minute examination of Bible passages on which he based his narrow views, affected his engineering work, for while exact in matters of detail, he often passed over broad questions of construction and organisation.

For instance he once sent me for revision a design he had made in elaborate detail for a church, but the walls were not strong enough to support the roof, and the timber was of a kind we could not obtain locally.

In his division were several small military stations, in all of which (except Kasauli) European subordinates were in charge. Major Beckett travelled between these places and it would have been well if he had gone about more than he did, for his subordinates were an unscrupulous lot of scoundrels, all more or less hand-in-glove with the native contractors.

My work was to assist Major Beckett in the preparation of designs and estimates. After the free and easy independence I had enjoyed I found these petty details most irksome, and asked for an independent charge. The Major demurred a little but said he would try to arrange it.

In October I visited Simla for the first time, riding by a bridle path which had been used before the cart-road was made. In the forty-five miles from Kasauli the hills are bare and uninteresting, but when one reached Simla, the scene changed.

First one rode through a wood of holm oaks and rhododendrons, with views here and there of wooded ridges covered with deodars, and in the background the mighty snowy range. Then gradually the road wound in and out of villa gardens, if such a name can be applied to the 'compounds' of the chalet-like houses where dwelt the high officials of Government, and then one reached the busier parts of the station where fair ladies were being wheeled along in <u>jinrickshaws</u> and young men cantered alongside on hill ponies.

I only stayed a couple of days in Simla that time. I had gone simply to be photographed! My mother had expressed a wish to see a likeness of me after four years' absence, so I had made this little expedition to Simla for that purpose. I went almost immediately afterwards back to Peshawar again for my examination in Pushtu, as I have mentioned before. This was my last visit to that part of the frontier.

On returning to Kasauli I received orders to go to Jutogh and take over charge of the sub-division there from Mr Hoeruli, the Assistant Engineer, who was being transferred to the Civil Buildings and Roads Branch of the PWD.

I reached Jutogh on the 15th November. It is a charming little station built near the top of a hill with two peaks, distant some four miles from Simla, with which place it is connected by a good cart road winding along the hillside. It is an entirely military station and quite distinct from Simla, yet near enough to enable one to go in and take part in any social or other function that might be going on there. During the Afghan business it was decided to increase the garrison by 300 infantry, so new huts were built for the infantry men, the original Goorkha officers' houses were being done up as officers' quarters and mess, and new quarters were being made for the men of the artillery, which was now being re-organised. This entailed a great deal of work on the engineers, and about half of it had been completed before I arrived.

Mr Hoeruli was the son of a CMS (German) missionary who had been educated partly in Germany, partly in India. He had received his first appointment in the PWD after going through the usual course of instruction at the Thomason CE College at Roorkee. He was an excellent engineer in all that concerned office work, accounts etc so that I found everything in the shape of documents and returns in perfect order. But the cost at which work was being done startled me considerably. I had had no experience of barrack building, yet the rates for various classes of work were so much higher than those which I had been accustomed to on the frontier, that I felt sure something must be wrong, especially as there were ample supplies of material at hand. The stone was quarried close to the site of the works, the mortar was all made of materials locally manufactured, the timber came from the market in Simla, everything in fact tended to economy and put me at once on my guard.

Fortunately for me the first work I had to do was the construction of a longish piece of hill road with a number of small bridges and retaining walls in it. The contract was ready to be given out to tender, but, knowing myself to be on familiar ground when it was a question of road making, I intimated that I would be my own contractor and make the road myself. This was not only interesting, but I found that I saved about twenty-five per cent of the estimate. The surplus I applied to making another road. This was of course utterly irregular - I never asked for any sanction from higher authority, and, quite innocently, thereby infringed one of the primary regulations of the Department. Beckett was aghast when I told him, with some pride, what I had done, but he acknowledged that the money was well spent. The experience thus gained was very useful, for it showed me how extravagant the estimates had been. Of course I could not interfere with existing contracts, but as the works gradually became complete, I sent the contractors about their business and gradually became my own contractor for everything. I saved the

State far more than my pay and that of all my subordinates by this means, and had the satisfaction of having it officially reported by the Superintending Engineer that the work was not only cheaper, but better done than formerly.

Hoeruli was, like Major Beckett, a very exclusive Plymouth Brother. I did not see very much of him, but the little acquaintance I had impressed me a great deal with the devotion and earnestness of that sect. Subsequently I became great friends with Beckett and derived much benefit from his unworldly conversation, though we differed much in many matters. The lives of such men as he and Hoeruli were a strong protest against the prevailing frivolity and godlessness of so large a proportion of society in the hill stations in India.

But there were many who were not so exclusive in their views as Beckett and Hoeruli, but who were equally steadfast in their adherence to the old truths of the Gospel. Among the many people I met in Simla there was a circle of most delightful Christians, who lived apart from the prevailing tone of society, and who were yet not averse to mirth and amusement. Among these my greatest and best friends were Captain 'Jim' Hutchinson and his wife - dear 'Mrs Jim'. Then there was Archdeacon Matthew and his wife, both cultured, refined, deeply taught in the Bible and full of good works. He was one of the best preachers I ever heard and his early Sunday services were the nearest ideal I ever came across to perfect worship. I rarely missed riding in to them. The Presbyterian minister, Mr John Fordyce, was also a man whom it was a great pleasure to know, and there were many others too numerous to mention. The winter society in Simla is peculiar in that the preponderance of ladies is very noticeable. The husbands being in the plains, frequently travelling about with the Viceroy or the Commander-in-Chief at his inspections, the ladies remained at their mountain homes during the winter months. To one who like myself had been knocking about without any ladies' society at all, the change was very agreeable.

There was a rink where we used to meet frequently - roller skating, which had been the absorbing fashionable amusement a few years before at home, had not grown out-of-date in India then, and every evening and especially on three evenings in the week (when certain ladies provided tea) all the beauty and fashion of Simla gathered to skate. It was capital fun for we all knew each other and used to have great games. It was fully six miles from Jutogh, but one thought nothing of that and I generally used to stay and dine, either at the club, or with some friends and then ride home in the glorious frosty starlight. When the moon was shining what magnificent views there were!

After I had been a short time at Jutogh a mountain battery of artillery, commanded by a Major Douglas, marched in. It had been all through the Afghan war including the Kandahar march, and was very smart and efficient. With this battery for the next two years I was very intimately associated, for I had to build the barracks for them, and as the mountain battery was an entirely new organisation, there were no type of standard plans for their buildings, and I had therefore, in consultation with Douglas, to work out what was suitable. Poor Douglas however took ill immediately after the battery arrived and lingered on for some two or three months getting worse and worse. He had abscess of the liver and in spite of all the medical skill available, he died in February 1881. I sat up with him till within a few hours of his death.

The winter 1880-81 passed away pleasantly in interesting work, shooting big game in the hills to the westward and small game in a charming little trip I took to the plains, and in making many friends in Simla. With the advent of spring I took my three months' Afghan leave and went home, a delightful trip. I met my sisters in Rome after a brief visit to Naples. We then went on by Pisa and Turin to Paris whence we came to England. It was a charming change and one fraught with consequences to me ever since in renewing my acquaintances with the Naemoor* household: I returned to India and Jutogh at the end of June after a pretty hot journey.

My friend Duperier had become engaged to Mrs Lang's eldest unmarried daughter and I was bidden to be best man at the wedding which took place in the pretty church at Kasauli on September 1st. A very happy wedding it was, the bride and bridegroom being both universal favourites.

The Viceroy then was Lord Ripon, the Commander-in-Chief, Sir Donald Stewart. I went to dinner parties and other social functions at both 'Peterhoff', the then Viceregal Lodge, and 'Snowdon' which was the 'chiefs' residence, meeting at both places many distinguished men and women, but, being only a subaltern, I did not mix much in the great world of statesmen and warriors who then ruled our Indian Empire. Men such as the saintly Bishop French of Lahore, Sir Charles Aitcheson, and General Brownlow I got to know a little more intimately and to admire. At one dinner party I met a man with whom I afterwards was on the most intimate terms - Colonel James Browne.

The circumstances of our meeting were somewhat peculiar and have left a vivid impression on my mind. It was on an evening during the rains and as I usually did, I sent my dress clothes to the club at Simla and rode there from Jutogh. After dressing I mounted by pony to ride about a mile to the house where I was to dine and I remember distinctly looking at the sky to see whether rain were likely to come on and whether I should unbuckle the waterproofs in front of my saddle. It looked all right and I started. But before I got halfway, down came the rain in sheets and in

---

* See footnote on page 125.

spite of my unbuckling the waterproofs I was so drenched on arrival that my dress shoes were simply full of water! A gentleman staying in the house offered me nether garments which I gladly accepted, but as they were about six inches too long for me I had to appear in the drawing room 'reefed', as sailors would say! This of course created some amusement among other guests, among whom were Colonel and Mrs Browne. He kept the company in a roar with a succession of amusing stories, chiefly against himself. I did not have much conversation with him and I did not think he would afterwards have remembered me, but in that I was wrong.

Another notable point about that dinner was that my next neighbour - a Colonel Firebrace - strongly advised me to leave Military Works and apply for Railways. When I said I would have done so long before, but did not think the railway people would have me, he told me that was quite a mistake and that they would be very glad indeed if I went in for that branch of the Public Works. Accordingly I applied for Railways as soon as possible and got a reply that as soon as I could be spared from the Military Works branch, I would be transferred to Railways. This change has probably affected my whole future, although it did not take effect till about seven months later.

Almost immediately afterwards General Innes, the Inspector General of Military Works, sent for me and said that if I would withdraw my application for Railways he would appoint me executive engineer of the Quetta Division. This was a very high compliment, as this division was perhaps the most important in India, and the pay was far beyond anything I was then getting. However I had made up my mind on the subject and declined his offer with thanks.

My work at Jutogh was nearly at an end. I had had a very pleasant time there. I was practically my own master, had designed as well as built almost all the works round, and these were of great variety, barracks, hospitals, guard rooms, stables, and finally a church which I designed but did not actually build, though I chose the site of it. The experience was very useful to me in afterdays when I went home.

I was also comfortably housed. I had a charming cottage, with my office under the same roof, surrounded by a little garden. But in spite of these advantages I was not sorry to move, because the long residence at such a high altitude seemed to have a bad effect on me. Though not actually ill, I seldom slept more than three or four hours a night, and this resulted in weariness and low spirits.

I put in for a week's leave, but before it could be granted, I suddenly got orders to proceed to Bareilly and then to Lucknow, to be Executive Engineer at that important military station.

One of the many friends I made at Simla was a young clergyman, Maitland, a Cambridge graduate of independent means. He had been persuaded by Bishop French of Lahore to devote his life to serving Christ in the mission field. I was present at his ordination as deacon at Simla, the only other candidate being an intensely dark Indian, it was unutterably solemn and touching to see the two young men kneeling together, to receive the laying on of hands for the work to which both had been called. I saw a good deal of Maitland after that, especially at the Hutchinsons' where he stayed.

With these dear friends I spent my last Sunday in Simla, shortly after my twenty-seventh birthday, and started early next day 8th October 1882, for Lucknow.

Mussoorie, showing the Camel's Back and Roller Skating Rink

10
Lucknow

The circumstances under which I was sent to Lucknow were no doubt complimentary to me, but they were far from agreeable. The officer who was acting executive engineer there - a man considerably my senior, but still a subaltern - had acted with great discourtesy towards the officer temporarily in command of the division, a very senior colonel. The engineer had the rights of the case in dispute on his side, but had expressed himself in so rude a way that he was instantly reported, and orders were issued from headquarters that he was to be relieved of his duties at once. I was sent to do this, and found myself in the disagreeable position of being successor to a man who had rubbed up all other officials who had dealt with him, the wrong way, and who at the same time was carrying on very important works very successfully.

The division is large and important, comprising Lucknow itself, Faizabad and Sitapur, with a total garrison of four cavalry regiments, eight infantry battalions and four batteries of artillery. The executive engineer was usually a major, and I was probably the youngest ever to be given the job, but as I was only <u>locum tenens</u> till a more senior man should come from home, I could not introduce much change. Although the post was responsible it did not carry much extra pay, so with a big house to keep up I was really worse off than before. For part of the time of my occupancy I sub-let parts of the house, though after Christmas I had various guests to stay, including Uncle Colin and his wife, and Miss Albright her cousin.

I was Engineering Adviser to the general commanding the division, and had to attend various committees on defence. I had a number of big works in progress to supervise, and a large office staff, native and european. My first assistant was Lieutenant EC Stanton, who at the time of my arrival was on leave in Kashmir.

Lucknow was very different from anything I had met in India hitherto. The people of the district were unlike either the Sikhs or Pathans of the Punjab. The very trees and fruits were new to me, as were the social customs. Everything pointed to a longer European occupancy than the less luxurious style of the Punjab.

Lucknow itself was most interesting and beautiful. It is divided into 1) the Native City and Civil Lines, and 2) the Cantonments, sometimes called Dilkusha (Hearts' Delight) from an old hunting palace of the Kings of Oudh in one of the gardens. The main road was an avenue shaded by mango trees, and called the Mall, with officers' bungalows on either side, and behind them the barracks. The whole occupied a tract of land as large as Paris, seven miles by four.

The place abounded in public gardens, one of them round the Dilkusha Palace, where Havelock died. Round the famous Residency whose ruined walls still stood marked with shot and shell exactly as they had been left after the Mutiny, lay an exquisite garden. A former pleasure ground of the Oudh kings, a lovely piece of turf, was used for cricket etc and surrounded by magnificent trees. Beyond the river Goomti was a delightful wilderness called Paradise, a four mile ride from the cantonments - a charming tangle of woods, shrubs and lanes.

Along the river bank were some fine old buildings, though not of a very high architectural order, as art had deteriorated since the days of the Mughal Emperors. One of these had been turned into a comfortable and well-appointed club, and here I stayed during the next hot weather.

The Goomti was not a very inviting stream. It wound in 'links' through the old city and was spanned by many bridges, among them a notable one of cast iron built in the early 19th century. Many boats floated on the river and during the hot weather and the rains I often went out in one.

Of course there was plenty of society. The General, on whose staff I was, was an anglo-indian soldier of the old school named Cureton. He had raised a cavalry regiment during the Mutiny and was a very fine cavalry leader, but he knew no other arm and did not interest himself much in anything but cavalry and artillery. He was very kind to me personally though I fancy he was rather disappointed when he found how young I was. His wife was not living with him, but he kept a very hospitable house and was a great favourite in society. There were also many notable civilians, judges, magistrates, barristers, bankers etc, many of whom I knew more or less intimately. Although at first I felt very lonely and strange I soon found congenial friends, especially Major Ellis, the Brigade Major of the garrison, who had heard of me from the Pringles. As he was living alone, he suggested that I should come and share his bungalow which I did for a month or two and let my own palatial residence. Ellis introduced me to the CMS missionaries and the Zenana mission ladies. It was a great pleasure to know them and I often used to go to the mission church on Sundays. We got up a little Bible reading afterwards which was a great stimulus to us all.

I had of course to go periodically to Faizabad and to Sitapur. The former was some eighty miles by rail from Lucknow, a beautifully situated little station on the banks of the Gogra river, with very fine trees and public gardens and most excellent pig-sticking in the rough ground near the bed of the river. I had frequently to go there on committees of various kinds, as well as to supervise work but there was not much of importance of the latter in progress. The Commander of the troops there was a Colonel Burn, who, as it turned out had been a great friend of my father's and was extremely kind to me, always putting me up with him whenever I came. He was a fine old soldier - like General Cureton one of the old school of anglo-indians. He always rose before dawn and used to go for a ride or walk returning when most other people were just getting out of bed. He was very keen about lawn-tennis, which was then a most fashionable game, and the courts in the gardens at Faizabad were kept in beautiful order.

Sitapur, also a charming place, was not then connected by rail with Lucknow, so one had to go by the now almost obsolete dak ghari. I was always very hospitably entertained there by a Major Burton of the 1st Bengal Cavalry, whom I had frequently met in Afghanistan - now stationed at Sitapur with his regiment and the staff officer of the station. I had not, however, very much to do there.

At Lucknow I had no lack of work. We were building new infantry barracks on a very big scale and had a lot of other less important works in full swing. There was a brickfield entirely under my control, and workshops of a very extensive nature, so that I was entirely my own contractor for everything except labour. The quality of the work was of the very best and I have never seen it surpassed anywhere.

Stanton my assistant turned up from Kashmir in due course having been seriously ill there with pleurisy. He had not much work at Lucknow and between us we got through it very easily.

The Chatter Manzil, Lucknow; used as a Club

**   **   **   **   **

During that winter the Viceroy came to Lucknow for some little time and held court in royal state. His camp was pitched in one of the many beautiful parks and was itself a magnificent scene. It consisted of a double row or street of immense tents, with a broad carriage road passing up between them and at the end a huge tent for levees, <u>durbars</u>, etc with a tall flagstaff in front.

In this big tent a <u>durbar</u> of the <u>talukdars</u> or 'barons' of Oudh was held. They are wealthy landowners of long descent, whose rights and privileges as well as duties, are a constantly recurring subject of solicitude to the rulers of the country. I had the privilege of a front seat at this <u>durbar</u> on account of my official position, and so I saw the proceedings very well.

The <u>talukdars</u> themselves were in very handsome eastern dress; they were not however men of prepossessing appearance, and seemed to be coarse, and arrogant, with an exalted idea of their own importance and yet without the dignity that I had so often seen among the Muslim chiefs of the Frontier. Lord Ripon wore the insignia of the Star of India, and occupied a throne at the end of the tent. He made them a speech in English, which was translated into Urdu by his Foreign Secretary, after which the various <u>talukdars</u> defiled before him and shook hands, offering gifts which were touched and returned. Then <u>attar</u> or scent and <u>pan</u> (a sort of leaf) were handed round and the ceremony ended.

While the Viceroy was at Lucknow a review of the whole garrison was held, partly in honour of the Viceroy, partly to inaugurate the cold weather manoeuvres and partly to distribute medals to the troops who had earned them. I saw rather a striking effect at this review. It was held in the morning about 9.30, and a thick mist hung all over the parade ground. I was standing close to the flagstaff when the Viceroy's carriage and four horses drove up. Lord Ripon is a nervous man about horses, so he had the horses taken out of the carriage and there he was sitting, shrouded in mist and not a soldier in sight. A gun - the first of the royal salute - boomed out, and suddenly as if a curtain had been lifted, the whole mist cleared away and revealed an army of men, two brigades of infantry, and one of cavalry with horse and field artillery, all standing in line, motionless.

At Christmas time Stanton and I had a charming little shooting trip for three or four days. We went to the valley (or 'Kadir' as it is called) of the Ganges, where there are many little lakes and swamps, left by the river at various times, and which in the cold weather are much frequented by wild fowl. We had excellent sport, chiefly ducks and snipe, but with a fair sprinkling of other sorts of game as well.

Not long after Christmas I had the great pleasure of a visit from Uncle Colin and his wife and her cousin Miss Albright. He had just retired from the service, his last appointment having been Chief Engineer of Burma. Before leaving India he was making a tour of the principal places and thus came to do Lucknow. He spoke to me about his future, said it was strange to be his own master for the first time in his life and how, on his return to England he proposed to take up some philanthropic work in connection with Irish emigration. He little knew how much philanthropic work lay before him in the immediate future in Egypt, and how he would gain himself a name famous in Europe as the one who brought back prosperity to that down-trodden people.*

Miss Albright and I had some charming rides together. I borrowed a lady's saddle for her and mounted her on Jenny, a little mare I had recently purchased - a very well bred, nice-tempered animal, and the most marvellous jumper I ever rode; she could literally jump anything she could put her nose over. The weather was delightful and we had some very pleasant gallops. With my guests I visited all the various Mutiny scenes, the Alambagh with Havelock's tomb and its long-winded epitaph, the Residency where Sir Henry Lawrence's tomb has a brief epitaph in striking contrast to the other, and the fort with its huge Imambara or great hall - one of the largest rooms in the world. The ladies were unaccustomed to military life and the one Sunday they spent with me was perhaps as interesting to them as anything else, for at church every man was in uniform; even the chaplain had medals and a VC outside his surplice.

After they had stayed with me a few days we all spent a day at Cawnpore, going over the sad story of the massacre, visiting the garden and the well with its beautiful statue and memorial screen, as well as the ghat where the treachery of the Nana had displayed itself. I was interested to see there the old church where in 1847 my aunt Eliza had married her cousin Robert Christie. She had been married from the house of another cousin Mrs Spiers, but my father was the only member of her own family who was present at the wedding. She died within a year of her marriage with her infant child, at Meerut.

I parted from Uncle Colin and his party at Cawnpore - but rejoined them about ten days later at Agra and spent a couple of days there. I had not been there before so it was a great pleasure to us all exploring the beauties of the place. The Taj is of course the best of the wonders of Agra and is undoubtedly a marvellous work 'designed by Titans and finished by Jewellers', as Bishop Heber described it. We went there in the evening and waited till the full moonlight made the polished marble even

---

* Sir Colin's main work in Egypt (1883-92) was twofold: 1) the construction of the Nile Barrage, and 2) the abolition of the corvée or system of forced labour - a form of slavery.

more exquisite in appearance. But beautiful as the Taj is, I think I enjoyed even more the buildings inside the Fort where the combination of red sandstone and black and white marble, aided by the natural beauty of outline in Saracenic architecture, in arabesques and inscriptions in Arabic and Persian, is exceedingly chaste and beautiful. There is in the fort a perfect gem of a mosque called the Moti Musjid (Pearl Mosque) - all of the purest white marble, which is beautiful beyond description. We had not time to go to Fatehpur Sikri, which is a night's journey from Agra, but is I believe even more beautiful. I left the party at Agra and returned to Lucknow while they journeyed south-west towards Bombay.

Not long after this my friend Stanton got smallpox. It had been raging in the native town, but he had foolishly gone about without taking any precautions and the consequence was he caught the disease and nearly died of it. He and another brother officer, Jerome, were living in the same bungalow. Jerome and I took turns to sit with him, and we got a soldier's wife to help also in nursing him. Various ladies sent delicacies of all sorts for the sick man, but of course the disease was so much dreaded that we (Jerome and I) had to keep quite apart from everybody while we attended him. I kept a special suit of clothes to wear in his house, and had these always disinfected so I could hardly have carried much infection with me. I have never, before or since, seen a smallpox patient and certainly had no idea of the horrible nature of the disease. Poor Stanton was simply one mass of swollen sores from head to foot, his eyes were completely closed by the swelling of his face, and his lips were black, swollen and distorted. He got better, but was fearfully disfigured.

He was invalided home, leaving with me a horse which he had recently purchased, but which just before his illness he had managed to let down with the result that its knees were badly broken. He was so much cast down with the idea of having to sell the horse at a very great loss that I volunteered to take him over and try and doctor him a bit. He consented to this and the horse which was a real good waler came into my stables. I broke him to harness, rode him regularly hunting (where he acquitted himself so well that the colonel of the 10th Hussars advised me to enter him for the chief steeplechase of the year) and I finally sold him for nearly as much as Stanton gave for him originally.

About that time there arrived from home with the Seaforth Highlanders - one of the infantry regiments in the garrison - Lieutenant Colonel and Mrs Forbes, with whom I subsequently became very great friends. Mrs Forbes had been anxious to see some spiritual work begun in the regiment and it happened that just at that time my cousin Robert Pringle came to stay a day or two with me and always anxious to do good among the soldiers asked permission to hold some meetings in the barracks of the Seaforths. This was readily granted, Mrs Forbes doing all she could to further the matter. The meetings were so well attended that Dr Pringle urged me to try and keep them up. I did this with the help of

Major Ellis, the Brigade Major, and I believe they were kept up for years afterwards to the great advantage and blessing of the men.

Shortly after this (March 1883) a Captain Brookes RE came to relieve me as Executive Engineer of the Lucknow Division and I was transferred to the Railway Branch as Deputy Consulting Engineer for Guaranteed Railways - a very grand title, but one which carried with it no great responsibility and no better pay than I had at Jutogh.

The Government of India had guaranteed interest of 5% on all capital subscribed, and to ensure equitable expenditure had appointed a Consulting Engineer, with one or more assistants. They had to inspect all railway lines in the district every half-year, test and pass all new bridges etc and investigate and report on accidents. The work was varied, enabling one to get an insight into all branches of railway management. I used to attend at the engine workshops to learn all I could about locomotives and driving; I also read several books on the subject.

The travelling was managed as luxuriously as possible, though at best it was rather trying in the hot weather. The Consulting Engineer had a private carriage very comfortably furnished, with a small kitchen and a bathroom, and as he (the CE) was away in the hills nearly all the hot weather I had the exclusive use of this carriage and could take it out whenever I liked.

I shifted my quarters from the large official residence of the ex-Engineer, to the Chatter Manzil Club, previously described, where I had a nice suite of rooms and lived very comfortably during the hot weather. The cooking was excellent, there was a swimming bath attached to the Club, which I used daily, and it was close to my office.

During the hot weather we had plenty of amusement. For part of the time I kept one of my horses at Faizabad and used to go there periodically for the hunting of the mighty boar, but one day riding hard for a first-spear over the most awful ground I managed to lame my steed, and after that did not send another to replace her. (She got all right again but I did not hunt her again that season). Then every Thursday at Lucknow the 10th Hussars used to have a hunt of some sort. Sometimes it was a paper-chase, when, the colonel of the regiment being master of hounds, the hares were NCO's well mounted, and the field comprised as many of the men as had good characters and could ride well. Every officer also without exception used to turn out. The result was we had a field of about sixty or seventy and as the line chosen was often a fairly stiff one, we sometimes had some grief - in fact I once had a pretty bad fall myself. I generally rode 'Sir John', Stanton's horse, a very good hunter.

We also had the so-called "Prince of Wales' Own Royal Staghounds," something not unlike stag-hunting in England.

** ** ** ** **

Among the places which I had officially to visit was Benares, 200 miles from Lucknow, where at that time a very big bridge was being built over the Ganges. I had periodically to visit and report upon this work and it was not only in itself interesting, but it took me to a very interesting place - chiefly on personal grounds for it was there that my father had died in 1865. I went to see his grave and found it in very good order. It was surrounded by rose bushes, from which I gathered some flowers and leaves and sent them to my mother, to her great pleasure. The cemetery is a sad lonely place, and although it is well kept it proclaims the idea of exile to a degree which is painful. I saw the house my parents had occupied and even came across some of the character references my mother had given to the native servants when she left.

I also called on a remarkable old lady, a Mrs Kennedy, at that time aged ninety-five. She had lived at Benares since the year 1847 when her husband was General there. She had known my parents very well and in fact she seemed to think that if my father had only taken her advice and not gone for his morning ride in a forage cap, he would not have died. Her faculties were quite clear and she walked with a light tripping step, but she was getting very blind.

The native town at Benares is a wonderful, but very sad sight. It is most pathetic to see the sick people being brought to the brink of the sacred muddy stream to die, and the corpses of those who have died brought to be burnt at the water's edge. Towering over all are the minarets of a mosque built by one of the Mughal Emperors who determined to build a Muslim place of worship that would overlook all the temples. If the Hindus were allowed they would not let that mosque remain there a day.

There is however evidence at Benares that Hinduism in its best form is above the degradations of the popular worship and that some of its followers study nature in a way that has truth for its guide. There is an ancient observatory there with many curious instruments in it, in which much useful work has been done, in fact the old pundits were able by means of it to foretell eclipses.

In July I visited, for the first time and for a few days, Calcutta, the capital of the country. I went there to be examined in the Persian language, in which I passed the Higher Standard. Of course it was not a good time of year to visit Calcutta, but it was an interesting visit and I am glad I did it.

In October I went for a few days to Mussoorie again to see my cousins the Pringles. Four years had passed since I had visited them before - their children were now growing up, and they themselves were just preparing to go home for good. It was very pleasant being with them again and the weather was lovely - the views of the snowy range being most magnificent.

Just before the end of the hot weather I got a telegram one morning from Colonel Browne at Simla saying he had been appointed Engineer-in-Chief of the Kandahar State Railway, which had been abandoned in 1880 but was now to be begun again, and asking me to be his personal assistant. My seven years of service in India were now nearly at an end and I was thinking of reverting to the home establishment, but this offer was too good to be refused, so I accepted it at once.

I lived for the last three weeks of my time at Lucknow with the Forbes' and a truly delightful time it was. The weather was glorious - the first fresh cold weather. Mrs Forbes was an excellent rider and every morning early we went for a ride together in some of the pretty country beyond the city. I had one or two pleasant shooting trips, and there was a Soldiers Exhibition, on the Committee of which, both Colonel and Mrs Forbes and I were members. It was a great success and many of the exhibits (which were open to all soldiers in north India) were remarkably good.

The only drawback was Colonel Forbes' health. Every now and then he used to get severe internal pains, which we thought little of at the time, but they were undoubtedly the first symptoms of the complaint (cancer) of which he died fifteen months afterwards.

I handed over my duties to a civil engineer named McGeorge on November 7th, and started off the same evening. It took four days' and four nights' continuous travelling (via Ambala, Lahore, and Sukkur where I ferried across the Indus) to reach Sibi, a small town at the desert's edge facing barren rocky hills. Here General Browne was waiting for me, to take me on a trolly up to the Narrai Gorge, the base of the new railway line.

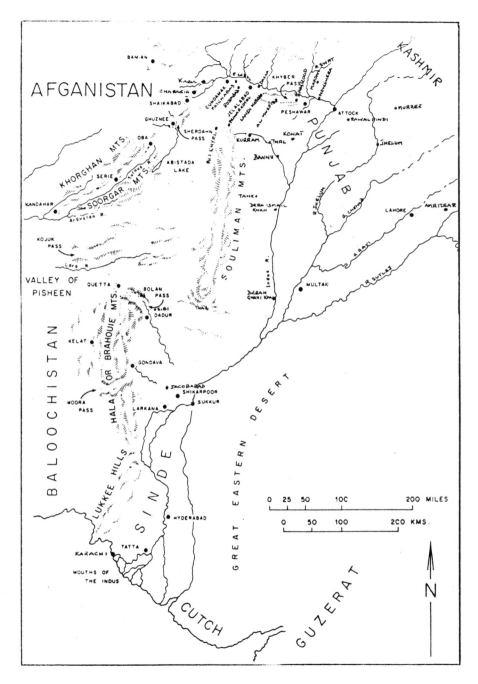

11
Sinde-Peshin Railway

The man under whom I now found myself serving and with whom I soon came to be very friendly - Colonel James Browne - was no ordinary character. In height he was about the average, but he looked rather below it on account of the great breadth and thickness of his exceptionally powerful body. He had a very mobile face; usually his broad features - at least so much as was visible above a thick beard - wore a cheery jovial look; but when he was grave, or stern, or angry he looked quite a different man. He was full of humour, an admirable raconteur, blessed with a memory that produced an infinite series of good yarns, and an absence of all egotism which frequently resulted in the point of the story being against himself. He was an admirable linguist and spoke fluently several European as well as Asiatic languages. He was a brave and determined soldier as had been proved in several campaigns, and a bold and skilful engineer as I very soon discovered. But he was notably a ruler of men, he knew how to get the best work out of his subordinates, not by pushing them unduly but by absolute straight dealing. He trusted his lieutenants, treated them with sympathy, and managed to infect the dullest with a little of his own buoyant energy. He was a man of great talent, singular force of character and genuine unaffected piety.

As to himself and his own personal comfort, Browne was wholly indifferent. He neither cared what he ate, how he was clad, or where he lived. His horses were characteristic of the man. One was a splendid big English mare that he had ridden at the battle of Tel-el-Kebir, and which he kept simply for that reason, for she was of little use to him in the hill country where we were now serving; another was an ill-natured but useful shaggy hill pony called 'Jock' that did a great deal of honest work, and the third was 'Placid Joe', a pony with every fault imaginable, but kept by its master because he liked to laugh at its propensities for falling asleep at any time, and over eating itself on all occasions.

Browne was not a good horseman and did not ride for the pleasure of it. After a while he took to riding a camel with a wild dirty Beluch sitting in front of him. It was not very dignified, but he didn't mind that in the least.

Another notable character whom I was then much thrown in contact with, was my servant, whose real name I believe was Mahommad Sadiq, but who was universally known as 'Haji', as he had done the pilgrimage to Mecca called the 'Haj'. Whether this pilgrimage gave him the privilege of doing what he liked subsequently, or not, I cannot say, anyhow he seemed to view all the ordinary Muslim prejudices with contempt. Possibly this was because he had seen more of the world than his contemporaries. Born in Teheran, he had become a muleteer in the Abyssinian Expedition in 1868 and there had attracted the attention of a Captain Clarke RE who took him to India as his servant. After he had served him for some years they parted and Lieutenant Ronald Maxwell took him on with him in 1880 to Kabul where I knew the man as a most excellent servant. I found him at Lucknow without a situation and when I offered to take him he jumped at the idea, and served me most faithfully for two years until I left India in July 1885. He was much more like a European than any servant I ever had; for one thing he could turn his hand to anything; and adventure, especially if combined with a little profit, was apparently very congenial to him. In appearance he was a broad shouldered swarthy man with thick black eyebrows, short black beard and brawny arms. I always spoke to him in his native tongue, and as few other people understood Persian, I could converse freely with him without fear of eavesdroppers.

The country where we had now to work was as exceptional and uncompromising as the nature of that work itself. Nari, the railway headquarters, was situated where the Nari river (about forty-eight yards wide in ordinary and 400 yards in rainy seasons) emerges from a rocky gorge. Apart from the scanty irrigation of this river the country's population is sparse indeed. Sibi, seven miles behind us, was at the edge of absolute desert. Before us there was no trace of vegetation till, some fifteen miles distant, the Narrai Gorge ended at a place called Baberkach. Here Browne and I camped during the cold weather. Beyond it, though the country became a little less precipitous, no vegetation or cultivation appeared until near Harnai, forty miles further on.

The work before us teemed with difficulties. A railway line, begun during the first Afghan War, had been abandoned. Now the home Government, alarmed at Russian advance, had sent secret orders to resume the work, only now instead of 'Kandahar State Railway' the line was to be called the 'Harnai Road Improvement Scheme'. The gradients and curves were without parallel in the history of the railway construction. The line had to rise from 700 ft above sea level at Sibi, to 5,400 ft at the summit about 120 miles away.

As regards staff, Colonel Browne had one RE Captain (lent by the Military Works Deptartment) and five Bengal Sapper companies, each of which had several very junior subalterns attached. These, though excellent material and afterwards admirable officers, were of little use, having all their work to learn. Two men however had been sent for and were on their way, Captains Hoskyns and Buchanan Scott, each of them a tower of strength. Some civil engineers joined us later.

At first I was jack of all trades, store superintendent, engineering instructor, recruiting officer, sanitary engineer, veterinary surgeon etc. Every day I was up early, and generally went up the line with my chief discussing plans of action with him and laying out such portions of the work (cuttings, bridges etc) as were possible in the absence of accurate survey instruments. Then I returned to office, worked away at correspondence, sent in large demands for all sorts of stores and endeavoured generally to produce some sort of order out of chaos.

I was lucky enough to pick up two excellent horses by chance. An officer belonging to the Intelligence Branch at Simla had been ordered to carry out a reconnaissance in the Beluch country, and had telegraphed to the OC Sind Horse at Jacobabad to collect some of the best Beluch mares from the neighbouring chiefs in the district. He had done this and chose two from among the number, which he had taken with him to Sibi. The very first time he mounted one of them she had thrown him and broke his leg. So he was lying there with a tedious trouble, poor fellow, and the two horses on his hands. I went in to see him, asked him if he was willing to part with the two mares (which he was delighted to do) and I accordingly bought them both at a very cheap figure. I found that both were very quiet tractable creatures, and that the reason why one had thrown her rider was that she had a sore back, which of course accounted at once for her restiveness. They were both beautiful animals, and I was much envied by my brother officers for my possession of them. My three mares -which I called after my three sisters - were by far the best animals possessed by any officer on the line. When I went home I sold them all at an excellent profit. The training and breaking in of Beluch mares however, had taken me some time.

By the beginning of December (1883) we had got three divisions of the line started, one under Davidson (Captain RE) one under Scott, one under Hoskyns. There were great difficulties in making a start, for the whole place was full of needy and more or less dishonest adventurers whose one idea was to do as little work as possible for as much money as possible. I think we made out that nine languages were spoken on the works.

Towards the end of December, we shifted our headquarters from Nari Gorge (where we lived in houses) to a camp on a plateau some fourteen miles off at the upper end of the gorge and close to the site of some very big works. This place was called Baberkach. We (my chief and I) spent Christmas Day there quietly and pleasantly. The sapper companies celebrated the afternoon by having sports at which he gave the prizes. I met there several native officers and NCOs who had served under me (and some British NCOs also) all of whom gave me warm greeting.

** ** ** ** **

Almost immediately afterwards I was sent off on a very interesting exploring trip. There was a blank space on the map between the Harnai Valley and Quetta, which was evidently occupied by rocky mountains and passes, but which had never been surveyed. Before finally deciding on the Chappar Rift route which the line eventually took, Browne decided to send an officer to explore this unknown region and report on the practicability of taking a railway through it. This was a service of considerable danger, both because the region in question was infested by lawless robbers, and because in winter there was every chance of being snowed up. But of course I accepted the job with pleasure.

I left my chief on the 29th. His parting words, accompanied by a knowing twinkle in his eye, were 'keep your weather eye open and look out for squalls.' I marched for two days up the Harnai Valley through pleasant scenery, and past cultivated fields and gardens to a little post called Sharigh lying at the foot of a huge mountain 12,000 feet high called Kalipat.

The last day of the year I spent in exploring the hills and ravines on one side of the main valley, and then on New Year's Day 1884 I set out on my journey into the unmapped region beyond. My party consisted of Haji and another servant, a trustworthy guide named Khyroo, who had acted as such for Colonel Browne during the Afghan War and knew every pass between Sibi and Kandahar, and an escort of six mountaineers, wild lawless vagabonds, but to a certain extent amenable to orders. The baggage was carried on eight mules, and as there was no sort of path to be traversed I took with us a few tools for smoothing away obstacles. During the next few days I found them useful, for more than once we had to halt for a long time while a path was being made. Once a mule fell into a deep pool in a stream. He had my portmanteau on his back which was rather a bad bit of luck for me.

Our route lay first across a mountain pass, then up a wild and lonely valley full of immense boulders of conglomerate, among which flowed a stream of water with a somewhat brackish taste, not at all quenching to the thirst. Our progress was entirely governed by the rate of advance of the mules. I generally went on a bit ahead with the guide, taking observations to known mountain peaks, and otherwise noting information which I could afterwards reproduce on a plan. I also could see how the mules could best follow. On the 3rd January the valley abruptly ended in a great barrier of rock over which the stream fell in a cataract 430 feet in height. To get to the top we had to make a considerable detour, but there was a well defined path and I thought we might leave the mules to follow the guide and myself. We went on some little distance and as they did not appear in sight we retraced our steps to the edge of the precipitous portion and gazed down the steep path into the valley below, still without seeing any signs of them.

My guide here showed wonderful intelligence. He cast about like a hound that has lost the scent of a fox, till at last he found a small piece of chopped straw which he held up in triumph as it was evidently fallen from the mule that carried the fodder for the others. Following up the track thus indicated we worked off along another line and before very long found the whole of the mules, with the servants, baggage and escort in a regular cul de sac out of which they could only go out by the way they came in. We retraced our steps, and got on to the proper line again, and though the actual length of our march was not very great, we did not pitch camp until it was quite late and I felt extremely thankful that we had not been left without tents, food, or baggage as very nearly was the case.

On the 4th I started very early, as it looked very like snow and I had a big pass before me some seventeen miles off. The route fortunately was not very stiff and I got across the pass - which was 8410 feet above sea-level-about 4 o'clock. On my left towered a mighty mass of precipices, behind me was a grand panorama of peaks running from 10,000 to 12,000 feet high, and in front were the picturesque ranges round the valley of Quetta. The pass was fairly wooded with old juniper trees. My camp that night was pitched in a snug ravine among the pines, I had a roaring fire and made myself very comfortable, the more so at feeling that I had got across the worst of the journey and had only downhill now to go. It was hard frost and my dogs, poor beasts, would have been very glad to have got into my bed, had I permitted them.

Next day I descended the valley towards Quetta, without any incident except a mule tumbling down a hillside and taking some time to put right again. In the afternoon I walked into Quetta, at that time a collection of very new houses and barracks scattered over a wide stony plain with a sort of castle or citadel built on the top of a low hill in the centre.

My journey had been successfully accomplished, much to the disgust, I heard, of the tribesmen, who did not expect that an Englishman would traverse their domain in the depth of winter. My success was possibly due to the fact that my outward appearance was very like that of a native. I wore a light turban on my head, and had let my beard grow. My face was tanned by exposure to sun and wind. My outer coat was the poshteen or sheepskin coat, with the wool inside, worn by all Afghans, and as it reached to my knees, only my nether garments (which were pretty well concealed) were of European cut. On the last day of my journey I was sitting by the wayside resting, with two of my escort, when a lad came up and I had a little conversation with him in Pushtu. "Who is he?" asked the lad of one of the men afterwards. "He is a Khan", replied the man, and the lad went away thinking I was a chief of a northern tribe.

Whether I was thus disguised or not, and thus safe, I cannot say, but the melancholy fact remains that the next Englishman who penetrated that region a few months later, was murdered.

In Quetta I stayed for a few days with some brother officers, having interviews with the chief military, medical, engineering and other authorities. The weather was bitterly cold and I was glad of the shelter of a house.

I started on my return journey by another route from that which I had come by, returning to the upper regions of the Harnai Valley at a place called Kach, a lonely desolate spot among wild picturesque mountain gorges - but which would soon echo to the whistle of the locomotive.

Shewing effect of a small flood on a temporary bridge

12
Work on the Railway

After my exploring trip ended at Quetta early in 1884, I returned along the proposed railway line towards General Browne's headquarters (Narrai).

The first day's march was down along a valley leading towards the famous Chappar Rift, with a small stream tumbling over a rocky bed at the foot. Sheep grazing on the hillsides and a few coveys of hill partridges were the only living creatures to be seen. Lower down, the valley seemed to rise in front of me, strangely enough, with no exit for the stream along which I was travelling, nor for another that was coming to meet it.

At the point of junction, however, I saw a cleft a few feet wide, down which the streams disappeared. I rode down here with precipices towering on either side. The rift opened out soon into a sort of amphitheatre, bounded by cliffs with huge boulders tumbled at the bottom. The path led on into another narrow gorge and finally into a valley beyond. Constructing a railway line here, but that I knew of my chief's indomitable perseverance, I should have thought impossible.

A few more days' marching brought me back to General Browne. His headquarters were now at Baberkach, in a central position from which he could supervise the big bridges or tunnels on either side. I made out my report and then, having little to do, volunteered to work under my old friend Captain Scott.

We had to excavate for the foundations of a bridge pier, in an exposed site in the Narrai River. I had to make a big dam round it and keep pumping out the water while the workmen got the shingle out. After six weeks working day and night, Sundays and weekdays, rock bottom was reached and the pier could be built.

Elsewhere the work was progressing steadily. By the end of March the weather was getting very hot. I was sent to collect camels and arrange for sending the sappers further up the line and the pioneers back to India. This I found a very congenial task. It meant scouring the country and bargaining with the local people for their animals. I remember one day being eleven hours in the saddle doing this sort of work.

But moving the troops was a small matter compared to the exodus of the civil workmen, who numbered about 20,000, a vast army indeed. Of course they made all their own arrangements for transport and camps, but we had to see about feeding them and preventing them from spreading sickness. It was a most serious difficulty, for 500 camel loads of flour were consumed daily on the works, and the country produced absolutely nil.

However by the middle of April all this difficulty was overcome and my chief and I shifted our headquarters to a place called Mangi, close to the Chappar Rift. There were camped there four companies of the Bengal Sappers, as well as the headquarter offices of the line. At one side of the camp there was a lofty range of hills, pierced by the Rift, at the other side - northward - was another equally lofty and rugged mass of mountains and on either side the valley stretched, rising in both directions. It was a somewhat picturesque place, but it proved to be far from healthy.

The first thing to be done was to consider how to attack the problem of taking the line through the Rift. For this purpose a very careful survey of the whole site had to be made and no fewer than eight subalterns were employed, under Scott, on this work. After much consultation the chief decided on the line to be adopted, involving about a mile of tunnels, and one great bridge across the chasm, 290 feet above the gorge below.

I never saw this completed. It was finally finished in March 1887 and formally opened by the Duchess of Connaught (the Duke being then Commander-in-Chief in Bombay) and named after her the 'Louise Margaret' Bridge.

The tunnels, with some few exceptions, could be worked at from several points at once, by excavating small galleries or passages from the vertical faces of the cliffs until the true position of the tunnel was reached and then working right and left to meet one another. This was of course work that required very careful and accurate observation, as well as considerable cool-headedness, for the workmen had to be lowered on platforms from the tops of the precipices until they reached the required spot. There they worked away blasting the rock until they got a little passage made. As the Rift was often filled with water, from floods, from one side to the other, a path had to be made along the face of the rock above high water mark. This was done by driving bars into the rock face and resting planks upon them, an operation which sounds easy enough, but was really very difficult.

As for myself I had a survey to do of a rough ugly place far up the valley, called Mud Gorge. Here the rough irregularities of the ground were such that the exact location of the line was a matter of much consideration. The soil was a muddy clay interspersed with huge detached rocks and boulders, with apparently every indication of landslips and other disturbances. The length of this portion was about five miles. I surveyed, and laid out a line which I thought was the best, and I do not know that anyone has ever suggested an improvement, but that one bit of line has caused more trouble since then than all the rest of the railway put together, and I believe that it has caused the whole of the railway to be, if not exactly abandoned, at least only used as a secondary means of approach. The reason is that the soil is continually on the move in rainy weather, and there is never any certainty that some part of the rails will not have diverged so much as to obstruct the whole line.

I had also to set my younger brother officers to work at survey on the highest parts of the line, where it crosses the summit 6400 feet above sea level. In doing this we had an adventure one day which might have been serious. Our camp was at Kach up among the mountains, and we had to go next day (and return next night) to a place some ten miles off, with a gang of coolies and some wagons to form an advanced depot, and I had to point out also where the survey operations were to be carried out. It was a cold cloudy day, with snow showers occasionally but with nothing to impede our progress, until we reached the scene of our survey work. There we were overtaken by such heavy rain that we got inside some caves for shelter, until the rain ceased which it did after some hours.

We went out again and worked for a while till the heavy clouds gathering again warned us to go home. We had at least ten miles to go. I knew that each little watercourse which we had crossed in the morning would be a fair-sized stream owing to the first rain, and if more heavy rain came on it might possibly be a raging torrent, so I told my companions to push on as fast as possible. We galloped on mile after mile crossing many streams, drenched with the rain that was now pouring in sheets. When we got within a mile or two of our camp we found ourselves faced by a broad roaring river which had been a dry watercourse in the morning. I pushed my mare into it; she was swept off her legs instantly but swam gallantly across. I signalled to my companions to try lower down, but they both followed in the exact place where I had been, and were both swept off their horses. One of them a strong young fellow, got clear of his steed and swam out all right. The other got under his horse and to my horror when he did come up he was apparently stunned and incapable of doing anything for himself. I rode down to a bend just below and was going in after him, when he was washed ashore more dead than alive - to my intense relief.

Our native followers seem to have been unable to get in at all and they did not stay as I thought they would in the caves above mentioned, so that they had a terrible night of privation. Much to my grief, one of them was frozen to death.

I had another little exploring trip later on, which only lasted however for two days. In a valley to the north of the mountain range north of our camp there is a native town or village called Kawas, which was at that time a nest of robbers and bad characters of all sorts. It was intended to send a regiment of infantry from Quetta to be camped in the neighbourhood, to keep these folk in order, and the question arose whether it would be possible to establish signalling communication between the two valleys across the intervening mountain. I volunteered to find this out and started with my little guide who had been with me on the former occasion. He carried a blanket for me and food enough for two days, and I also took my rifle as I thought I might get a shot at some of the wild goats of the mountains.

We had at first a long stiff climb over bare rocky crags, at the top of which we halted and had a splendid view of the wild mountainous scenery all round, the highest peaks being about 12,000 feet above sea level. There was a long winding lake among the mountains, formed by a landslip which had blocked one of the valleys. From the water vertical cliffs rose all round giving it a very weird gloomy appearance. We spent all that day roaming about among the highest parts of the mountains, which were fairly well clothed with vegetation, heaths and small bushes being predominant, and with many noble trees, either pines or cypresses. I saw no game however and in place of wild goats came upon some flocks of sheep under shepherds whose entire clothing consisted of a sheepskin cloak and a pair of loose cotton trousers.

As night fell we lit a fire under a tree near one of the shepherd's bivouacs and proceeded to bivouac ourselves. I gathered a lot of heath and scrub for a bed and pillow, and slept comfortably till the early morning when the air became very cold. My guide and this shepherd were much interested in seeing me kneel in prayer before I slept. Muslims are quite accustomed to this, but I don't think they had ever seen a Christian do it before.

I went on with my guide to Kawas, but he would not let me go into the village or even near it, as he said my life would not be safe. I examined it easily with my telescope however, and came to the conclusion that it would be very difficult to establish communication across the mountain by signalling unless there were three or four signal stations, which would not have been practicable. I therefore returned by a different route to the camp at Mangi which I reached in the afternoon after a most pleasant ramble.

**   **   **   **   **

At the beginning of June all the RE officers in the district gathered together at Quetta for a week's gaiety. We challenged the garrison of Quetta to play polo, lawn-tennis, cricket (RA and RE v Quetta garrison) and billiards. We invited the beauty and fashion of Quetta to a ball. We gave various dinners, and we had an RE dinner for ourselves on the same night as the Corps dinner in London. It was a great success. We numbered I think twenty, of whom the large majority were subalterns. There was one field officer (Major Tomkins). Of course there were a few absentees, ie those officers who were obliged to remain on duty with troops or on the works.

I took part in the polo match and in the cricket. The polo was a splendid game, and though we were pitted against a large garrison containing many good players, we very nearly won. We REs wore our Corps jerseys (blue and red stripes), the others wore white. I think we had the faster ponies, and were as good players, but our ponies were rather out of hand. In the second twenty minutes, one of our players (Jerome) was run off with, and out of the game, and during that time they managed to get two goals, and it was by this amount that they won. I think we otherwise had the best of it. The cricket was very good fun - a most excellent match, with big scoring on both sides. It is not often that one can play a cricket match in India in June all day long.

At the RE dinner we sent a telegram home to HRH the Colonel of the Corps wishing him and the Corps all success. We got a reply in a few hours.

There was however one drawback to our pleasure - we were all, more or less, in poor condition. The hard work and rough fare had impoverished one's blood, and the result was that a trivial cut or scratch did not heal but became a very ugly sore. Both my hands were crippled with these ulcers, and when I went - after the polo match - to a doctor to get them dressed, he said I ought to go away on leave. I had however no intention of doing so then.

Shortly after my return to Mangi I had to lay out a road over the Chappar mountain, a very interesting bit of work. General Browne had been away since the end of April on three months' leave, and his work was carried out by Major Tomkins the Superintending Engineer at Quetta. I really did all the ordinary work, and only referred to Tomkins in important matters. Now Tomkins was very anxious to get a road made and ordered me to undertake it, on the ground that the railway works had blocked up the old route through the Rift. This I think was reasonable, but General Browne was very much annoyed when he came back that a work of this sort had been done without his knowledge and public money spent on a work which, when the railway was complete, would be of no further use. However I think the road was really very much required and it was rather a nice piece of engineering.

Our life at Mangi was hard but pleasant enough. We had a fairly good little mess, we had cricket and polo, and a small steeplechase course which I made, and we all pulled well together. But sickness began to break out. The men got knocked up with fever, and scurvy began to make its appearance. The variations in temperature between day and night were very trying. In my tent the range was as much as 50° (Fahrenheit) in twelve hours. One day I woke up with severe pains in my back, and thought at first I had strained some muscles playing at polo or cricket. It did not wear off however and I realised that I was suffering from lumbago and sciatica. I had arranged to go to Quetta for a day to consult Tomkins about some matter, and after putting it off for a day or two I thought I was better and sent off my luggage by easy stages, intending to ride the forty five miles in one day. When I started I felt very unfit but I did not like to back out, and off I went.

The last ten miles gave me terrible agony. Instead of staying for one night I stayed for three weeks, laid up all that time with great pain. Major and Mrs Tomkins were most kind and hospitable - they must have been rather put out by my very long visit, but they treated me with the greatest kindness.

During this time General Browne wrote to say I was to take up a survey division for the laying out of the line in to Quetta - from the end of the mountainous portion - a distance of thirty-three miles. I was to begin as soon as possible, assisted by Mr 'Bob' Egerton a civil engineer and a very nice fellow, who was then at another division. The country we had to work through was different from that through which the rest of the line had been made. The first part was over undulating moorland, not unlike the Highlands of Scotland, then, coming futher down the valley, one came upon a region of cultivated fields, with villages, groves of trees, wells, brooks and fertility. Some eight miles from Quetta one crossed a stream, turned the corner of a mountain and then came straight into the cantonment.

The work was of a pleasant and interesting nature. I got my baggage and camp equipment ready at Quetta and as soon as I was able to travel marched by easy stages to the end of the then existing line at a place called Garkhai, where a company of sappers was then encamped, engaged in blasting the rocks for the construction of some big cuttings, and there I awaited Egerton's arrival.

While there I used to go out as far as the very imperfect state of my health permitted, to prospect the country over which we were now to lay out a line. While engaged on this one evening I had a very narrow escape.

I was returning to my camp at Garkhai, which lay a short distance up a narrow valley where the men were busy blasting rocks. when walking along the path I heard shouts bidding me run for the mines had just been lighted. Running was impossible for me, as I was lame on both legs and could only hobble with the aid of two sticks. To return the way I came would be as dangerous as to go on, so I just walked on trusting the Lord to keep me. In a few minutes I was surrounded by showers of stones. One huge rock landed on the path just behind me and made my heart jump! However not one touched me.

Egerton came in due time, and for two months or so we had a most pleasant time together. He was better up to his work than I was, and I sometimes let him decide where the line should go in opposition to my own judgement, but on the whole we generally acquiesced in the location we adopted. General Browne came to see us once or twice and gave us general directions and advice. Egerton was somewhat more affected by the heat of the sun than I was, so he generally did his share of the outdoor work in the early part of the day, while I relieved him when the sun got too powerful for him. Our camps were usually pitched in groves of trees, not far from villages, while we worked in the adjacent country.

The climate was at first hot, but as the months wore on, it became much cooler. With the advent of cooler weather, however, came fever. First our servants were attacked, then Egerton got turns of it, and finally I got knocked over. We finished the work however by the middle of October laying out the line and completing the plans - including that of an important junction - for the thirty-three miles in less than three months, which was good going.

QUETTA.

13
Three Months Leave

I then applied for three months' leave. I had been corresponding with my old school-fellow (and subsequently my brother-in-law) Jack Moubray;* who said he might very possibly join me on a shooting and exploring expedition during the cold weather. I wrote to him to meet me in Simla, whence we would start about the end of October for the beautiful valley of Kulu, in the heart of the Himalayas. I started from Quetta about the middle of the month, riding down the Bolan Pass on a camel. The distance is eighty miles and it took me two days. I had rather a nasty fall at one place and got my face cut a little, but otherwise there was no incident in my journey worth recording. From the mouth of the Bolan I went by rail to Ambala and thence by dak and tonga to Simla where I put up at the Club.

It was very interesting to be back at Simla after two years' absence. There were a good many people there whom I knew, and I received many invitations to dinners, garden parties etc. Everybody said I was looking very thin and ill, and I suppose I must have been, for a photo taken at that period makes me look rather lean. I only weighed about nine stone.

I lost my faithful companion Bunger, a brown spaniel, at this time. He had been with me for six years, a constant friend, and as I think he recognised the place when he arrived at Simla, he must have jogged off to his old quarters at Jutogh, for the last I heard of him was that he had been seen going off in that direction. Very probably the poor brute was carried off by leopards, which infest the woods to the west of Simla.

While waiting thus at Simla I got a letter from Jack Moubray to say he could not see his way to coming out from Home. This was disappointing, though perhaps as matters afterwards turned out, it was just as well, for I was really not fit to do any hard marching. The weather

---

*Jack Moubray's home was Naemoor (now called Lendrickmuir) a house in Kinross-shire. It is alluded to in GKSM's account of his leave in 1881, p.99, when he was invited to stay with his old school-friend, and met the latter's three sisters. The youngest of these became GKSM's wife in July 1886.

had grown colder and, at the very pressing invitation of some friends, Mr and Mrs Molesworth Macpherson, I shifted my abode from the Club to their house, a very pretty and beautifully situated villa, but a house where I felt the cold very much. I still purposed to march to Kulu and made all my arrangements to start, having written ahead to engage porters, shikaris etc, hired baggage animals, and purchased all the necessary stores. I was to set forth on a certain Tuesday, but on the Sunday during service at church I was seized with the shivering fit which experience had taught me was the precursor of fever. Before I could get back to my house I had the fever on me in full force and for nearly a week I was in bed. When I got up I was so weak and seedy that marching further into the hills was out of the question and I resolved to march to the plains by easy stages, go to Roorkee and do some quiet shooting and fishing in the neighbourhood of that lovely place.

It was however a great disappointment to give up exploration in the grand mountains, not to mention the chances of excellent sport in Kulu, then much frequented. After a few days in Roorkee, which I found beautiful as ever, but altered a good deal in that the trees were grown much bigger I went off to Hardwar some eighteen miles off, where the Ganges issues from the hills, and where there are many temples sacred to various Hindu deities. I stayed here in one of the bungalows belonging to the Government and kept up for the officers of the Irrigation Department, for it is at Hardwar that the great Ganges Canal makes its first beginning - a mighty artificial river. The bungalow where I lived was situated in a most beautiful spot, with the bright clear rushing stream before one, in the middle distance the temples above mentioned, and the low wooded hills close behind them, while in the background was the great snowy range rising pure and beautiful against the blue sky. Here I lived for some days, sharing the bungalow with an old friend in my Corps named Onslow. During the day we generally did some fishing, and sometimes had excellent sport. One morning before breakfast Onslow got a 12lb mahseer and I got a 17lb the biggest fish I ever caught. I hooked him in a rapid below a bridge and landed him on a gravel bank about a quarter-of-a-mile mile down after a gallant fight. My tackle broke at the last minute but I got into the water and had the fish in my arms before he could get away.

Onslow had soon to return to Roorkee, while I went on to Dehra Dun - the valley bounded on one side by the Himalayas, on the south-west by the low rocky range of the Sewaliks, and on the east and west by the Ganges and Jumna respectively. Here I spent some idle weeks gradually getting back health and strength, doing a little fishing in the streams, and going out to look for big game in the surrounding woods. The scenery was very beautiful, and the climate delicious, but the sport was poor. A few years before there had been plenty of game, tigers, leopards, and deer of various sorts, but it had been much shot over by the ex-Amir Yakub Khan and his followers. He was then a political prisoner at Dehra.

While I was there a mountain battery from Jutogh turned up doing their 'cold weather march' several old friends among them. For some days I stayed with them, then I went off by myself into the Sewalik mountains to look for deer and do some fishing. I stayed here in a forest bungalow in the heart of the jungle.

A tiger was said to be prowling in the neighbourhood, but though I sat up one night in a ravine where he frequently passed, I never saw him. This was disappointing, but on returning to Roorkee my luck turned and I got a fine leopard, whose skin since then has formed a familiar plaything for my children.

I spent Christmas pleasantly at Roorkee in the old RE mess. From there I went to Delhi and spent a few days with my friend Maitland, who was now an SPG missionary, and a delightful companion. It would be impossible to describe all the sights we saw in this most wonderful and interesting place, but I must mention the visit we paid to the Kutab. This is one minaret of a mosque that was never finished, and is built of red sandstone with bands of black and white marble, and with balconies at intervals all round, possibly one of the most beautiful towers in the world. It is situated eleven miles from the city and for the whole distance one drove through country covered with ruins of what had once been splendid buildings, now overgrown with thorns and grass. At the top of the Kutab, which one reaches by an inner stair, there is a low railing, which I was glad of, as I have no head for great heights. Outside the railing was a ledge about six inches wide, on which my companion volunteered to walk round! I told him he might do so if he liked, but I should prefer not to see him fall the 300 odd feet down and would therefore descend before he began his acrobatic feats! Needless to say he did not attempt it.

It would be impossible now to mention all the other sights we saw together at Delhi. The fort there with its magnificent throne room and various halls, the great Jama Masjid or principal mosque, a truly magnificent building of the same red, white and black stones, were duly visited and admired, and many others. The great mosque, by the way, was only open to Muslims, till after the Mutiny, when anyone was allowed inside. No Hindu, however, as a rule dares to go in alone, as the feeling is so bitter against them. I took in with me a lad, who had been my faithful attendant when I was at Jutogh, a hill Rajput, a Hindu. He was much impressed. He said when he got back to his people and told them what he had seen they would not believe him! In the great quadrangle of the mosque I found some very ragged strange looking men. I spoke to them in Persian and found they were natives of Bokhara, who were making the pilgrimage to Mecca, but had come first to Delhi attracted by the fame of the magnificent mosque.

**   **   **   **   **

I went from Delhi by train to Jaipur in Rajputana. I had heard much of the beauty of that place, which was. and is still no doubt, one of the most civilised of the native states. I had a letter of introduction to the Resident Engineer, a Colonel Jacob, who received me very kindly and showed me many interesting things. He had under construction a huge waterworks reservoir, in which he used the Maharaja's elephants for consolidating the earthwork - a novel expedient - a series of cotton presses, gas works, a lovely museum of marble, quite in Oriental style, but with copies of architectural masterpieces from many parts of India, a School of Art etc. The streets were broad, well paved and watered, lighted with gas, and lined with strong substantial houses.

In one street there was a curious sight, viz:- a cage with seven compartments right across, and in each compartment a full grown tiger. One of them was an enormous brute, not long caught, full of fury. He had to have double bars on his cage.

The Maharaja's stables and palace were an interesting sight. In the former there were about 300 beautiful horses of all sorts, most of them of Indian breeds, and all of them fat as butter from high feeding and little exercise. Some were being taught to prance in a peculiar way which is thought by Orientals to be ornamental. The palace and gardens were far superior to what one generally finds in native dwellings, though my experience of such is small.

At the same hotel with me were staying some notable foreigners. Don Carlos, the claimant of the Spanish throne and his suite, and the Duke and Duchess of Mecklenburg-Strelitz. The Duke was a big red-bearded man who knew hardly any English - nor did Don Carlos - but the Duchess, a charmingly pretty and clever looking woman, spoke it almost without any accent, and interpreted for the party generally.

I spent one most interesting day at the old capital of Jaipur, called Amber. We first drove some five or six miles to the foot of a low hill where some of the Maharaja's elephants were waiting for us. On these we slowly climbed the rocky path which led to a depression in the hill, and from the top beheld a most picturesque sight, a lake lying among hills, with a temple on an island in it, and towering above it, a most beautiful ancient castle of exquisite design. Eventually we found our way there. Guides had preceded us and showed us all over this grand palace of the old Rajput kings, designed grandly and finished exquisitely, but now - like our English Haddon Hall - a monument of the past, wholly uninhabited. In my desire for searching out the hidden parts of it I was going down a dark passage, but my guide said I had better not, as a leopard had been rearing a littler of cubs in that part! It reminded one of the descriptions of deserted Babylon in Isaiah. 'Thorns shall grow on her palaces, nettles and brambles in the fortresses thereof, it shall be an habitation of dragons, a dwelling place for owls.'

From Jaipur I went, having still some leave left, on a wandering tour through a little frequented part of the Punjab from Hansi to Karnal. I had an idea I would get some good shooting, but although I got enough for the pot, I had not much sport. The distance was about seven or eight marches which I did on foot, getting a bullock cart to take my luggage.

My route lay along the banks of the Western Jumna Canal, a work which was carried out some 300 years ago by the engineers of the Emperor Akbar. They seemed to have an eye to the picturesque, for there are few straight reaches, and the canal winding in and out of wooded banks, and under quaint old masonry bridges, has little in its appearance of the artificial. Unfortunately the original engineers had very little idea of the proper survey and alignment of so great a work, and the result was that it had so interfered with the natural drainage of the country that in places it had created large swamps, full of malaria. This was one reason why Karnal, at one time a very large garrison, had to be abandoned, and the comparatively modern cantonment of Ambala constructed.

I used to put up in the canal inspection houses at night, as a rule. They were very comfortable, well furnished, and had generally a fair stock of readable books. One day I had a somewhat amazing adventure. I was marching along the canal as usual with a bullock cart taking my luggage, coming a little behind me. My faithful spaniel, Don, was much excited at large troops of monkeys that were jumping about from tree to tree, or swinging over the picturesque stream, and he was incessantly running after them and barking. Some of the monkeys came very close to the bullock cart, which brought Don at them with a rush, which so frightened the bullocks (especially the leading one of a team of three) that he wheeled round, and as we were then going along a road at the top of a small embankment, the whole cart, baggage and my servant seated on the top, were precipitated over the bank with a terrible crash. No one was hurt, but the cart was badly smashed and I could not go on without having it mended. So I sent for a carpenter from the nearest village, about a mile off, and sat down on the canal bank, telling my servant meantime to get my breakfast. Soon he had all his pots and pans out, a kettle and mud-cooking range erected, and he began to make <u>chupatties</u> or scones for my meal. Meantime the monkeys who were the original cause of the disaster watched the scene with interested eyes. Gradually they stole down to the cooking place and although the servant drove them away once or twice, they got bolder and bolder and at last one snatched off a <u>chupatti</u> and bolted off chuckling up the tree. This was rather too much, and so I put a cartridge of fine shot in my gun and fired at part of his body which was not likely to be mortally injured. The effect was very laughable. He had evidently been stung severely by the shot, and clapping his hand on the injured part, he rushed at the nearest small monkey, cuffed him and drove him away, then drove the others off, making maledictory remarks in his own language all the while. I had my breakfast unmolested.

It was not till late in the afternoon however that I got the repairs finished, and I had a good long march before me. My destination was a place called Jhind, the capital of a small state of the same name, and I had an official introduction to the Raja, who was no doubt quite ready for me, though I could not say the exact date of my proposed visit.

It was quite dark before we got there. I had intended to go to one of the canal bungalows, but we (I and my faithful henchman, the hill Rajput) missed our way and having become separated from the baggage cart, as I had been in pursuit of game, we thought the baggage would be in before us. At last we found our way to the town which was, like many Eastern towns, walled all round, and the gates shut at night. It was quite dark, and after shouting a good deal we were admitted into a dark narrow street, the gate keeper meantime sending a message to the kotwal or head policeman who promptly took us, much to my amusement and my henchman's indignation, to the lock-up! After being in durance vile for a short time, the kotwal returned with an English-speaking native, who questioned me as to who I was and whence I came. I replied, of course, without any delay that I had a letter to the Raja and told him who I was. He then said 'Sir, I think you must be one of the high British officials.' I replied that modesty would prevent me from describing myself in those terms. He then explained to the kotwal that I was a sahib of high rank who had lost my way, whereat the kotwal apologised profusely and took me out of the lock-up to a room of the Raja's - very dirty it is true -when he asked if I would like to have a sheep killed for my dinner! I said that my appetite did not demand such an amount of meat, but if he could get me anything on a smaller scale I would be glad to have it.

Eventually scones and omelettes and rice, and milk were brought, on which I dined comfortably - they brought me also a bedstead and a quilt and pillow for my comfort at night, on which I slept well. Next morning there was a large gathering assembled to do me honour and we trooped out of the town, an ordinary Englishman in shooting clothes and a gun, with a long tail of ragamuffin natives on ponies of sorts, mostly thin and bad tempered. I soon found my servants and bade adieu to my rag, tag and bobtail escort.

A few days afterwards I reached a canal bungalow near Karnal, in heavy rain. It was occupied by the Executive Engineer, a Mr Yates and his wife, with his assistant Mr Scratchley. I spent a pleasant evening with them and next day we tried snipe shooting, but the rain had been too heavy. I stayed at Karnal however for three or four days, met several old friends there and occupied my time pleasantly between the fine stud of General Parrot, which I had visited four years before and the pursuit of game in which I was very fairly successful, making some good bags of snipe and duck.

14
Floods and Fever

My leave however was now at an end and I returned to Narrai about the middle of January, to resume my work on the railway. I found my mare Jenny who had been in the charge of Mr Campion, in excellent form and it was a great pleasure to have a gallop on her again, bounding under me like a deer. I was put in charge of the Nari Division as a temporary measure. There had been two executive engineers there during my absence but they had both succumbed to the work and had gone off on leave or transfer - to Sir James Browne's disgust - and so he put me in their place. It was a big and responsible charge. I had two big bridges, one of five spans of 150ft each, the other of four spans of 150ft and the girder erection was in full swing. Then I had about twenty smaller bridges and culverts, besides retaining walls and tunnel lining etc. All this time trains were running daily over the line the whole way.

It was however only intended that I should do this work until another man could come to take it up. Eventually I was relieved by a Captain Connor of the Staff Corps, Eurasian, a nice gentle sort of fellow, but weak in body and mind and generally quite unfit to tackle such work. He had to go in a few weeks on leave, after making some fearful blunders and causing much delay to the works.

Lady Browne was in camp with her husband at Baberkach and she had with her a little baby boy about nine months old. Our menage therefore was on rather a more refined scale than it had been the year before, and the opening up of the railway had enabled us to get many little luxuries to which we had been formerly strangers.

My work was varied as usual. I was military staff officer to the troops under my chief (the 23rd and 32nd Punjab Pioneers, the 4th Madras Pioneers and about five companies of sappers) then I had the whole of the stores for the works to arrange for, various construction projects to examine, and general assistance to give to any executive engineer who needed it. Among other jobs I had to do was the loading of an immense mine with gunpowder for the blowing up of a very large mass of rock. This was a somewhat risky operation, involving as it did the handling, inside a very narrow tunnel, of upwards of a ton of gunpowder. I did it all with my own hands and I am glad to say the explosion was quite successful.

As the weather was now beginning to get very hot Sir James Browne resolved to send his wife and child to Karachi, there to wait a little before going home so that she might reach England in spring. I escorted them to Karachi (not travelling in the same carriage of course. My experiences of travelling with babies had not then begun). It was delightful at Karachi, the weather was most balmy and the seaside breezes most invigorating. I stayed for two or three days, in a hotel, just enjoying a rest, going out sailing, or driving with Lady Browne. By the time I got back to the railway I found I had again to take up construction work, as Captain Connor was far from well.

About that time we were honoured with a visit from the Commander-in-Chief of the Bombay Army, Sir Arthur Hardinge. I had to go down to meet him one evening at Sibi, and escort him next day up the line to meet my general. His ADC Captain Hardinge of the Scots Fusiliers, whom I then met for the first time, was afterwards at the Curragh, at Aldershot, and at Chatham with us - a gallant soldier and hard rider. (He was killed by a fall from his horse riding quietly one day in Hyde Park.)

Those were stirring times in the political world. The fall of Khartoum and the death of Gordon, the fighting in the Sudan and on the Red Sea had diverted public attention from the Afghan Boundary Commission, until we were startled by hearing that the Russians and the Afghans had had a fight which as nearly as possible involved us in war with Russia. Two army corps were mobilised in India and all orders were issued for their assembly at Quetta. My chief wrote to the Government offering to take his brigade at once, as it stood, straight to Herat, and I remember he and I sat up till late one night arranging all the details of the march. Orders were received to weed out all the sickly men and send them back to India, and to concentrate the remainder in Peshin, on the plain where I had surveyed the line in the previous autumn.

The Amir was at that time paying a state visit to the Viceroy of India at Rawal Pindi. Rain had fallen all over the Punjab, and in our part of the country it fell in torrents, washing away much of the line and making communication difficult.

Just then I was at Baberkach fourteen miles from the end of the line at Narrai, my chief being up at the Chappar Rift. Hearing that things were in a bad way at Narrai I resolved to find my way there, both because I felt I would be of use there and also because I would be in telegraphic communication there with the outer world. I had a most difficult scramble over the hills and reached Narrai of course with no baggage other than what I carried on my person. I found matters very bad at Narrai. A terrible accident had just happened. The rain had undermined the foundations of a small railway culvert one night, and early in the morning a big train with two heavy engines had come up the line. Both engines were upset and the train smashed to pieces. Both engine drivers and one of the firemen were killed.

Then one of the pioneer camps was completely cut off by the floods. I got a telegram from the officer commanding to say. "No food. we are starving". With much difficulty I got together a train of bullocks laden with food and sent them off to him by paths above flood level and by boats. I heard to my wrath that he had really plenty of food, and that he had sent me the telegram by way of a joke. the idiot!

I had been two days at Narrai, slaving away, never changing my clothes (of course having none to change!) day or night when one morning (Easter Sunday, 5th April 1885) a man woke me to say a huge flood was coming down. Up I jumped and saw a sight such as I never saw before and hope never to see again - a truly awful flood. Huge brown waves leaping and roaring, whirling timber and corpses, spreading over everything. Rain was falling heavily. I warned all the people in the little community at Narrai to be ready to leave their houses and get into the hills, while I had all movable stores removed to the highest places. Then I watched a gauge anxiously to see how the waters were rising. Much to my relief the rain ceased and the water gradually fell. In the afternoon all was comparatively quiet and I summoned all the Europeans together and unitedly we thanked God, reading the prayers for Easter Day. I must have looked a queer parson in my dirty clothes and unshaven face, but I am sure no congregation on that Easter Day had more reason to offer grateful thanks to God for all His mercies.

When the floods subsided there was a tremendous amount of work to be done to put the line in order again. Many of my culverts had been knocked to pieces. and several landslips had occurred. Then I had to arrange for camel transport for all the troops. This was a very difficult matter for I had to use moral persuasion to induce the camel owners to go to what both they and I considered was war. I collected about 800 of them and spent a whole day in bargaining. At last they struck for more wages than I felt disposed to give, and I told them they could go about their business. It was a bit of bluff on my part and it succeeded for when some hours had passed. they agreed to my terms and went quietly away to the places I had ordered. I telegraphed the result of my negotiations to my chief and got back a very characteristic congratulation. As soon as the troops had got well on their way I followed and finally reached the Peshin Valley about the beginning of May to find them all quietly settled there, with not twenty sick out of the whole 2000.

But my work was done. The constant rain and exposure had told on me and very nearly finished me entirely. I found myself at Quetta in a wet tent with wet clothes on wet ground, and far from well.

Sir Robert Sandeman the chief political officer found me in this state and very kindly asked me to come to his house which I gladly did. I had however to go out again with Major Shepherd RE who was to take up the construction of the line which I had surveyed in the previous year, and point out to him the place, explaining various points. We were away for three or four days, and I found that my feet were swelling and in great pain. I went to the doctor of the 4th Madras Pioneers who bandaged them for me and advised me to go in to Quetta as soon as possible. I rode back in my stockings (for I could not get a boot on) in great agony and went straight to bed in Sir R Sandeman's house. The swelling in my feet spread to my knees and hands and the pain became excruciating. I had got rheumatic fever.

For the next six weeks I lay in great pain. Nothing could exceed the kindness of Sir R and Lady Sandeman, and of Dr Fullerton, the Residency Surgeon. He used to come every evening at 10 to inject morphia into me, and thus enable me to get a few hours of blessed sleep. My Persian servant Haji was most faithful and kind in his care of me. And when my dear old chief came to see me, he (Sir James Browne) was almost crying.

Lord Dufferin, then Viceroy, sent me a very kind message of sympathy, which cheered me very much.

To add to Sir James Browne's difficulties, cholera had broken out. It raged up the line carrying off some of the best men, and it came into Quetta attacking my good host Sir R Sandeman. I used to hear the Dead March and volleys from my sick bed, where I lay realising how I was kept in God's gracious hands, and if it were His will to carry me through I knew no disease could harm me. Thus the month of June passed away.

By the beginning of July I was a little better. Lady Sandeman got a pair of crutches made for me and I was able to crawl about the house a little. A board of doctors had decided that when I was fit to be moved, I should go home.

I spent a day or two with Lady Sandeman in a little country house they had in the Hanna Valley. I had to be carried there and back in a litter, but I think it did me good.

At last on the 11th or 12th of July I was sent off driving at first in Sir R Sandeman's carriage to the head of the Bolan Pass, then carried in a litter through the Pass. I had to spend one awful day of heat at a place called Kundilani half way down the Pass, where the temperature must have been about 110° in the bungalow. Next morning I reached the terminus of the railway and found two brother officers there, Ronald Maxwell and Oldfield working cheerily in spite of cholera raging all round. The former came with me to Karachi and saw me off.

I had to spend two or three days at Sukkur on the Indus to get my accounts squared up. I lived with the Examiner of Accounts, Mr Braddon, a good Christian man, who was very kind. But the heat was terrible, day and night. At Karachi I also put up with kind friends Mr & Mrs Whiting. Their house was near the sea and the delicious cool breezes were indeed a treat after the terrible heat of the journey. On the 19th July they and Ronald Maxwell saw me on board a coasting steamer to Bombay. It was very rough and the steamer was very dirty, so I was glad when I reached Bombay and was carried on board a P & O ship for Suez.

I had a trying journey home, which by the way I did not reach till October. I went first to Suez, took the train thence to Alexandria, then took ship to Venice, being kindly cared for on that part of my voyage by two brother officers, Courtney and Lawson, returning from the Egyptian War. From Venice I went via Milan to Lucerne, where I found a large party of relatives, Aunt Joanna and her children (except George), Uncle David and his wife and two daughters. I thence went, by medical advice, to Baden near Zurich where I spent about six weeks doing the 'cure' much to my benefit. I could not walk five yards when I went there, but when I left could manage to totter a few steps. My sister, Janie, joined me there and we spent a pleasant time together. Finally, we travelled with Uncle David's party down the Rhine and so via Ostend to Dover and so home.

Bolan Pass

Epilogue

When Scott Moncrieff left India in 1885 as a young man with rheumatic fever he returned to England to recuperate. But this was not to be the end of his connection with India. He married Helen Morin in 1886 and for the next four years commanded the 12th Field Co. RE at Colchester, Aldershot and the Curragh. Between 1890 and 98 he was instructor at the School of Military Engineering, Chatham and then returned to India to supervise military works in the Punjab, with his headquarters in Peshawar. In 1901 he commanded the RE at the Relief of Peking, and by the time he left India in 1904 he had been promoted Lieutenant Colonel CIE. Two years later he was made a full Colonel and was Assistant Director of Fortifications and Works at the War Office in Whitehall. After a period as Chief Engineer at Aldershot he became Director of Fortifications and Works at the War Office and was appointed Major-General. He was also awarded the KCB and the KCMG. Although officially retired in 1917 he had to stay on because his appointed successor was ill, and he worked until the Armistice in November 1918. During his retirement Scott Moncrieff showed the same energy and enthusiasms as he had done during his working life. He was a member of the RE Old Comrades Association, the Central Asian Society, the Church Missionary Society, the British and Foreign Bible Society and other religious bodies. He still enjoyed sport, including fishing and golf. Six daughters were born to him and Helen, two of whom are still alive today.

His death was in keeping with the life of this adventurous and humanitarian man. On his way to Warsaw in June 1924 to give technical help and advice to a charitable organisation interested in the welfare of Jews, he suddenly died from heart-failure in a railway carriage at a Frontier Station between Germany and Poland. His body was later returned to Scotland and buried beside that of his wife at Fossoway, Kinross-shire.

Major-General Sir George Scott Moncrieff, KCB, KCMG, CIE, RE,
at the end of his long career (taken about 1912)

Appendix
The Frontier Railways of India

To the west of the great plains of the Punjab, and parallel to the greatest of its rivers, the Indus, there lies a range of mountains, or rather a series of ranges and valleys, an offshoot from the great northern barrier of the Hindu Kush and Himalayas. This mountainous country divides the plains of India from the great central valley of Afghanistan, in which lie Kabul, Ghazni, and Kandahar, and from the deserts of Baluchistan to the south. It reaches from the great backbone of Asia, 'the Roof of the World,' down to the coast of the Arabian Sea, between the Persian Gulf and the mouths of the Indus. This mountainous region, through which have passed from time immemorial vast armies bent upon the spoil and plunder of the rich cities and plains of India, seems destined in these modern times to become famous as one of the most important political frontiers in the world, as the place where the two great Powers of Asia are eventually to meet. It is in width about 150 miles, more or less, the mountain peaks reaching from 10,000 to 16,000 feet in height, and it is intersected by very many passes, the names of some of which are very familiar to most Englishmen. From a political and military point of view, only that part of the frontier which separates Afghanistan proper from the Punjab is of any importance; it is, indeed, the only vulnerable point on the frontier of the Indian Empire. The more southerly portion, which separates Baluchistan from Sinde, need scarcely be taken into consideration.

Our attention, then, is concentrated on the Afghan frontier from Kelat, in the south, to Peshawar, in the north. Between those two points there are a number of passes, of which some four or five are the most important. Beginning at the north, we have the Khyber and Kuram routes, leading to and converging on Kabul, the capital of the country; half-way down there is the Gomal Pass from Dera Ismail Khan to Ghami, a pass much used by traders, but of no great military importance. Further on, there is the Thal Chutiali route from Dera Ghazi Khan to Kandahar, through the Bori Valley, by which Sir M Biddulph's division came from Kandahar in 1879. And furthest south, there are the twin routes of the Bolan and Harnai passes, both starting from Sibi and meeting again in Peshin, beyond Quetta.

A British army engaged in active operations on or beyond the Afghan frontier must necessarily move by one or other of these passes; and the object of the frontier railways of India is either to traverse these passes, or where this is not possible, to bring troops and stores close to the mouth of the pass.

On the outbreak of hostilities in Afghanistan, in 1878, the system of frontier railways may scarcely be said to have begun, except on paper. In the north the Punjab Northern State Railway had been completed from Lahore as far as Jhelum. This line had, up to the end of 1877, been made on the metre gauge, but in 1878 the gauge was altered to the broad gauge, five feet six inches, uniformly with other main lines throughout India. A break of gauge, which would, of course, bring disastrous confusion in time of war, was thus happily avoided. Although the line had only been completed to Jhelum, surveys and estimates had been made in 1877-78 for the extension to Peshawar, on the broad gauge.

During the campaigns of 1878-80, the work of constructing the line beyond Jhelum was pushed on with the utmost energy and resolution; but, for all practical purposes, Jhelum, 180 miles from Peshawar and 260 miles from Thal, the frontier post on the Kuram line, was the railway terminus during the whole of the campaigns. This, it must be remembered, was the line of communication for armies operating on two divergent lines, ie, by the Khyber Pass and the Kuram Valley, the point of divergence being Rawal Pindi. There is a first-rate military road leading from Jhelum to Peshawar, and a fair road from Rawal Pindi to Kohat and Thal, and during the war enormous trains of carts were kept up on these roads for the conveyance of warlike stores to the front, but the difficulties attending the organisation of such a train were enormous. It was only by dint of very great exertion that this transport was able to cope with the quantities of stores of all sorts that poured in at the railway base; and, further, the roads got unequal to the increased strain on them, and got cut up and worn with the continual traffic. It was, therefore, of the utmost importance to push on the railway as far as possible. Before the close of the campaign the line was opened for some twenty miles beyond Jhelum, but this did not very appreciably relieve the difficulties of the ordinary cart transport.

Rawal Pindi, sixty-eight miles beyond Jhelum, is a first-class military station and fortress, the headquarters of a division, and one of the most important strategical points in the whole of India. It was here that in April 1885, the Viceroy of India had an interview with the Amir Abdur-rahman Khan, of Kabul. The railway was opened to Pindi on the 1st of October 1880, by which time the Afghan war had just ended. The country between Jhelum and Pindi is extremely difficult, and the construction of the line there was a very troublesome and tedious job. The whole district is a tangled mass of ravines, and even using 1 in 50 as a maximum gradient, and curves of 1000 feet minimum radius, the work was not completed till, as we have seen, the campaign had been ended.

Meantime work had been going on steadily from Rawal Pindi to Peshawar. a distance of 100 miles. through a country which. although not so difficult as that from Jhelum to Pindi. is still troublesome to work in and with many natural obstacles. The ruling gradient on this portion of the line is 1 in 100, and the minimum radius of curves 1000 feet. As the work had gone steadily during 1879-80. the portion from Rawal Pindi to Peshawar was opened in 1881, with one gap at the great bridge at Attock. over the Indus. This was not finished till May, 1883, and when this was complete, through railway communication was established between Calcutta and Peshawar. from one end of the Empire to the other. At Peshawar the terminus for the military route to Kabul. via the Khyber Pass, now remains. The line might be taken, if necessary. eight miles beyond Peshawar to the mouth of the Khyber Pass, Jumrood, and this could be done at any time without difficulty, if necessary. A line was also surveyed during the war, through the Khyber Pass, some forty miles beyond Jumrood; but it is very unlikely that anything further will be done there unless the Amir wishes the work to be executed for his own advantage. From Peshawar to Kabul an excellent military road was constructed. under the supervision of officers of our Corps. during the Afghan campaign. and I hear that the Amir is very wisely keeping this road in good repair.

Previously to the completion of the main line from Jhelum to Peshawar. two branch lines were constructed. or rather begun. Of these one is from Rawal Pindi to Khushalgarh. on the Indus. a distance of some fifty miles. This is purely a military line. and was intended as a feeder to troops operating on the Thal-Kuram line. It has never been much used since it was made. for the war was over before it was opened. and commercially it has been a failure. Had the Kuram Valley been annexed. and a large cantonment formed there at a place called Shalozan. as was at that time contemplated. this branch line would have been more useful than it now is. I may mention that surveys were made for extending this line, via Kohat and Thal. eighty miles. and thence up the valley of the Kuram river. Here, again, it is very unlikely that anything will be done.

The other branch I alluded to above was at first simply for bringing in salt from the salt mines at Pind Dadan Khan. joining the main line at Lala Musa. By extending this branch, however, it has assumed a strategical value of the first importance. It has been extended throughout the country lying between the rivers Indus and Jhelum, commonly called the Sinde Sagar Doab, and has been brought opposite the important frontier posts of Dera Ismail Khan and Dera Ghazi Khan. The former, as we have seen above, is opposite the mouth of the Gomal Pass. leading to Ghazni. and the latter is at the eastern end of the Thal Chutiali route to Kandahar. A military road is at present under construction on this route from Dera Ghazi Khan, through the Bori Valley, to Peshin, and will be. when finished, a most important strategic route. By this Sinde Sagar Doab line of railway. therefore. troops will be enabled to arrive from the great garrisons of northern India. at Dera Ismail Khan. and at Dera Ghazi

Khan, and proceed by the quickest route to Kandahar, without troubling the Sinde Peshin Railway at all, and thus leaving it free for other work. There is another point, too, of immense importance. The desert which is crossed by the Sinde Peshin Railway between Jacobabad and Sibi is by some supposed to be the old bed of the river Indus. In any case, a branch of that mighty river would in time of flood undoubtedly flow that way if it were permitted to do so. It is prevented from so doing by a great dam, called the Kusmore Bund, to the north of Jacobabad. Now, if a very heavy flood were to occur in the Indus, this dam might burst. It has stood very well for years, but still the thing is possible; and if this occurred, the waters would sweep over the desert and cut off communication between Sibi and Jacobabad. This, in time of war, would be a most appalling disaster. Hence the supreme importance of having, in the Sinde Sagar Doab branch of the Punjab Northern Line, an alternative communication with Kandahar, independent of the bursting of dams or other such mishaps.

To give a description of the works on the Punjab Northern State Railway and its branches, would occupy more time than is at my disposal; but it may be interesting to state what works there are, without going into details.

Between Lahore and Peshawar there are four enormous bridges, spanning the rivers Ravi, Chenab, Jhelum, and Indus. The Chenab bridge is two miles long, and was, at the time of its erection, the longest bridge in the world. The bridge over the Indus at Attock is one of the greatest engineering works in India. The great difficulty here was the depth and velocity of the stream. The river here rushes through a rocky gorge, and is liable to sudden floods of greatly increased volume. The height of the bridge has been made 110 feet above ordinary low-water (ie winter) level, in order to keep the line well above floods. The highest known flood was, I believe, ninety-two feet, which occurred after the waters had been pent up by a landslip in the Himalayas. However, every hot season, when the heat of summer melts the glaciers, the volume of water coming down is enormous, and there is always a chance of a sudden rise. The bridge consists of two spans of 308 feet, and three spans of 257 feet. The girders, which are of steel, are so arranged that they carry a military road below, and a railway above. All the girders rest on wrought iron trestle piers, the centre pier being founded on an island, or partially submerged rock, in mid-channel. The founding of the pier on this rock was a matter of much difficulty, as it was discovered that the rock was honey-combed by the water, and it would have been unsafe to trust a great weight upon it. An oblong excavation in the rock had, therefore, to be made until solid material could be secured, and the whole filled with Portland cement concrete. The erection of the great girders across the rapid channel, and at so great a height, was also a matter of much difficulty. The staging was of wooden beams on the cantilever principle, working out from the pier, supported by timber struts and tied back by chains.

There is of course an enormous amount of earthwork in the hilly country between Jhelum and Peshawar, and there are a few tunnels. Of these the most important are Margalla, 900 feet long, and three others some 600 feet each.

Having thus briefly glanced at the works on the northern portion of the frontier, let us turn to the very important section further south, to which I desire to devote the greatest attention. This southern portion is more important, from a political and military point of view, because it lies at the most vulnerable point of the Empire, where, in event of war, all attention would be concentrated. And it is important from an engineering point of view, for the nature of the country there renders the construction of a railway a far more difficult task than it would be in almost any other part of the world.

At the beginning of the Afghan war of 1878-80, the communications were worse in the south than they were in the north. There was, it is true, through communication between Lahore and the sea at Karachi, but it was broken in two places, viz:- at the crossing of the Sutlej at Adamwahan, and at the crossing of the Indus at Sukkur. The bridge over the Sutlej has since been completed, but the Sukkur bridge is still unfinished, though it ought to be ready before long.

At the time I speak of (November, 1878) the branch line from Ruk to Jacobabad and to Sibi was then not under construction except for a very short portion of its length; it was therefore no practical use to the two divisions under Sir Donald Stewart, who advanced against Kandahar in the winter of 1878-79. But the line had been surveyed, and it was put in hand without delay. Colonel Lindsay, RE was Engineer-in-Chief, and under his orders the rails were speedily laid across the desert separating Sinde from the Afghan mountains. The materials were collected from every part of India, and the line advanced at the unprecedented rate of a mile a day. The arrangements for supplies, water, tools, etc were admirable, and in spite of the burning heat of the desert, casualties were few. By the month of June 1880, the advanced terminus was established at Sibi, thirteen miles from Ruk junction. The long and terrible march across the Sinde Desert, which has been so graphically described by Sir Thomas Seaton and other writers, was thus dispensed with; and when the troops were withdrawn from Afghanistan in 1880-81, this railway doubtless saved many lives.

On the upper section of this line, which was then called the 'Kandahar State Railway,' surveys were put in hand and completed from Sibi to Peshin and Quetta. A careful reconnaissance was first made as to whether the Harnai route or the Bolan route should be chosen, and the Governor of Bombay, Sir Richard Temple, himself traversed both routes, and reported, in December 1879, on this subject to the Government of India. The Harnai route was finally chosen, because, although it is longer than the Bolan route, it would be possible to find a line with a maximum gradient of 1 in 45 on the former route, as against 1 in 25 on the latter. This would of course make a vast difference in a line whose very raison d'etre is the supply of heavy stores and munitions of war to an army in the field. It was therefore decided to make the line by Harnai, though many distinguished men were against this view. Detailed surveys were made from Sibi to Garkhai on the Peshin plateau, and reconnaissances were made as far as Kandahar. It is true that the line indicated in these surveys had afterwards entirely to be altered, but it must be remembered that the work was done in an enemy's country, under pressure of war, when any line is better than none, and when men had not leisure for selecting the best possible alignment. The limiting radius of curves was then fixed at 600 feet, which still continues to be the minimum.

A beginning was made on the construction of this line in 1880. Some quarters were built for the engineers, some of the earthwork was started, one tunnel was begun. But the disastrous affair of Maiwand brought matters to a conclusion. The troops had to be withdrawn that protected the line, and whose presence alone made work possible. With the advance of the troops towards Kandahar, the working parties and the treasure had to be sent back towards India under a small escort. The marauding tribes, not slow to take advantage of any retrograde movement, were at once on the alert, and on August 6th 1880, a massacre occurred at Kochali, at which a large number of defenceless men were butchered, and a great quantity of treasure stolen. An expedition went out after the guilty tribe some two months afterwards, under the command of Sir Charles Macgregor, the ringleaders were caught and punished. and part of the treasure recovered. But the bad effect of the raid continued for long afterwards, and indeed has scarcely died out yet.

Not long after this, in October, 1880, the British Government resolved to abandon Kandahar, and to stop all operations on the Kandahar State Railway. The line from Ruk to Sibi however continued to bear the name until 1884.

The money spent on the line up to that time was swallowed up in the war expenses, but I believe it came to about half a million sterling. For the most part this was money entirely thrown away. A good deal of work had been begun, but had not sufficiently advanced to have any permanent value; and most of the stores collected at great expense had to be sold at considerable loss.

Some three years passed away, and what little work had been done was gradually falling to pieces from want of repair. The Harnai pass resumed its former quietness, and except at little forts at intervals up the valley there appeared no sign of the British occupation. However, about the middle of 1883 the Government seems to have become alive to the fact that the stoppage of the works was a mistake. Orders were sent to the Government of India to re-commence the work in the following cold weather, and to this end a force of two half-battalions of pioneers and five companies of sappers was to be ordered to proceed to Sibi in October. An engineer officer of railway experience was to be made Engineer-in-Chief, he was to command the troops, and to have such an executive staff of officers for carrying out the works as the railway department could spare for him. Colonel James Browne, RE was nominated for this command. Work was to begin as early as possible on the most difficult parts of the line. The old surveys made in 1879-80 would show where these difficult points were, and the consulting engineer to the Government of India (Mr Molesworth, whose name is familiar to all engineers), would go over the line and give his advice on the subject. The work, however, was not to be called the Kandahar State Railway, it was to be known as the Harnai Road Improvement Scheme. Possibly it was hoped that by this means the British public would not notice the change of face that had been made by their rulers. This circumstance would be hardly worth mentioning but for the fact that still further to keep up the fiction of the road, as opposed to the railway, all expenditure on rails or rolling-stock was forbidden. Now many of the heavy works - all of them in fact - lay at a very considerable distance from the base of operations, and all stores had to be carried from that base either on the backs of camels, or (in case of heavy articles) dragged on wheels up the bed of rivers. It was the wish of the Engineer-in-Chief to lay rails at once, in a temporary fashion, as far up the pass as possible, and this might quite well have been done for at least twelve miles up the pass in January and February, 1884. But the orders of the Government would not permit him to do so, although it is a first principle of engineering to secure the best and easiest method of communication to the works, in all cases. It is probable that if permission to lay rails had been granted, a temporary line might easily have been made in 1883-4, from Narrai to Gundakinduff, eighteen miles, but even if it had only got as far as Kelat-i-kila, twelve miles, the moving forward of the base to that point would have caused an enormous saving in the item of transport. It was calculated that this saving for one item alone, viz:-Portland cement, would have amounted to £30,000 in twelve months. Probably £100,000 more than was necessary was thus spent on camel transport. I mention this in vindication of the progress of the platelaying and carrying power of the line. It was not the fault of the engineers that the carrying power of the line was not utilised as it might have been.

I have seen it stated that girders and rails for the work were collected at Sibi in 1880, and were there when work recommenced in 1883. This is not the case. The only rails found were a few metre-gauge rails, which had been handed over to the Military Works Depot; and as for girders, there were none. The earthwork too that had been done in 1880 consisted only of a few banks, scarcely any cuttings, and certainly not one bank or cutting of any size or importance.

The troops ordered to the works on this occasion were half-battalion 1st Madras Pioneers, half-battalion 23rd Punjab Pioneers, and Nos 4, 5, 7, 9 and 10 Companies of the Bengal Sappers and Miners. I may, perhaps, mention here the difference between pioneers and sappers, terms which in India are not identical as they are in some European armies. The unit of the sappers is the company about 100 strong, with one or two European officers (from the Corps of RE), and five British non-commissioned officers. The Punjab Pioneers are simply battalions of infantry of the line, who, being recruited from a caste (Muzbi Sikhs) accustomed to the use of tools and to digging, have been set apart specially for engineering works. Each man carries a tool of some sort with him, and though they are not skilful artisans, they make very useful labourers. They are admirable soldiers - sinewy, powerful men, and very valuable as fighting material. They are not, however, so amenable to discipline as the high-class Sikh, who, in addition to his other good qualities, is a most docile soldier.

The Bengal Sappers are recruited from all the warlike castes of northern India. The Madras Pioneers were recently formed by Sir F Roberts from two infantry regiments who did good service in the Afghan War. The men are recruited from the usual class of Southern India Railways, and, though inferior physically, are superior mentally to the Sikhs of northern India. The officers of the pioneer regiments are infantry officers, and are not specially selected for engineering knowledge. There are no European non-commissioned officers.

By the end of 1883, the troops for the work had arrived at the scene of operations, and were distributed as follows:- the whole of the pioneers at Kelat-i-kila, two companies of sappers at Baberkach, one company at Gundakinduff, one company at Kochali, and one at Spintangi.

There were many difficulties, however, in getting the work started. There were at first no directing officers of any railway experience, except the Engineer-in-Chief himself. Gradually executive officers began to come in, one by one, as they were relieved of duties elsewhere. A batch of young lieutenants, fresh from England, were appointed as assistants, and thus the engineering staff was gradually organised. Another difficulty was the want of survey instruments. All those that had been used formerly had been sent away, and in the railway stores at Sibi there was not even a chain or a levelling staff. Many expedients had to be resorted to to lay out and stake off work, and it was a long time before an adequate supply of instruments arrived on the scene. Work may be said to have fairly begun by the middle of December.

In addition to the troops, large numbers of civil labourers came for employment. Some of these came in republican gangs, where each man got a share of the profits, and each man worked, but for the most part they were brought by native contractors, who undertook contract work at rates settled by the Engineer-in-Chief. These contractors generally made all arrangements for feeding their men, which was a great thing, as it would otherwise have been a dreadful burden to the engineers, and in some few cases they brought their own tools. As a rule, however, each executive engineer had to supply tools to the contractors in his division. In some cases water had to be supplied by the engineers. This was done by paying the contractors an extra rate, and supplying them with empty casks for the storage of this precious fluid.

Work went on without interruption from December 1883, to the end of March, 1884, on the lower section, ie, from Narrai to Spintangi. By the end of March the headings of three new tunnels, Baberkach, Gundakinduff, and Spintangi, had been driven. The Narrai tunnel had been lined with brickwork. The foundations of seven of the most difficult bridge piers had been laid secure against all contingencies. An enormous quantity of earthwork, especially in heavy rock cuttings, had been finished. In one place 400 men of the 23rd Pioneers were engaged on one rock cutting for five months, working steadily every day except Sundays.

By the end of March 1884, the weather got so hot that it was considered advisable to move the troops at once to the upper parts of the line. The 23rd Pioneers were ordered back to the Punjab. Of the remainder, the 1st Madras Pioneers were sent to Kach, and, being joined by the other half-battalion, were quartered there for the summer months. The 14th Company Bengal Sappers went to Garkhai, and the remaining companies to Mangi, at the head of the Chappar Rift, for tunnel work. The garrison at Mangi was afterwards increased by two companies of Bombay Sappers, who came from Quetta in July 1884, and stayed till April 1885.

Of course, when the troops moved, it was necessary to move everything else, stores, offices, tools, plant and the whole body of workpeople, some 14,000 or 15,000. The management of this vast exodus was a work of considerable anxiety and difficulty. A sudden influx of people such as this into a desolate and barren land naturally caused a famine. Everything was eaten up, and for some days the matter of supplies was the burning question of the hour. Some idea of the quantity required may be gained when I state that 500 camel loads of food were consumed daily on the works.

Meantime events were rapidly developing in the outside world. In February the Russians had occupied Merv, and the British public began to turn their attention towards the East. The Liberal Ministry announced that in consequence of the encroachments of Russia the Quetta Railway would again be commenced. This announcement was made in May, the date of Lord Kimberley's despatch being 24th April. This had the effect of changing the title of our work from 'The Harnai Road Improvement Scheme' to 'The Sinde Peshin State Railway.' which title it bears to this day.

The early months of the summer of 1884 were occupied for the most part in survey work. The alignment was entirely re-surveyed and altered from Nasak to Garkhai, and great was the improvement thereby effected.

Work was begun generally all along from Harnai to Garkhai in July, but unfortunately in August and September sickness, fever, scurvy etc, broke out with such virulence that great numbers of the workmen died, and those that remained were unable to do much work. In one gang twenty-nine out of forty-two died of scurvy. All that medical skill and care could do was done, but even among the soldiers, better clad, better fed and cared for than the civil labourers, only a very few were fit for duty. At Mangi at one time sixty per cent of the sappers were in hospital. At Kach the Madras Pioneers were completely knocked to pieces. The officers, too, all along the line fared as badly as the men. Everyone suffered more or less, and several laid up a store of fever and sickness which they have since had much difficulty in getting rid of.

Some of the troops were withdrawn during the autumn for the campaign in the Zhob Valley, and these did not return to the works. The remaining troops, except two companies of Bombay Sappers, stayed on till the cold weather had fairly set in, and they then returned to cantonments in India, much weakened by sickness.

Meantime orders had been issued to start the work during the cold weather on a very much larger scale. Several new executive divisions were formed, and work went on uniformly along the line from Narrai to Chappar. Three regiments of pioneers were sent to the works viz:- the 4th Madras, and the 23rd and 32nd Punjab Pioneers. These were formed into a brigade under the command of Colonel James Browne RE, the Engineer-in-Chief of the line, who was given the rank of Brigadier-General, and who had thus, in addition to his heavy engineering duties and responsibility, the command of a very strong brigade of regular troops. This giving of a military command in time of peace to a Public Works officer, though most necessary in this and similar cases, was a new departure in Indian procedure. With the exception, however, of the Brigadier-General Commanding and his staff-officer (whose duties, like those of his chief, were both civil and military), the officers of the Royal Engineers on the line (not with native sappers) were in every respect civil officers. They had no command of troops, and had precisely the same duties to perform as civil engineers. The RE officers attached to companies of native sappers performed certain civil duties also, for which they received extra pay, but it was not found in every case that this mixing of civil and military work was satisfactory, and it is, I think, admitted that it is better to keep the duties distinct.

Work was again fairly begun on the lower section in November 1884, but it had hardly been started when a severe outbreak of cholera occurred. Everything that could possibly be done was done to keep the camps of the workpeople clean, but these were so large, and the numbers of labourers so great, that there was much difficulty in the strict enforcing of sanitary laws. There were a few cases of cholera among the troops. Troop trains were kept waiting near their camps ready to carry off a whole regiment at a time to a distance, if the disease should break out at any time with violence. Camps were arranged along the line to which troops might be sent. These troop trains were not required, and, perhaps, the worst result of the cholera was the stoppage of the works by the desertion of labour. All the Afghan workmen bolted to a man! The less noisy Punjabis and Sindis and Mekranis, from the coast of the Persian Gulf, stuck to their work well, as did also the Hindus from the east. The working season on the lower section is a short five months, viz:- from November to March. The cholera epidemic effectively stopped the full swing of the work for the first month. During December a good deal was done all along the line, but in January, February, and March there were long and most serious interruptions from floods. The rainfall this year (1885) was most exceptional. Usually, the total amount for the first four months of the year is about three inches; in 1883 it was 2.28 inches; in 1884, 4.89 inches. This year it was 19-27 inches, nearly six times as much as usual. When it is remembered that twelve large bridges were under construction, it will be understood what a terribly serious hindrance these repeated floods were. The last great floods lasted from the 30th March to the 5th April 1885, and were the cause of much disaster. Old natives said there had been nothing like them for sixty years, and certainly the flood levels were far above previous records. A terrible accident occurred on the 1st April. A heavy goods train, with two 48-ton engines, was coming up to Narrai with stores, in the early morning. One of the culverts on the old part of the line between Narrai and Sibi had had its foundations scoured out by the flood, and the rails and sleepers were simply hanging by the fish-plates. The train came along over it at ten miles an hour, with the result that both engines were upset and smashed, and about a dozen waggons knocked to pieces. Three men were killed, and one severely wounded. It took nearly a month to put right the damage caused by this flood. However, it is unlikely such a flood will occur again, and so the worst is known.

The troops were moved up to the cooler regions in the Gwal Valley in April. They had some difficulties on the march from wet and stormy weather, but the health of the whole brigade was excellent, only some six or eight men out of 2,000 being in hospital at the beginning of May.

The threatened war with Russia in March, April, and May 1885, had its effect on the works. The orders of Government were to push on with increased energy throughout the hot weather at all parts of the line. A new temporary railway was begun in the Bolan. The Transport and Commissariat Departments collected large quantities of stores and followers at the mouth of the Bolan, and among the crowds of natives thus gathered together, cholera broke out in May. It spread up the Bolan with great rapidity, and spared neither great nor small, european or asiatic. Among other victims was Captain Ewen Cameron, RE, an officer of great skill and experience, and one whose kind and genial nature had endeared him to all who knew him.

At first the cholera did not spread up the railway works on the Harnai route, and we hoped that we might escape it altogether. About the end of May, however, it appeared and spread like a raging fire up the whole line. The workpeople were panic-stricken. Many of the minor Government officials, such as clerks, postmasters, etc, abandoned their posts and fled without warning. The native clerks in one office left one day en masse. In spite of every care, the death-rate spread with fearful rapidity; some of the best men on the works, both european and asiatic, fell victims. The Europeans connected with the management of the three most important sections of the work, viz:- bridging, tunnelling, and platelaying, all fell victims to disease. The bridging contract was in the hands of Mr Sullivan, a gentleman who had great skill and experience in girder erection. He worked with great pluck and perseverance, but he was obliged to leave the works in June, and he died on his journey home. The tunnelling apparatus was worked by an American, Mr Phillips, who had just arrived, specially for the work, from New York, who died after he had been a fortnight on the works. The platelaying was under a contractor, Mr Baness, a man of great railway experience, who had just finished another large platelaying contract with success; he died of cholera in June. The intense heat of the weather added much to the general collapse. At the end of June the fire of disease seemed to have burned itself out, but not until in one month 2,000 men out of 10,000 had died. And the works on the lower part of the line had completely stopped; men could not be found to face the over-powering and combined force of heat and disease.

By the end of June the state of the works was the line completely finished for twenty miles beyond Sibi, for the next forty miles everything finished but rails and bridge girders, and beyond that all earthwork, with a few exceptions.

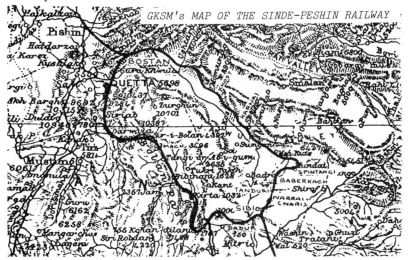

GKSM's MAP OF THE SINDE-PESHIN RAILWAY

**   **   **   **   **

I propose now to give some account of the engineering works on the Sinde Peshin Railway, which was constructed under the circumstances formerly narrated.

I have selected this line among all the frontier railways for lengthy description, partly because having been there since the work was started I know it better than I do any other line, and partly also because it presents more difficulties from an engineering point of view than any other frontier line. Indeed, I may say that of all the mountain railways I have ever seen or read of, I do not know of any which on the whole presents greater difficulties. It is therefore, I think, for purely engineering reasons, if on no other grounds, a fit object for study by engineer officers.

In the first place, in considering this line, it must be remembered that it passes in a very short distance over a very great height. It rises from 300 feet above sea level at Sibi to 6,500 feet above sea level beyond Kach, or 6,000 feet in 120 miles. Now in Europe the summit level of the St Gothard railway is only 3,500 feet. There are railways in America, both in North America and the Andes, that rise to a greater height, but not, I believe, to such a height in so short a distance, nor with as broad a gauge (the gauge of the Sinde Peshin Railway is 5 feet 6 inches). Now the effect of the rapid rise in a climate like that of south Afghanistan is that the changes of temperature from the lower portion of the line to the highest are at all times inconceivably great. The natives have a proverb that owing to the existence of Sibi there was no necessity for the infernal regions. Again, on the upper portion of the line the cold of winter is positively Arctic in its rigour. The bitterness of the cold seems worse than the most severe winter in Great Britain. During the months of January and February the north wind blowing from the frozen uplands of Central Asia seems to freeze the very marrow in one's bones. When this wind is blowing, often camels and horses simply refuse to face it, and as the narrow mountain gorges often cause its force to be concentrated in violent gusts, it may be imagined what a serious matter it is for the passage of caravans over mountain passes. These facts made the carrying on of work on the upper portions of the line during the winter, and on the lower portions of the line during the summer, almost impossible. Men would not face the cold on the one hand and the heat on the other.

In addition to these difficulties of climate, there was the difficulty of working in an absolutely barren land. Everything had to be imported for the works, hardly anything could be obtained locally. Even lime and building stone were only in a very few places procurable. A few spars for building huts in the upper section was all that the surrounding country could supply in the way of timber. It is true that the Engineer-in-Chief arranged for the supply of some sleepers from a juniper forest to the north of the line, but the political authorities here stepped in and promptly vetoed this, as likely to cause quarrels among the Afghan tribes, so that even what might have been utilised in the country was not allowed to be used. All materials, tools, plant, cement, timber and even labour, had to be imported from India or northern Afghanistan. The variety of races employed as workmen was very great, and it was reckoned at one time that nine different languages were spoken on the works. In a barren and thinly inhabited country such as the one I am describing, all food supplies had to be brought from India, which of course had its effect in increasing the cost of labour. All stores had to be brought on camels or other pack animals, and an enormous number of these were constantly in use. There are no roads in the country, nor is it like a sandy desert where pack animals can go anywhere. There was a regular caravan path available for all pack animals, but this was often rendered impassable by floods, though it was the only means of communication. The camels were supplied to us by the Powindahs, a race of Afghan carriers who used to do the great carrying trade between Central Asia and India, and who still do a very fair amount of business. They had some magnificent camels. It may appear incredible, but many of these used to carry loads of 800lbs up the pass. Generally a camel's load is about 400lbs. The cost of this camel transport was enormous, and unfortunately we were very dependent on it - a strike among the camel men meant a complete stoppage of the works.

When it is remembered that operations were carried on in a country which had the reputation of being peopled by a savage and blood-thirsty race of robbers, it will be admitted that, as compared with other railways, this line has a unique position in the matter of initial difficulties. Climate, material, supplies, transport, population, were all adverse to work, so that apart from difficulties of engineering, pure and simple, there were great opposing forces to work and fight against. The engineering difficulties themselves were by no means trifling.

There are four parts of the line which present special engineering difficulties. The first is the Narrai gorge from Narrai to Baberkach, a distance of fourteen miles. The second is the Kochali defile from Gundakinduff to Kochali, five miles long. The third is the Chappar Rift, some three miles long; and the fourth is the summit of the pass, a portion some twenty-five miles in length from Mud gorge to Garkhai. With the exception of these the remainder of the line is in no way more difficult than any ordinary line through a mountainous country.

With regard to the first of these difficult places - in the Narrai gorge the Narrai river breaks through the mountain barrier which skirts the desert for some hundreds of miles along the frontier. All the drainage of a very large portion of country stretching right back to the Bori and Zhob valleys to the north, in all some 24,000 square miles, is pent up behind this mountain range. The Narrai gorge is the only important outlet for the waters between Sibi and Dera Ghazi Khan. At Baberkach, which is at the upper end of this gorge, three rivers join, and half a mile lower down another river, the Bheji, comes in. The turmoil of waters at this part of the gorge during a flood is quite indescribable. The combined waters force their way through the mountains by a wild and rocky gorge which ends at Narrai, seven miles from Sibi. The hills there consist of sandstone, indurated clay, and conglomerate layers, tilted at an angle of about 28" to the horizon. They are absolutely barren. The general direction of the river is at right angles to the ridges, which are very clearly defined; the river has cut for itself a narrow gorge, leaving the mountains on both sides in a series of sharp serrated ridges. The appearance of this gorge is very wild, and it has a bold fantastic beauty of its own. In carrying the railway up this gorge, every care has been taken to avoid, as far as possible, the expensive and difficult bridge work involved in crossing and re-crossing the river. Tunnels have been made in various places, and many heavy cuttings and banks. But with all precautions, it has been found necessary to cross the river six times in the whole distance of fifteen miles, and it is a matter of some doubt whether two additional bridges will not be found necessary.

On leaving the station at Narrai, the line does not cross and re-cross the river, but in order to save two bridges, keeps close under the base of the perpendicular cliffs, which have here been cut back en bloc, to allow room for the line, and with their debris afford a foundation for it. Then the line passes through a tunnel, which was driven in 1880 but not lined. In the three years which followed much of the roof of the tunnel fell in, and there were some blocks of rock loose and just ready to fall. the removal of which was a dangerous and delicate operation. It has now been lined throughout with brickwork in cement. After leaving this tunnel the line again passes under one of the perpendicular cliffs, which it has been necessary to cut back. All this cliff cutting and the tunnel, and some length of line, might have been avoided if the line had been taken across the river and back again in a straight line. It would have given a shorter, better, and safer line, but the enormous cost of the two bridges deterred the engineers, although I think it is very likely that eventually these bridges will have to be made.

The first of the present bridges across the Narrai is at a place called Tanduri, six and a half miles from Narrai. Tanduri means an oven, and the name is singularly appropriate, for the heat there in summer is terrific. This bridge was originally of five spans, since increased to six spans, each of 150 feet. This work was begun by Captain Davidson RE, in January 1884 and finished in March 1885. It has presented no great difficulty; the piers are not very high nor the foundation rock very deep. A good sandstone quarry near the site supplied stone for piers and abutments, and the general position is sufficiently open to make all the accessories for the work easily laid out and arranged. There is a small rectangular fort near at hand, in which are quarters for the men employed on the work, and stores of all kinds for use on the bridges are kept.

After this the gorge widens a little, and the line crosses an open plain for a mile or two, and plunging through a rocky spur of the hills at Kelat-i-kila. again meets the river, and crosses it on a bridge of four spans of 150 feet and one of 40 feet. The site of this bridge is narrow and awkward; the average height of the piers is 45 feet; they were built of stone from a quarry some two and a half miles off. Great difficulty was experienced in securing these foundations, owing to repeated floods, but Lieutenant Thackwell RE who was in charge, was very successful in overcoming all difficulties. The work was begun in December 1884 and the last girders were rivetted up in June, 1885, so no time was lost, in spite of the disastrous floods in January, March, and April.

In the next three miles there are no fewer than four bridges, all of the same character, each with five spans, generally of 150 feet, and with piers of about 28 feet average height. The foundations of some of these piers gave much trouble; and in the absence of anything like good building stone (which was not procurable), or of fuel to burn bricks, the piers and abutments were all built of Portland cement concrete in blocks, which will be hereafter more fully described. These four bridges were for the most part entirely built in the winter of 1884-85, but four of the most troublesome of the river pier foundations were secured during the early months of 1884. The girders had not been erected on any of these bridges in June 1885, but all the masonry was quite ready to receive them. Near the last of these four bridges is the meeting place of all the waters alluded to above. Much difficulty was experienced in keeping the line and banks free from the destroying action of the waves. At the extreme end of the gorge there stands the great Baberkach rock, round which in time of flood the waves whirl and roar with much fury. The line passes through this rock in a tunnel some 250 feet long. It was proposed at one time to blow up the whole mass of rock, which is made of hard conglomerate. Mining galleries were laid out and driven by the sappers of the 7th and 10th Companies Bengal Sappers and Miners. The charge required was about 60 tons of gunpowder. The idea, however, of this great blast was abandoned in favour of a tunnel, because some preliminary mines that were fired gave unsatisfactory results.

The second difficult portion of the line is the Kochali defile, some three miles beyond Baberkach. Here for five miles we have a narrow and winding ravine, through which, in time of flood, a river comes with sudden and great violence, passing between steep hills that rise almost vertically on both sides. The longitudinal slope of the ravine is greater than the maximum gradient of the line, and so the line has to enter the lower end at a considerable height. The soil is clay shale of a very treacherous nature. The cuttings on this part are perhaps the most troublesome on the whole line, some of them being as much as 100 feet in depth. Heavy revetment walls have been required to support the slopes of the embankments, as the width of the defile does not admit in most cases of the slope reaching the ground in the ordinary way. There are three very heavy bridges, each of an average length of 300 feet. The first of these rises to a considerable height, the piers being 67 feet high. Between the first two bridges is a tunnel 540 feet long, passing through a neck in the hills. The heading of this tunnel was made in the early months of 1884 by the 5th Company of Bengal Sappers, under Lieutenant King RE. It was taken out to full width and lined with brickwork during the cold weather of 1884-85. The danger in this work from the falling of earth and shale was very great, and many lives were lost. There is another small tunnel towards the upper end of the defile, but it is only 120 feet long. It was begun and completed last winter (1884-85), under Lieutenant Capper.

From Kochali to the Chappar Rift there is no great difficulty to be encountered. There are two heavy bridges at Zindagi-Ab, between Kochali and Spintangi; there is another over the Garmi river at Spintangi, and three between Spintangi and Harnai. There is one tunnel through white marble rock at Spintangi. But there is no exceptional difficulty about any works until the Chappar Rift is reached, and this is the crux of the whole line from Sibi to Peshin.

The Chappar Rift is an extraordinary freak of nature. Imagine, if possible, a mountain range broken asunder at right angles to its contours. Down the chasm thus formed, a mountain torrent forces its way through enormous boulders, the quantity of water in summer being a mere trickle, but in time of rain a boiling torrent completely filling up the rift from wall to wall and effectually preventing anything from passing up and down. The main caravan route from Kandahar to Sibi via Harnai led through this rift, and in 1880 the roadway was improved and made passable for artillery. But every flood destroyed this road, and recently a road has been made over the top of the mountain; the existence of this upper road was rendered necessary on account of the quantity of debris which was then being shot over the edge to the bottom of the rift by the railway tunnel and cutting works. The longitudinal slope of the rift is about 1 in 20. The maximum gradient of the railway is 1 in 45. Hence, to effect an exit at the upper end it is evident that the entrance at the lower end must be at a very high level. To gain this height was one of the engineering problems that presented itself. It was managed as follows:- the stream through the rift joins at its lower end a valley at right angles to the rift reaching towards Khost. The railway coming up from Khost was kept on the side of that valley opposite to the mouth of the rift, and continued up and past the mouth until it had met naturally the stream coming down, then it described a complete semi-circle, and, crossing the stream, skirted along the face of the rock towards the rift. The next question was how best to take it along the face of the rock. An embankment on the face of a rock with a cross slope of 1 in 2 was out of the question, for the lower end of the bank would be in the air. A cutting was objectionable because of the violent storms of rain which occasionally fall. The water pouring off the rock above into the cutting would turn it into a water-course. It was suggested to drive iron standards into the rock and lay girders on them. This would allow the rain water from above to pass below the line, but if a train got derailed it would have nothing to save it from utter destruction. It was finally decided, therefore, to make what in Persia and Afghanistan is known as a karez ie, a tunnel passing just under the surface and connected by many shafts. These karezes are made largely by the natives to bring water from springs at the hills to irrigate their fields. By adopting this principle to the railway, the surface water would readily get away over the line, and yet the train would be quite safe in case of accidents.

This covered passage, or karez, is divided into two parts, the first having eight shafts and a length of 817 feet, the second twelve shafts and a length of 1400 feet.

After passing through these karezes it has been found necessary to tunnel through a jutting portion of the mountain. This tunnel is 645 feet long; it was a very troublesome heading to drive, owing to difficulty of access to it.

The line then reaches the edge of the rift, and has to leap across to the opposite rocky wall of the chasm. The bridge which takes the line across is 200 feet above the bed of the torrent below; it will consist of two spans of 150 feet, and some two or three spans of 40 feet. The line then immediately plunges again into a tunnel 542 feet, curving round to the left. Emerging from this, it enters the core or heart of the rift, where the chasm widens out to an oval shape, a high wall of rocks all round the edges, and the sides formed of debris of rocks and shale. The railway winds up the eastern side of this, in cutting and bank alternately, until it has to penetrate the rock afresh at the place where the rift again narrows in. This tunnel (No 3) is 1251 feet long, but it has presented in some respects less difficulty than some of the others, as it has been possible to have no fewer than seven adits leading into it from the face of the rift. There is beyond it a somewhat heavy rock cutting, and then the line finally plunges through the last of the rift tunnels 437 feet long, and emerges into the upper valley at Mangi. The tunnels aggregate a mile altogether.

Taken as a whole the work on the Chappar Rift is a very bold piece of engineering. It was planned by Brigadier-General Browne, working in constant consultation with Captain B Scott RE, who has continued in charge of the works as Executive Engineer since their first commencement. The starting of the work was a matter of no small difficulty. A very careful survey of this most precipitous ground had first to be made, then the levels had to be fixed and the line located, then work had to be begun, all of which operations were not only difficult, but extremely dangerous, involving a very steady head and good nerves. When the position of the line had been fixed, men had to be lowered from the summit of the crags on cradles or platforms, and from this position had to make foot-holds for themselves on the smooth vertical face of the cliffs. Nor was this all. Violent floods so frequently prevented all ingress and egress to the rift, that Captain Scott saw it was necessary to make a high level road that should be independent of all floods. This was done by taking advantage of ledges and shelves of rocks; and where no such ledges existed, iron bars were driven horizontally into the vertical rock face, and supported a roadway of planks or chesses. This upper road enabled the working parties to come and go independently of the weather. Of course this high level road is merely for foot passengers. For all animals, and for the regular heavy traffic of the country, a road has been made, as I have already mentioned, over the top of the mountain.

So carefully and well was the work on the Chappar Rift organised, that in spite of bitter cold it went on steadily all last winter (1884-85), although occasionally there were difficulties of supplies, both of food and stores. The work was then placed in the immediate charge of Mr Rose, a civil engineer, working under Captain Scott's direction. It is hoped that the tunnels will all be completed in December, 1885. They were begun in June 1884.

Much credit is due, let me here state, to the men of the Bengal Sappers and Miners, especially the 5th, 9th and 10th Companies, for the way they began these works, especially in the construction of the high level road, and in beginning the adits. These men worked fearlessly and well in positions of much danger, and they accepted the difficulties of the work in a proper soldier-like spirit as a compliment to their skill and aptitude.

We have so far glanced at three out of the four difficult portions of the line. The fourth is the 'summit' section, which may be said to extend from Mud gorge to Garkhai, a distance of about eighteen miles. Mr Molesworth, indeed, considered Mud Gorge (a place half-way between the Chappar Rift and Kach) a more serious engineering difficulty than even the Chappar Rift. It is a wild and precipitous glen, about three miles long, with a longitudinal slope at first of about 1 in 30, gradually lessening to 1 in 70. The soil is extremely soft and treacherous; it has the appearance of loose mud - whence the name of the place - and at first it seemed necessary to make two large tunnels and some four or five high level bridges. However an alteration in the alignment got rid of all these works, and a huge cutting 75 feet deep and 1200 feet long is now the most formidable operation to be undertaken, and it is possible that some revetting or lining will be required to protect the sides of the cutting. There is also a short bank 105 feet high. But even these heavy works are far better than the tunnels and bridges for which they have been substituted.

Much care and attention was bestowed on the selection of the alignment on this 'summit' portion. The country through which the line here passes is very broken and mountainous, and on the old plans there appear some terribly heavy works, such as a 60 feet bank for nearly a mile, a bridge 120 feet high etc. Careful survey eliminated all these difficulties. Under Captain Hoskyns and Lieutenants C Cowie and Petrie, an entirely new line was selected, which might, I think, be taken as a model for the adapting of a line to the contours of a country. In one place there is a 'corkscrew', or spiral, a device which is common enough on such mountain lines as the St Gothard, but unknown either in this country or in India. The line takes a complete turn under itself. The whole alignment on this section was laid out with such care and such a light line, comparatively speaking, selected, that the whole of the earthwork was completed in five months. This rapid work was the result of Captain Hoskyns' organisation, and when he went away to active service in the Zhob Valley Expedition, the work was well sustained by Lieutenant Thackwell, who was placed in temporary charge.

From Garkhai to Quetta there are no engineering difficulties. The country is quite open, and the line lies along the surface. There is one tunnel through hard lime-stone rock, and a bridge of four spans of 40 feet over the Quetta Lora river. At Bostan there is the junction of the main line from Sibi to Peshin, and the branch to Quetta. Bostan is a little village surrounded by fields on the left bank of the stream called the Kakar Lora. It will doubtless be a place of some importance, not only as a railway junction on the Peshin plateau, but because it is proposed to put workshops, locomotive sheds, and staff quarters there. It is proposed to fortify the site and to protect the adjacent bridge also by a <u>tete</u> <u>du</u> <u>pont</u>. The climate is temperate, and the garrison there will not be <u>badly off</u>.

After leaving Bostan the line passes through a low range of hills, and five miles from Bostan reaches the new cantonment of Peshin. The destination of the line after this is uncertain. It may cross the Peshin plain to Kila Abdulla, and tunnel through the Khojak range to Chaman. This would have the advantage of giving a direct route, but one attended with extraordinary difficulties. Three miles of viaducts and a tunnel two miles, perhaps four miles, long would be necessary, and as the soil is indurated clay, like the Kochali tunnel, this would add to the difficulty of the undertaking, as it would have to be lined throughout. There would be great delay and difficulty in starting a tunnel at such a distance from the base.

Again, even if the line did reach Chaman, it could not go direct to Kandahar. There are some fifteen miles of slope below Chaman, and the line would have to zigzag down this glacis, and then travel westward to a point to the south of Kandahar.

An alternative scheme for the extension of the line is to take it along the Quetta branch as far as the Quetta Lora bridge, and then, instead of striking south-east to Quetta, take it almost due south towards Nushki, which is quite clear of the Gwaja Amran range. It may be remembered that the Afghan Boundary Commission last year went via Nushki. Taking the comparative lengths of the two lines via Chaman and via Nushki, it appears that, measured from Bostan, the latter route is the longer, but it would cost less than the Kila Abdulla line, and could be started at once. Strategically it would be a better line, as it would run parallel to the frontier, and in rear of the important military position on the Gwaja Amran range. Another line could, moreover, be taken from Nushki to Gawaja Sultan, on the banks of the Helmand, whence the communications between Herat and Kandahar would be threatened. The Nushki line would not only be cheaper, but could be finished more quickly than the other. Nearly the whole length is surface railway; there is but one tunnel, 300 feet long, and 600 feet of bridging. The ruling gradient is 1 in 100, as against 1 in 45 on the other line. Thus the Nushki line would be completed in half the time, and carry about double the traffic. The only objection to the Nushki line is that it passes through a portion of the Amir's territory, between the Registan Desert and the Amran range.

At Bostan, however, the first great stage on the road is reached. The great watershed between the Indus and Afghanistan has been crossed. With the railway thus in the great upland plain of Afghanistan, we can wait further development of events.

The line will probably be open for through traffic to Peshin by the end of the financial year 1886-87, ie three and a half years from the commencement of the works in October 1883; and had it not been for the exceptional floods and sickness that have so fatally hindered the work hitherto, probably this estimate of time would have been reduced by at least six months. It is most annoying to reflect that the years 1881-83, when the works were stopped, were years of exceptionally good weather, and of very healthy seasons.

There is another very important line, the temporary Bolan line, of which a brief description may be interesting.

I have already pointed out that the reason the Harnai route was chosen instead of the Bolan as the place for a permanent line, was that on the Bolan it was not possible to get a grade of 1 in 45, whereas it is possible to do this on the Harnai route. On the other hand, a glance at the map will show that the Bolan route is by far the shorter to Quetta and Peshin. A military road was constructed up the Bolan Pass in 1882 - 84 as far as Quetta, with a ruling gradient of 1 in 20. This road was a work of very considerable difficulty, but it was admirably made, and will always be of the greatest value as a military communication. In July 1884, the question was raised by the Government of India whether it would be possible to supplement the work of the Sinde Peshin Railway by constructing a line for part of the way up the Bolan. It was then well known that the railway by Harnai would take some time to construct, and as difficulties with Russia appeared threatening, it would be as well to know how far existing communications might be utilised or added to. It was thought that rails might be laid on the already existing military road up the Bolan. This matter was referred to the Superintending Engineer at Quetta, with the reply that a railway might be made up the Bolan in continuation of that already existing, as far as Mach, half-way up the

Pass, and forty miles from Quetta; that for eighteen miles beyond Mach the steepness of the gradient would prevent a railway being made, the gradient there being 1 in 20; that for the last twenty-two miles into Quetta it would again be possible to construct a line on the 1 in 45 grade, and at Quetta a line so constructed would join the Bostan Quetta branch of the Sinde Peshin Railway.

In March 1885, it appeared as if war with Russia was absolutely certain. Orders were given to the Commissariat and Transport and other departments to collect vast quantities of warlike stores at Quetta, and very extensive arrangements were made for establishing a transport train of carts, camels, and other pack animals, from Rindli, the terminus at the mouth of the Bolan, to Quetta. The station at Rindli was at once enlarged, new sidings were put in, and very complete arrangements begun for the increased traffic. The amount of material of all kinds that kept pouring in along the Sinde Peshin Railway was enormous. A glance at the map will show how difficult it was for the single line across the desert to bear the strain of traffic pouring in from two directions. From the Punjab by Multan and Sukkur, and from Bombay via Karachi and Sinde, trains of stores and troops came daily for the front to Ruk, and these had to be despatched along the single line from Ruk to Rindli. In fact, this single line was called upon to do the work of a double line. That it was able at all to cope with this double burden of military traffic, without delay or accident, and yet send on ordinary stores as well, was greatly to the credit of the manager, an officer of our Corps. I have mentioned this because I saw lately a paragraph in a newspaper making calumnious and sweeping assertions against the Corps in general, and this officer in particular, with regard to their efficiency as railway managers.

At the beginning of April it was resolved by Government to extend the line up the Bolan somewhat in the manner proposed the previous summer, in order to ease the difficulties of transport; for, of course, the railway brought five or six times as much in the way of stores as the transport train and camels could carry away. This railway up the Bolan was to be entirely a temporary arrangement. It was not laid on the military road, as at first proposed. The reasons for this, doubtless, were that the road required all its width for ordinary purposes, and that no reduction of that width could be afforded. Also, that it would never do to obstruct the traffic with railway working parties. Further, the road lies above the highest possible flood level, and hence at all the road bridges, railway bridges also above floor level would be required, and the construction of these would take a great deal of time, and defeat the aim of the whole work, a quick temporary line. So the rails were simply to be laid in the bed of the river, which is wide and straggling, and has at most seasons but little water in it. Heavy floods would, of course, knock it to pieces, but these are not, as a rule, of common occurrence, and the line might take its chance of them. Where it has been necessary to cross the river, low crib bridges have been made, ie, cribs of sleepers weighed with boulders, and protected as much as possible by stone pitching. At these crossings the line has been laid as low as possible, so as to present as little surface as possible to the action of a flood. Of course, during a rainy season it might be impossible for an engine to get over one of these crossings for a week or a fortnight, even supposing the pier foundations remained sound. Still, one must accept a certain amount of risk in all works constructed in war, and a state of war or extreme danger would, in the opinion of those best qualified to judge, alone justify the construction of such a line.

Colonel Lindsay RE was at first nominated to be Engineer-in-Chief of this line, and he started the work in April. and continued in charge till the end of May, when he met with a serious accident which obliged him to go to England. He was succeeded by Mr O'Callaghan, a Civil Engineer of great skill and experience, by whom the great bridge at Attock was built. Under him was a large staff of engineers, chiefly civilians. There were among them two captains in the Corps, and the only reason that there were not more is that the Government of India had, up to a recent date, given few facilities to officers of the Corps for entering the railway branch of the Public Works Department, and hence there are not many officers of the Corps in that branch under the rank of Major. Nearly every one of these was engaged on the Sinde Peshin line already, so there were no more for the Bolan.

The work on this line, constructed on the temporary principle indicated above, was carried on during the whole of the summer months, and was completed as far as Mach by the 1st of November 1885. It is impossible to describe adequately the difficulties and privations under which this work, like the other, was carried on. Cholera and other fatal diseases carried off thousands, sparing neither high nor low, european or native. The heat in the lower Bolan, too, is beyond all description; and. hence, though the engineering was not of the same character on this line as it was on the other route, the initial difficulties were much the same, with one notable exception, that the presence of the first-rate Bolan road facilitated work there in a way that on the other pass was unknown.

Beyond Mach it was at one time proposed to haul trucks up the incline to Darwaza by means of stationary engines and wire ropes. but this idea has been abandoned. I understand that it is now proposed to lay a temporary narrow-gauge line (3 feet 3 inch gauge), with special rolling stock (Fairley engines and bogie trucks). One difficulty will be the supply of water, which in the upper Bolan is very deficient. I hear, however, that arrangements are being made to raise water from springs at Dozan (halfway up) by means of pumps, a height of 350 feet. A supply of iron pipes is being obtained from Suakim, where they are no longer required.

It is expected that the line will be open to the summit of the pass by the 1st of January, and into Quetta by the 1st April 1886, probably a year before it will be possible to arrive there by the other route.

The Bolan temporary line undoubtedly hindered the progress of the work on the Sinde Peshin State Railway by taking away numbers of the workpeople, who had got disheartened at the heavy difficulties and repeated floods, and who, moreover, always will leave an old work for a new one. But it will, it is hoped, help the Sinde Peshin State Railway in the future by bringing up material for the Quetta branch, and further.

Some writers in the Press, jealous of the Corps of Royal Engineers, have made invidious comparisons between the progress of the Bolan railway, on which the engineers are chiefly civilians and the Harnai line, on which the Corps had been so largely represented. But no engineer in his senses would think for a moment of comparing the two. There is no comparison between a permanent line, independent of floods, and a temporary line laid in the bed of a river.

We have, on the contrary, while giving our civilian brethren every credit for the work in the Bolan, good reason to be proud of the work done by the Corps on the Sibi Peshin line. It has been entirely under the direction of one of the most distinguished officers of the Corps, of whom I think I may be permitted to say that there are few men who, in the face of such difficulties as we have had, could have carried on such an undertaking with so much success, and all the difficult works on the line, without exception, have been either partly or altogether under Royal Engineer officers. From Narrai to Nasak, from Dargi to Quetta, there is no part that has not been under Royal Engineer executive engineers, and the only part that has been under civilian engineers is the easiest part of all, the only part, too, that enjoys a fairly temperate climate.

Baberkach Bridge

**   **   **   **   **

 Our attention has hitherto been directed to a description of the frontier railways in general, and to the Sinde Peshin State Railway in particular. Let us now turn to some details of engineering construction in the latter line.

 I must preface my remarks, however, by saying that probably many of the points to which I call attention, and many of the engineering details which I describe, are not by any means new. There are certain matters of engineering which are common to all railways, and for the matter of that to all large works; and these common points I shall endeavour to avoid. The details I am about to describe are those that were new to me personally, and to almost every officer in our Corps who joined the line while I was there. Many of us had had experience in the construction of barracks and forts, in the laying out of military roads and building of road bridges; some of us knew a little about canal engineering, which is even more precise and exact than railway work, but with two or three exceptions, the Royal Engineer officers sent up to the works knew nothing, practically, about the technicalities of railway engineering; did not know how to lay out curves or to set out bridges; did not know how to set out tunnels, and were quite ignorant on the subject of platelaying, and the peculiar circumstances of the country were so many, that even those officers who had had a great deal of railway experience found still that there was much to learn. This applies not only to our own people, but also to civilian engineers. Many of them were gentlemen of large railway experience, but they found that they had a great deal to pick up on this peculiar line.

 I shall, therefore, be glad if by relating our experience I can give some idea of how we set about this work. I shall try and point out the practical lessons which I, in common with others, learnt on this great work. It is better to have some idea, even if it only be in theory, of the work to be done, and not to have to learn it at the cost of disagreeable and humiliating failure as well as of valuable time.

 The first point in the construction of a line is the survey, location, and staking out. The general direction of the line, the points it is to pass, the stations, etc, are fixed by superior authority, and general instructions on this ground would be issued as a matter of course. As regards the special location of the line, technical orders of a precise nature would be issued by the Engineer-in-Chief, who in every case goes over the ground with the executive officers and issues orders to them as to the route, or the various alternative routes, he wishes to be laid out and levelled. The actual staking out, traversing, plotting, and levelling, almost invariably fall to the lot of a junior officer to carry out. The laying out of a line is in most cases simply a question of trial and error. Sometimes one can see at once the best place for a line to pass, but very often it is difficult to tell which of two or more alternative lines is the best, until they have been surveyed, marked out, and plotted on paper. As this is generally the first duty an officer has to do, it is very important for him to be thoroughly conversant with the laying out of curves and in taking levels.

As regards both these points, curves and levels, let me merely say that the American methods are far superior to the English. The English method of carrying out a curve is arbitrarily to fix a radius, or an apex angle, and to calculate therefrom the tangential angle by means of a regular formula. This involves a long arithmetical calculation, which carried on under most uncomfortable conditions, as it generally is, is almost certain to be wrong. It is pitiable to sit down on a rock, under a blazing sun or pelting rain, with a book of logarithms, to work out an angle which generally comes out in minutes, seconds, and fractions of a second, and which therefore has a further liability to error in the number of times it may have to be repeated round the curve. The American method is far simpler. In it the tangential angle is arbitrarily fixed, not the radius. All that one wants is a table of radii corresponding to even tangential angles, and from these one can select what would give a suitable curve, and then proceed to lay out the curve with accuracy and speed, and above all without loss of temper. I have not time to go into full details on this subject; it can be learnt from a small book entitled <u>A Practical Treatise on Railway Curves</u>, by a Mr Shunk, an American engineer.

The American method of levelling has a great advantage over our method, in that it is simpler, the books can be kept more neatly and checked more readily. The rule is a very simple one. To the reduced level of the starting point add the level of the backsight; this gives the level of the axis of the instrument. From this level all foresights are subtracted, whence the reduced levels of all the foresight positions are at once obtained.

Once a line has been determined upon and staked out, the next work is to lay out cuttings and embankments. It is generally advisable to calculate the cubic content of any piece of work before it is given out to one of the numerous petty contractors who are always to be found on such works. With regard to cuttings; the practice on our line generally was to mark out the exact formation width at first and let the sides be cut vertically, then afterwards to lay out the slopes, which were generally, though not always, $4/1$. In gravelly soil, curiously enough, it was found that the rain had less destructive effect upon vertical sides than upon $4/1$ slopes. As regards embankments, the formation levels and the edges on both sides should be marked out, and if possible profiles put up at regular intervals.

It is always customary to mark every tenth peg on the line with a small masonry pillar, and also to build a small pillar round the tangent peg of each curve.

The laying out of bridges is a matter requiring the greatest care and accuracy, and it is often a matter of no little difficulty, owing to the nature of the ground. This duty almost invariably falls to an assistant engineer, and it is well worth while to take pains and ensure accuracy at first, for a mistake in measurement, which perhaps will not be discovered till the girders have to be erected, may cause the whole work to be at fault, and render the labour of months useless.

The first thing to be done is to determine accurately the centre line of the bridge longitudinally. If the bridge is on the straight, which it generally is, the way to do this is to set up the theodolite on the tangent point of the nearest curve on one bank, and direct it on a pole or flag erected on the tangent point of the first curve on the opposite bank. This gives the vertical plane of the centre line. Mark out with pegs, in any convenient number, the centre line thus obtained, accurately across the bridge site; especially have some, if possible, in the bed of the stream. These pegs may be built round with masonry. The site of one abutment will probably be fixed by superior authority, and the position of the centre line on the face of this abutment must be marked. From this mark the measurement for the spans and piers must be taken. It should be remembered that when girders of a given span are to be used, this means the span in the clear, not the total length of the girder, and hence, in laying out a bridge the distance between the piers must be the given span plus the width of the pier. Thus, for instance, in a bridge of three spans of 150 feet, with piers 12 feet thick. the centre lines of the two piers would be 162 feet from each other, and 156 feet from the face of each adjacent abutment.

To measure these distances accurately, it is generally advisable to take a base in any convenient direction (one parallel to the centre line of the bridge is often most convenient), and measure the distances there with measuring rods, and with a steel tape, then fix the centre points of the piers by triangulation. Of course, if the site will admit of measuring the distance on the centre line of the bridge itself, so much the better, but it is always well to have an outside base as a check. The centre points of each pier being obtained, their centre lines are then laid out at right angles to the centre line of the bridge, or if the bridge is skewed, at the angle of the skew. The centre lines of each pier, and the faces of abutments, should have their positions fixed by pegs or masonry pillars, built at points up and down stream on sites above flood level, so that if a flood comes and destroys all the work, the line may be taken up again at once.

Having got these preliminaries settled, and the centre lines in both directions accurately fixed, the next thing to be done is to excavate the river bed for the foundations of the piers. This is generally a very difficult task. Some of the pier sites are certain to come in the water, and to get at these sites the first thing to be done is to divert the stream and build clay embankments round the site, high enough to resist a small flood. Of course, if a big flood comes, there is nothing to be done but try and save plant and tools, it is impossible to provide against every contingency. But the banks or dams ought to be high enough to resist a small flood. The site being cleared, the excavation through the sand and shingle of the river bed is begun. It is tedious troublesome work, and it will be found that progress is much hampered by water percolating through from the main stream. The deeper the excavation, of course the greater this percolation. This water must be kept out altogether, and to this end pumps generally have to be employed. Sometimes the water can be baled out by hand, sometimes the quantity is only moderate, and such as can be kept down by hand pumps. Very often, however, hand pumps are found insufficient, and then steam power has to be resorted to. Of course the expense and trouble of steam pumps is so great that they should not be used if manual labour can be utilised and is sufficient. At the same time the foundations must be absolutely dry, and no expense must be spared to ensure this.

A very convenient sort of pump in these situations is the pulsometer, the great advantage of which is that it does not require a portable engine with its staging and belting. The boiler to work the pulsometers is easily moved; it can be erected at a safe distance from the work. and one boiler will generally work two or three pumps.

These pumps, too, can be used in situations where it is not practicable or easy to use any other sort of pump - they can be lowered into a well, for instance.

If, however, the flow of water into the foundations is very great, pulsometers may not be strong enough, and then the only sort of pump to use is a centrifugal. This discharges a far greater volume of water than any other kind. The only objection is that it is rather troublesome to manage, a portable engine is necessary, with belting, and the bank adjacent whereon this engine stands has, of course, to be made very secure. The pump itself has to be on very strong staging over the water, otherwise the pull of the belting will overturn it. Then arrangement has to be made for the due disposal of the discharge water. Centrifugal pumps certainly have the great advantage of power, and for this reason are very largely employed in open foundations. It is unnecessary for me here, and it would be out of place, to enter into a detailed description of these pumps, as they can be seen on works in England. I would merely say that a thorough knowledge of the details and practical working of pumps is of great value to the railway engineer.

When the shingle of the river bed has all been taken out and the rock reached, the latter must be made ready for the reception of the concrete in the foundations. No time must now be lost, and every available man must be put on the works. Arrangements should be made for lighting the works, and for regular night reliefs, so that the work may go on day and night without interruption. A flood at this juncture will upset the labour of weeks. For instance, at the Kelat-i-kila bridge the foundations of two piers were swamped by floods twice, thus the work had to be done three times, and, of course, all the plant on the work, engines, boilers, pumps, etc, were completely ruined, where, indeed, they were not entirely lost.

The rock bed must be roughly levelled for the concrete. If there is a natural slope, stone-cutters must be set to work to cut it into steps with dovetail joggles, to give the concrete a firm hold. If it is naturally level, it is sufficient to clean the face and smooth off inequalities. Any honeycombing which may have taken place by the action of floods must be carefully removed until solid hard rock is reached. A low wall of boulders in mortar is built round the outside of the foundation site, and the concrete is then laid. The Engineer-in-Chief liked always to inspect the site before the concrete was put in, so that he might satisfy himself as to the thorough soundness of the rockbed on which the pier was to be built. The Portland cement concrete was commonly used in the following proportions:- one part cement, three parts sand, eight parts shingle or broken stone. For portions of the pier where the exposure was greater or more strength required, the proportion of cement was higher. The superstructure was always, where possible, built of ashlar masonry, with courses not less than 10 inches thick. But quarries were not always to be found; indeed, in the great majority of cases there was no building material near at hand, except the sand and shingle in the river beds. So it was decided to build the piers of concrete blocks of similar proportions to the concrete used in the foundations. The moulds of these blocks were 2 feet x $1\frac{1}{2}$ feet x 1 foot, and were simply wooden boards with wedge keys. The moulds were placed on the sandy ground near the work, and the concrete was then rammed into them and left for three or four days. The date was written on each, and after four days the concrete had attained sufficient hardness to admit of the boards being knocked away, and the block being carried to the work and laid in position. The blocks were laid like bricks, breaking joint and preserving a bond, all round the outside edges of the piers, and the inside of each layer was filled up with loose concrete. Thus the entire piers were built of concrete, rapidly and firmly. The concrete bridges near Baberkach had a very severe test in the floods of April, which occurred just after they had been completed. The result however was most satisfactory, no part of any pier showed signs of disintegration.

I may mention, that in mixing the concrete the Engineer-in-Chief directed that the sand and cement should first be measured and mixed dry, and then mixed with the measured shingle, also dry. During this second mixing water was sprinkled in very moderate quantity.

To raise the concrete blocks, and the large and heavy stones for the ashlar work, to their required positions on the works, one method, which seemed to be a favourite plan with native workmen, was to use inclined planes built of rails, and planks lashed across the rails. But a more scientific and satisfactory plan was to erect light derrick cranes at each pier. These cranes lifted weights up to about two tons, and were arranged so as to work in a horizontal and a vertical plane. The jibs were about 20 feet high, so the operations of the crane were limited to a hemisphere of 20 feet radius, with centre at the foot of the jib. To enable them to be used with piers of 40 feet or 50 feet, the cranes were erected on sand-bag platforms of sufficient height to enable the top of the jib to reach well above the highest point of the pier. Another method for lifting stones, etc, was to erect a sheers to reach above and over the pier, and have blocks and tackle with the running end of the fall round a windlass at the bottom of the pier, where there was plenty of room to work it with handspikes. But none of these ordinary methods were sufficient for raising the large stones required for the girder bed plates. At first these stones were obtained at enormous expense from quarries in the northern Punjab. Each was 7 feet long, 5 feet wide, and 2 feet thick, the total weight being 3 tons, more or less. They were transported to the site of the work with much difficulty, then holes had to be bored through them for the anchor bolts, and then special lifting arrangements had to be made before they could be raised into position. The expense and difficulty of all this proved to be so great that it was decided to make the bed plate blocks of Portland cement pure, or mixed with sand or fine shingle in small proportions. By this method the anchor bolts could be put in position before the cement was put in, there would be no trouble in raising the cement, and the whole mass would be thoroughly hard and homogenous. It would have plenty of time to set before the weight of the girders was brought on it.

The girders are all made and designed in England. The only work to be done in India is to put them up and rivet them together. With small girders up to 40 feet span, the invariable method was to rivet up the whole first, and lift it bodily into position by means of a single pole derrick. With large girders two single pole derricks were sometimes used, one at each end of the span, both ends being lifted together. In this case also the entire girder would be rivetted up before lifting. The most common method, however, for large girders was to build them up on staging. The staging used by Mr Sullivan, the contractor, consisted of short lengths of wrought iron pipes, fitted into sockets at each end, and tied together by iron bars; a very neat and portable, and yet very strong, arrangement. These groups of staging were founded on iron girders resting in the river bed, and were connected above with iron girders, on which were rails for a Wellington crane or traveller. This traveller worked longitudinally along the whole span, and transversely for its own length, viz, about 20 feet, so that it could lift into its required position any part of the whole girder. The time generally taken by this method to build up a 150 feet girder was eighteen days. The chief objection to this method is that a flood during the work will carry away the staging. Another objection is that with a Wellington crane native workmen have to be very carefully watched. With the usual carelessness of asiatics, they will, if allowed to do so, work the crane without preventer blocks or chains. On one occasion the whole crane tumbled over a pier into the next span, killing two men and wounding five. On the whole, however, this method of erecting girders is very rapid and efficient.

Before finally leaving the subject of girder erection, let me state that the knowledge of the manipulation of heavy weights in such artillery exercises as are taught at Woolwich and Shoeburyness, with the accompanying instruction in the use of ropes, chains, blocks, and tackle, is of the greatest value to the railway engineer, and I would strongly recommend to all who have the opportunity, and who wish to become efficient as railway engineers, to study by all means in their power this branch of practical mechanics, and the use of these appliances.

To turn to another subject of much importance in railway engineering - tunnels. Those on the Sinde Peshin line, as indeed on all lines, are of two sorts, viz, lined tunnels through soft soil. and unlined tunnels through rock. All the Chappar Rift tunnels, the Spintangi and the Quetta tunnels, are through rock quite solid enough to stand by itself. The other tunnels on the railway are lined. Lined tunnels are more dangerous in construction than tunnels through rock. though the latter take longer to construct, and require a greater expenditure of explosives. As regards the question where a cutting should end and give way to a tunnel, of course the reply varies very much with peculiar circumstances. but I think that, as far as possible, 80 feet was about the maximum depth that a cutting could be conveniently taken to. Anything beyond that should be a tunnel. The first tunnel on the Sinde Peshin line, at Narrai gorge, was driven through soft sandstone rock in 1880, but not lined till the beginning of 1884. It gave then the greatest trouble and caused enormous expense, chiefly because it was not lined at first. It is most dangerous to take a tunnel out to full width in soft soil, and allow, as in this particular case, trains to run through it. The vibration of passing trains may loosen large portions of soil, and cause the most serious accidents. In making a tunnel through soft or treacherous soil. the first thing to be done is to drive a heading through, about eight feet square, with sides and roof well shored with timber. This heading should be situated so as to be nearer the top than the bottom of the tunnel, as it will eventually be, because in widening it is easier to work when the heading is well above the floor. When the tunnel is enlarged to full size, small portions, about six feet in length, are done at one time, so as to lessen risk of landslips. With a single line of rails the cross section of the tunnel would naturally be somewhat oval, and the centreing used conforms to this oval shape. Moveable wooden centreings are usually employed, running on wheels with the widest possible track, and with sufficient space underneath to allow trucks to run between the wheels. The lining was generally of brick laid in Portland cement, and the space between the extrados of the arch and the ground above was filled up with coarse rubble masonry. Sometimes voussoir shaped concrete blocks, made in similar fashion to the blocks used on the bridges, and already described. were used for tunnel linings where brick was not forthcoming in sufficient quantities. As regards the direction of tunnels, in most cases it was possible to run a traverse from one mouth of the tunnel to the other. By reducing the triangulation thus obtained, and allowing for the curvature, if the tunnel was on a curve, it was generally possible to fix exactly the position and direction from both ends. But in some cases the nature of the ground was so difficult, and the mouths of tunnels so inaccessible, that the only thing to be done was to make a very careful trigonometrical survey, and plot the work on a large scale plan, from which the lengths and directions could be taken off by scale. This was the method followed at the Chappar Rift, and on the whole it was quite successful. In these tunnels at the rift it was a matter of much importance to have as many shafts, adits, or auxiliary galleries leading into the tunnels as possible, so as to be able to employ more and more hands at once. When a tunnel passed under a very high rock, or at some distance horizontally from the face of a cliff, it was not possible to use any auxiliary shafts or galleries, and the work, in such cases, had simply to go on from both ends. But as a rule it was quite possible to have either shafts or adits. The fixing of the direction of these, of the latter especially, was a matter of some nicety, but in nearly every case it was quite successful. The number of adits used in any place depended on the ascertained rate of progress in mining for the particular rock in which the work was going on; the object being to have as many adits as would enable all the galleries to meet at the same moment. The adits were, in cross section, about the same size as the main headings, viz, about eight feet square. When the headings met, the tunnels were taken out to full size, and the adits, which were left unaltered, were used for getting rid of the debris from the tunnels.

In blasting the rock to make these adits and tunnels - for every cubic inch had to be taken out by blasting - manual labour only was at first employed. Two gangs of labourers could stand side by side and 'jump' holes in the rock face, horizontally. A compound air rock perforator, that had formerly been used for the tunnels at Attock under the charge of some non-commissioned officers and men of the Royal Engineers, was sent to Sibi for use on the tunnels at Chappar. But it was found impossible to move this heavy machinery, one piece of which weighed eleven tons, across 100 miles of a roadless and difficult country, and so it never left Sibi. At the same time it was felt that progress with manual labour only was slow and crude, and so a light American machine, called Ingersoll's rock drill, was procured from New York. This was mounted on a sort of travelling carriage with wheels. It was infinitely lighter than the other, but even it required two elephants and a large gang of men to drag it up to Chappar - and one of the two elephants was never fit for any work afterwards. This machine works by compressed air which is conveyed in iron pipes to the various drills. I am sorry I never had an opportunity of seeing this work; it was first used last May and has been, I believe, very successful.

Dynamite and gunpowder were both used in the tunnels in very large quantities, in fact very special arrangements had to be made with the arsenals, and with Messrs Nobel and Co, the dynamite people, for the amount required. The officers in charge of the tunnel works as a rule preferred gunpowder to dynamite, because the latter shattered the rock into such fragments that it was troublesome to clear away. whereas a big block loosened by gunpowder could be lifted or tipped along with crowbars along the nearest adit over the cliff.

The fuses used were Bickford's ordinary black and land instantaneous. A few Bickford's subaqueous fuses were kept in store for use in damp localities. In firing groups of mines, in order to secure simultaneous action, a number of instantaneous fuses were fastened together in a bunch or knot above end, to which knot was also made fast an ordinary time fuse. The point at the knot was secured by gutta-percha and tin. Such groups of fuses can either be made up in store or obtained ready made from the manufacturer. The method of using was to put an instantaneous fuze in each mine, and to light the ordinary time fuse. When the latter burned as far as the point the whole of the mines would go off simultaneously, the fire being communicated along the instantaneous fuses to each mine. There were other arrangements, more or less ingenious, of different kinds of fuses, but it would be a waste of time to enlarge on this subject further.

In addition to gunpowder and dynamite, blasting gelatine was also used. It is said to have enormous explosive power, but I have had no experience of it myself, and am not aware how it has turned out.

Arrangements had to be made in all large tunnel headings to give light and ventilation. The former could only be given by reflection from a sheet of tin placed outside. Naked lights were forbidden where explosives were being used. Ventilation was conveyed through pipes from large bellows placed outside and kept constantly working.

While on this subject of mining it may be as well to describe the method of blowing up rocks with large charges. It was often desirable to blow out large portions of cliffs where a tunnel was either not practicable or unnecessary. A gallery would then be made about four feet square in section as far into the rock as the line of least resistance required, and then two branches of similar cross section, and somewhat less length, were made at right angles to the entrance gallery. The ends of these branches might be still further enlarged to receive the charges. The proportion of powder required for the charge varied with the nature of the soil, but for most ordinary soils $1/10$ LLR was found to be a formula giving very good results. The gunpowder used on the works was RLG, supplied from the Indian arsenals; it was sent in 50lb and 25lb barrels (which barrels, by the bye, came in very useful for a variety of temporary works). In loading the mines it was found better to take the powder out of the barrels and put in cloth bags, each capable of holding about 10lbs weight. By this means it could be packed better at the mine head. When all the charge had been loaded up, the powder hose was placed in the centre of each. Ordinary one-foot canvas piping was used for this, the powder poured in as tight as possible. In arranging the train of hose it was customary to lay one length of hose from one charge to the other, and then to have two lengths, one along each of the main gallery and meeting the other hose at the T head. At the points of junction the hoses were nailed together on a small piece of board, and some loose powder scattered over the joint. To protect the hose from the pressure of the tamping. it was placed inside hollow bamboos split in half longitudinally. After the hose had been placed in one half of the bamboo, the other half was laid over it, and the two tied together. Outside the mine the ends of the hose were brought together and nailed on a small board, to which also was fastened a suitable length of Bickford's fuse. Loose powder was also poured over this joint. The tamping of the mines was generally sand-bags, but here and there it was good to build a wall of mud bricks across the gallery, or boulders in clay might be used. It was worth while to take trouble with the tamping; a badly tamped mine always gives poor results. If, however, all precautions were taken the mines were invariably a success.

Electric fuses were not used, partly because of the uncertainty of their action, and because there were few cases in which a large number of simultaneous mines were required. In no case, either in tunnels or in other mining operations, did an accident occur that could have been prevented by the use of electric fuses.

Another very important branch of railway engineering is plate-laying, and of the special experience we had on the Sinde Peshin line I now desire to say a few words.

The pattern of sleeper sent out to the Sinde Peshin Railway is known as Denham and Olpherts' patent. I do not know by whom or on what principle this was selected as the type of sleeper, but it was certainly unsuitable in every way for a mountain railway. The sleeper and chair consisted of nine separate parts, cast iron plates and jaws for gripping the rail, and wrought iron ties, keys, etc, for keeping the whole together and preserving the gauge. The defects of this type of sleeper are very numerous. In the first place the multiplicity of parts caused endless worry and trouble. Next it was impossible to use the sleeper on bridges, or where check rails were required. Now it is generally laid down that every curve under 1000 feet radius ought to have a check rail, and as two-thirds of the curves on the line are of this description, this practically cuts out the larger portion of the line. And, again, this pattern of sleeper has very little grip on the ground, so that when laid on gradients (and it will be remembered that the greater portion of the line is on the heavy 1 in 45 gradient) there is a strong tendency to creep, ie be pulled down hill by trains passing over. The last objection to the sleeper is because of the brittle nature of the cast iron. The wandering Afghan or Baluch is a mischievous creature, and thinks the breaking of a piece of cast iron by dropping a stone on it, rather a nice amusement. This we have already found frequently by experience. So with this sleeper, constantly patrolling the line will be required to see that no tricks of this sort are being played.

The one advantage of this sort of sleeper is that it is made to gauge, and hence this does not depend on the platelayers. But unfortunately the sleepers sent out for the Sinde Peshin line were very badly made, tight to gauge, and of very rough workmanship. And so the one advantage was lost.

The rails used were of steel, 80lbs to the yard, and double headed. The fish plates were of the latest fashion, coming down over the lower flange of the rail but not below it, and secured by six fish bolts. All the permanent way, rails, sleepers, fish plates and bolts were sent out from England expressly for the line. The fish bolts were very badly made; very few indeed could be screwed home, and the whole of them had to be cut, shaped, and altered in workshops in India.

These defects in the permanent way simply show the absolute necessity there is for careful inspection in every detail before the articles are sent off from Home to a distant part of the world. These practical difficulties give an immense amount of worry and trouble, and they could quite well be obviated by a little care in the initial inspection.

A few words with regard to the actual platelaying. It was the wish of the Commander-in-Chief, a wish that was heartily responded to by the Brigadier-General commanding the Pioneer Brigade, that the men of those regiments should be employed as much as possible on platelaying, so as to give them an experience in this branch that would afterwards be a valuable military acquisition. Consequently the two Punjabi regiments were detailed for this work. One regiment would at one time have the platelaying and all temporary works in the immediate vicinity of the rail-head, while the other would be camped near the line a few miles further - on, making up the line and banks, and making diversions and temporary bridges. When the rails had advanced some distance beyond the regiment furthest to the rear, ie, that which has been doing the platelaying, that regiment would strike camp and march some few miles beyond the other. The latter would then take up the platelaying and the first regiment would take up works ahead. Thus, working alternately, both regiments were exercised in the work required. The men soon learnt what was to be done, and the officers took the keenest interest in their instruction. In one regiment each company in succession was exercised in the manipulation of the rails and sleepers; in the other regiment two companies were kept specially for platelaying, and the other companies were not taught it. The Brigadier-General did not interfere with the arrangements that each commanding officer chose to make in this respect, but he certainly considered the former method the better. There was one engineer officer told off to be with the working parties, and direct operations. It was his business to notify every morning to the traffic officer at the base what quantity of permanent way material would be required for the next day.

With this information, in the morning the traffic officer would load up at the base during the day the required amount of material complete, and have it made up into a train ready to be sent off early the following morning. so as to arrive at the rail-head by the time the men were paraded for work. On arrival the men would empty the train at once. Certain men would be told off to carry rails and lay them roughly parallel to the line; others would bring sleepers, and so on. As soon as the train was emptied it would move back again to the base for any other material duties. The working party would then go on with the laying of the rails in proper fashion, and work at it until it was fit for the passage of an engine the following day. The men worked in a very orderly manner, but there was no regular system of drill, which was, I think, a pity. There might have been some difficulty with the impracticable Denham and Olphert's sleeper, still some simple drill might have helped to accelerate matters with men accustomed to work in unison.

This system of platelaying seems, no doubt, very simple, but it required constant attention to details, and very often hitches occurred which interrupted the progress of the work. Chief among these troubles was the multiplicity of parts in the sleepers. If less than the exact number of each part in proportion to the whole was sent, the work was stopped for want of them. On the other hand, if more than necessary were sent, they got thrown aside, and might be forgotten next day, and then a pick-up train would have to go along and collect all the scattered pieces.

Generally, for military purposes, I think the old-fashioned wooden sleeper is, all round, the best. Soldiers very soon learn how to use it; it is very simple; can be used everywhere, ie, on bridges, curves, and all sorts of ground; and it comes in useful in a variety of ways besides its ordinary work. Thus temporary bridges of many kinds, scaffolding, staging, water-tank stands, and all that kind of work can be run up very quickly with wooden sleepers. and it may also be used for stockades, and any works of defence that may have to be made for protection of the railway. Its only defect is liability to be burnt, but even that is not so dangerous as the brittle tendency of cast iron sleepers.

Before concluding, let me just say a few words about river protective works. The violent floods we had last year made the protection of the banks. where exposed to the action of rivers, a question of pressing importance. It is customary to pave or pitch with large boulders banks exposed to water, but it was considered that this arrangement would not be sufficient in many cases. Two further protective methods were employed, both somewhat novel. In one place an arrangement was devised of protecting the toe of the slope with layers of concrete blocks chained together. Three chains were fastened securely to a small girder, which was buried in solid ground beyond the end of the bank on the up-stream side, and which, therefore, served as an anchor. The chains were then passed through empty Portland cement casks, laid in rows at the toe of the bank, and these casks were then filled with coarse Portland cement concrete. The chains thus passed through the centre of each block of concrete, and in order to connect each row or string of blocks, the chains were tied one to the other at intervals by smaller chains. The result of this was to present to the river a great shield, solid and yet flexible, like chain-armour. This protective work stood well in a heavy flood last March.

Another method was carried out on a very large scale by Captains Hoskyns and Whiteford, and consisted in a protection of the largest and heaviest boulders. and over them an enormous network of telegraph wires. The net was first made and laid with its lower edge in a trench at the bottom of the bank. This trench was filled up with boulders. so as to fasten the net below securely. Then all the pitching was duly placed in position, and when all was ready the net was turned over all and securely fastened down at the top. The effect of this great net was to keep the whole mass together. In the event of scour the whole would subside together.

I might say much more about details upon which I have not been able to touch, about concrete arches and culverts, retaining walls, diversions, temporary bridges; about station arrangements and rolling stock; but time does not admit of these details being enlarged upon, and I therefore conclude hoping that I may have given some idea of the work done on the Frontier Railways of India.

SINDH PESHIN STATE RAILWAY.
PLAN & SECTION OF TANDURI BRIDGE.

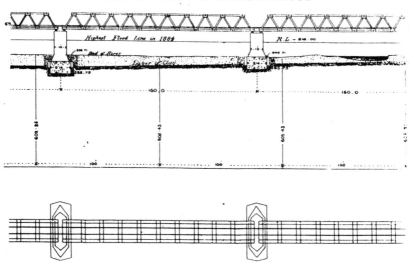